# BOYS IN RED COATS

## The Boy Battalions of the British Army 1797–1815

Owen W.H. Davis

Helion & Company Limited

**I would like to dedicate my first book to the memory of my Grandad Lawrence. Always thinking of you Grandad.**

Helion & Company Limited
Unit 8 Amherst Business Centre
Budbrooke Road
Warwick
CV34 5WE
England
Tel. 01926 499619
Email: info@helion.co.uk
Website: www.helion.co.uk
X (formerly Twitter): @Helionbooks
Facebook: @HelionBooks
Visit our blog at http://blog.helion.co.uk/

Published by Helion & Company 2026
Designed and typeset by Mach 3 Solutions (www.mach3solutions.co.uk)
Cover designed by Paul Hewitt, Battlefield Design (www.battlefield-design.co.uk)



ISBN 978-1-806722-61-7

British Library Cataloguing-in-Publication Data.
A catalogue record for this book is available from the British Library.

# Contents


Acknowledgments iv

Introduction vi

1 Evil under the Sun 9

2 Between Scylla and Charybdis 26

3 'To go for a soldier' 39

4 Discipline and Pranks 49

5 To the Cape 58

6 The Parting of the Ways 73

7 The Coming Tempest 81

8 Holkar Enters the Fray 99

9 Britannia at Bay 110

10 The Hunt for Holkar 122

11 'Who am I sent upon Fort-duty' 126

12 Pirates, Privateers, and Pindaris 143

13 There and Back Again 159

14 The Boys and Child Soldiery 166

Bibliography 170

# Acknowledgments

Discovering John Shipp's extraordinary memoirs in 2018, I became enthralled with his recollections of his military career in Africa and India. Amidst Shipp's anecdotes of animals he encountered and sieges he endured, I was captivated by his experience of serving amongst the ranks of a battalion of boy soldiers. Shipp and, as I was to discover, other boy recruits were part of an experimental approach to replenish manpower in the British Army. These boys subsequently found themselves fighting on the frontiers of Britain's growing Indian Empire. Pursuing this interest has led to the book before you. Over the course of its research, I have garnered several debts of gratitude to family and friends for their advice and support, and I cannot express enough my thanks to them. My parents were roped into helping edit and proofread this text, but any errors or mistakes contained within the book are naturally my own. I want to thank Paul Brunyee for encouraging me to present my initial research on the boy soldiers at the Waterloo Association's North-East Study Day. Paul's kind invitation and the enthusiastic response of the audience confirmed that a book was the right direction to tell these boys' stories. It was also at this event that I met Rob Griffith, who put me in contact with Duncan Rodgers who accepted my proposal. Rob's editorial support and advice with records have been invaluable, and I am grateful to Rob and Duncan for the opportunity to publish this book with Helion.

Numerous individuals and organisations have been indispensable whilst researching the boy soldiers, and I would like to extend my thanks to the staff of the National Archives, the British Library, especially the Asian and African Studies team, the Cheshire Military Museum, Clifton Park and Museum's York and Lancaster Regiment Archive, the National Army Museum and the Royal Irish Regiment Museum for their support with research queries and assistance with handling documents.

From my initial work preparing the proposal and writing the text, there are personal thanks I would like to extend to John Morewood, who, from the beginning, has offered advice on the proposal, how to navigate naval records, and image licences. It was John's and Gareth Glover's input that also helped refine the final title. I would also like to thank Gareth for his clarifying insights into why the Commander-in-Chief requested that the regiments complete the Statement of the Period of Service in 1806, which are now catalogued under WO 25 at The National Archives. For matters medical, Mick Crumplin and Martin R. Howard were a huge support; they both gave me a better understanding of medicine and tropical diseases in the early nineteenth century. I also greatly appreciated Mick's loan of his copy of Cantlie's *History of the*

*Army Medical Department*. The inclusion of the comparison between modern and turn of the eighteenth-century firearms owes itself to a chat with Mark Wardle about how a boy recruit might struggle with a Brown Bess. Whilst the invaluable data from WO 25 was suggested by Ian Chard.

Above all, I cannot thank my Mum and Dad enough; they have read through this book more than once, proofreading, challenging arguments and helping me to refine the final article. It would be safe to say that without their advice and support I would have been at sea!

# Introduction

One of the familiar images of the French Revolutionary and Napoleonic Wars is the drummer boy. Whether it is the bloodied collection of youths standing on the battlefield at Albuera in *Steady the Drums and Fifes* by Lady Elizabeth Butler, or the pensive expression of the rosy-cheeked boy in Richard Caton Woodville Jr.'s *Up, Guards and at them!* The image of the drummer boy or his naval counterparts, the youthful midshipman and the powder monkey, remains an oft-repeated leitmotif of the Napoleonic period. With good reason, these boys have become a fixture of the public's imagination and perception of the Revolutionary and Napoleonic Wars, as subsequent estimates have shown that for much of the wars, nearly 4 percent of the British Army was under 18, with up to 13,700 boys recruited between 1808 and 1815.[1] Whilst the drummer boy might be the popular image of children's engagement with Napoleonic warfare, it was not the only way they experienced the conflict.

The wars with France placed considerable strain on Britain's resources, stretching its financial, industrial and manpower reserves. While many historians have made a sound case for expanding the potentially nebulous concept of 'total war' to include France's mobilisation during the French Revolutionary War, there is an argument to extend some of these concepts to Britain. Over 800,000 men served in the British Army during the global conflict against France and her allies between 1793–1815. Recruiting men on this scale from the British public, which as a general rule remained wary if not outright cynical of army recruitment, encouraged the British government and army to develop alternative approaches for raising the recruits needed to fight France and man the frontiers of Britain's burgeoning empire.

One solution was the wholesale enlistment of boys under 16 years old in three British battalions. Whilst certainly controversial today, even at the time, this measure raised concerns that these youths were too young to handle a musket. The impetus to enlist boys owed its inception to two main drivers: the wholesale devastation of several infantry battalions caused by tropical diseases in the Caribbean and a seemingly philanthropic attempt to create a path for boys to take up a lifelong career as a soldier. This project was the brainchild of the Commander-in-Chief of the British Army, Prince Frederick, Duke of York and Albany, and his adjutant general, Sir William Fawcett. At the end of 1797, driven by the need to find recruits, they instituted a programme that resulted in over a thousand boys, from across Great Britain and Ireland, enlisting into regiments

1 Kevin Linch, *The British Army, 1783–1815* (Barnsley: Pen and Sword Military, 2024), p.181.

sometimes referred to as 'experimental battalions'. The resulting battalions, however, did not solely consist of the traditional ad hoc enlistment of drummer boys; rather, the Duke and Fawcett created a training ground for boys to take the King's shilling and enlist as private soldiers in the army. This fulfilled the practical purpose of raising the necessary soldiers for the depleted regiments returned from the West Indies. Beyond this necessity, they also took care to ensure these young boys received an education whilst they served in the army, a concept that paved the way for many of the army's subsequent educational programmes during the nineteenth century.

Almost akin to an apprenticeship scheme, the boy enlistment programme included time for the recruits to train for two to three years before they saw active service. Despite their young age, the idea was to create future battalions and not child soldiers thrown into the firing lines of Europe. The boys were a long-term investment and a way to produce the next generation of soldiers for the regiments who had enlisted them. Following their training in Britain, the Duke ordered the boy regiments to sail to India and the rapidly expanding dominion of the Honourable East India Company (HEIC), a lengthy journey which gave the boys time to mature. On their odyssey in the east, the boys faced Xhosa raiders at the foot of Africa, fierce ambushes in the hills of Sri Lanka, tenacious Jat and Maratha warriors in the ancient fortresses of India, Arabian pirates and French privateers, and their most insidious and ever-present foe, disease.

The boys' story reveals an obscure episode in the Great War with France and the history of the British Army. Some works have mentioned the story of these boy battalions, notably A.W. Cockerill in *Sons of the Brave*, which charts the history of all boy soldiers from ancient history to the Cold War, whilst Howard R. Clarke's *Redcoats in the Classroom* again provides an overview, which emphasises the boys' connection with education in the military. This is the first work wholly devoted to the boy battalions and their history, drawing on several first-hand accounts, including memoirs written by former boy soldiers, such as the indefatigable John Shipp and the laconic William Mansfield, with the latter's diary now housed in the Cheshire Military Museum. Observations of the boys were penned by several commanding officers, ranging from the glowing praise of Sir Hew Dalrymple to the admonishments of Sir William Fawcett. The text also includes accounts from civilian witnesses such as the keen diarist Lady Anne Barnard, who observed the boys during their first posting at the Cape of Good Hope. A wealth of statistical data has also been gleaned from the regimental records and muster rolls housed at the National Archives. Alongside this quantitative evidence, an invaluable glimpse into the lives of these battalions in India comes from the letters kept by the British Library in the India Office Records, including a never previously examined case of misconduct involving the 22nd (The Cheshire) Regiment of Foot. While contemporary newspaper copies held by the British Newspaper Archive provide glimpses of the boys' lives in the ranks through dispatches and articles.

Together, these records reveal a time of experimentation and innovation in the recruiting practices of the British Army, which had a major impact on the lives of these boys. They form part of a longer tradition of enlisting young people into the armed forces, which still survives to this day. The legacy of the boy battalions lives on through the many young boys and girls who can still enlist at or under 16 years old and the array of educational programmes that have sprung up in the British Army during the nineteenth century, in part to provide these young people with the skills they need for the ever-changing face of battle.

# 1

# Evil under the Sun

The plan for the boy soldier battalions was conceived in response to the difficult conditions many British regiments experienced during their deployment to the hot and humid climate of the Caribbean. British soldiers were dispatched to the West Indies following France's declaration of war on 1 February 1793. During the resulting War of the First Coalition (1792–1797), the British Army's role across the Atlantic was aimed at disrupting France's colonial trade and strangling her economy.[1] Within a few years of the opening of the conflict, the army was stretched to the limit distributing regiments across the globe to fulfil the British government's numerous enterprises in both Europe and in the colonies. This pressure was compounded by wastage through tropical diseases and eventually led to the collapse of several battalions by the end of the 1790s.

In the wake of France's declaration of war, Britain's first priority was to dispatch an expeditionary force to Flanders to help defend the United Provinces of the Netherlands and stop the deep-water ports of the Low Countries from being used as a launch-pad for an invasion of Great Britain.[2] Whilst Europe remained the main theatre of operations, the British government recognised that the French economy had to be disrupted. Accordingly, British strategy expanded to include an invasion of France's colonies on the numerous islands of the Caribbean. By the late eighteenth century, France had some of the wealthiest possessions in the West Indies, reaping the benefit of mass-producing luxury commodities, including sugar, coffee, cotton, and indigo.[3] The demand for these products was met by the slave plantocracies, which dominated the West Indian economy. These estates on both British and French islands were managed by a minority of white settlers, while the majority of the inhabitants were enslaved Africans or their descendants, who worked in the oppressive and brutal system of the plantations. At the outbreak of the war in 1793, France's Caribbean colonies consisted of Martinique, Guadeloupe, St Lucia, and Tobago in the Lesser Antilles, perched on the edge of the Atlantic. Whilst in the west,

1 Alexander Mikaberidze, *The Napoleonic Wars: A Global History* (New York: Oxford University Press, 2020), p.47.

2 Philip Ball, *Neither Up Nor Down: The British Army and the Flanders Campaign 1793–1795* (Warwick: Helion & Company, 2020), p.xv.

3 Laurent Dubois, *Avengers of the New World: The Story of the Haitian Revolution* (Cambridge, Massachusetts: The Belknap Press, 2004), pp.17–19.

at the heart of the Caribbean Sea lay *la perle des Antilles*, Saint-Domingue, now known as Haiti.[4] This colony consisted of a third of the island of Hispaniola, but its foreign trade far outstripped any of its Atlantic rivals – including the United States of America – making the Caribbean integral to the French economy and necessary to fund the nation's burgeoning war machine.[5] Intent on disrupting this source of French wealth, Prime Minister William Pitt the Younger, with the support of the Scottish statesman, Henry Dundas, Secretary of State for Home and the Colonies, launched an expedition to capture the islands. They planned to cut France off from this prosperous Atlantic trade route, whilst also staving off the threat of French forces launching their own attacks on Britain's Caribbean islands.[6]

While Britain was in prime position to rule the waves and dominate the Atlantic crossing through the size of her fleet and the skill of her crews, the same could not be said of her army. In 1793 the British Army was in a sorry state. In the decade since the end of the American War of Independence, the army had been ruthlessly cut to the bone with approximately 50,000 men under arms, scattered across the globe, forming garrisons in Great Britain, Ireland, the Caribbean and India.[7] An attack on France's colonies on the scale proposed by Dundas required a sizable injection of men into the West Indies, with some contemporary estimates proposing the dispatch of a force of 16,000 men. A taxing figure for the already diminutive British establishment, stretched thin to provide an expeditionary force for Europe.[8] Despite the odds, the army had to assent to Dundas' bold undertakings.

The eventual expeditionary force was cobbled together from garrisons across the Americas, Britain, and Ireland. One of the regiments drawn from the Caribbean garrison was the 9th (East Norfolk) Regiment of Foot, which had been stationed in St Christopher (St Kitts) since 1788. Regiments were also drawn from British Canada, including the 65th (2nd Yorkshire, North Riding) Regiment of Foot, which had garrisoned Fredericton since 1785. The 65th is a prime example of the unpreparedness of the British Army in 1793, as revealed by a monthly return of the regimental establishment taken on 24 May 1793. At the time, the battalion fielded roughly 309 rank and file available for duty, and another 20 in hospital. The battalion barely amounted to half the rank and file of the peacetime establishment set at 600 men.[9]

In addition to calling up battalions from garrisons across the Americas, Dundas also earmarked 14 regiments from Britain and Ireland to sail, as well as the flank companies from a further 14 battalions which were based in Ireland.[10] At the time, a typical British regiment consisted of a battalion divided into 10 companies. When the battalion was deployed in line for parade or battle, each company was arranged with eight companies in the centre and two on the flanks, with the grenadiers taking

4 Martin R. Howard, *Death Before Glory!* (Barnsley: Pen and Sword Military, 2015), p.31.
5 Michael Duffy, *Soldiers, Sugar, and Seapower* (Oxford: Clarendon Press, 1987), p.6.
6 Duffy, *Soldiers, Sugar, and Seapower*, p.5.
7 Linch, *The British Army*, pp.151–152.
8 Steve Brown, *By Fire and Bayonet* (Solihull: Helion & Company, 2018), p.35.
9 The National Archives (TNA): WO 17/185: 65th Foot Monthly Returns, 24 May 1793.
10 Brown, *By Fire and Bayonet*, p.35.

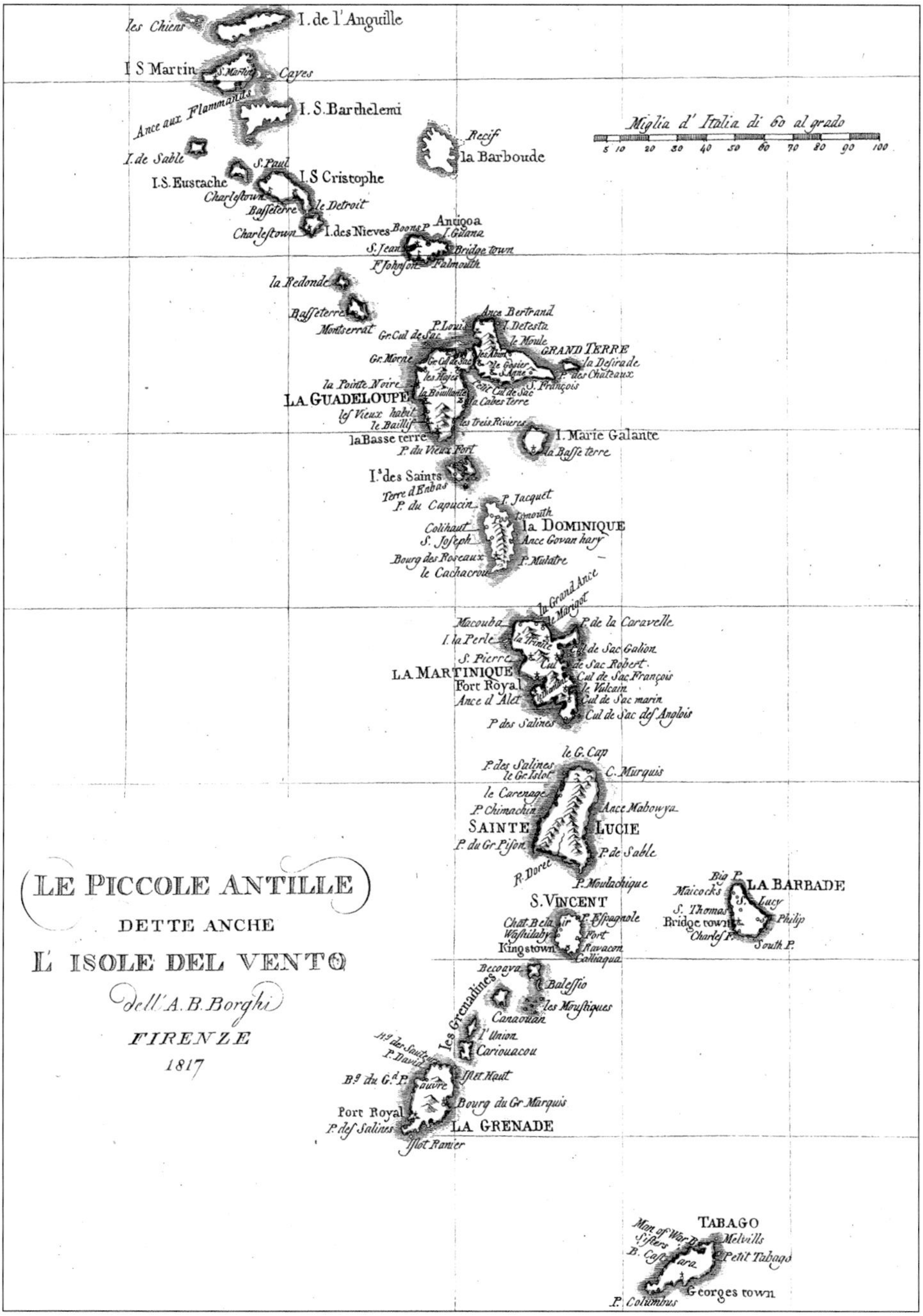


This map of the Lesser Antilles in 1817 provides a good idea of the relative proximity between French and British islands in the 1790s. (David Rumsey Historical Map Collection)

post on the extreme right, and the light company positioned on the extreme left.[11] The grenadiers and the light companies were both considered the best soldiers in their battalions, and it was common practice at the time to detach them from their parent regiments and form these companies into grenadier and light battalions composed of men from various regiments.[12] Of the 28 companies sent, three were particularly affected by their time in the West Indies; these included the 22nd (The Cheshire), 34th (Cumberland), and the 55th (Westmorland) Regiments of Foot. These companies had come from garrisons in Ireland and had no experience of combat or life in the tropics.[13] The five preceding regiments, the 9th, 22nd, 34th, 55th, and 65th, in addition to the 16th (Buckinghamshire) Regiment of Foot then stationed in Jamaica, all suffered such terrible wastage in manpower during their tenure in the Caribbean that they later became the first regiments to exclusively recruit boy soldiers. For now, they needed to survive beneath a blazing tropical sun, under the command of Lieutenant General Sir Charles 'No-flint' Grey.

Grey received command of Dundas' proposed expedition on 2 September 1793. He was a commander adept at daring raids, earning his nickname 'No-flint' for his penchant for rapid, stealthy advances, driven home at the point of a bayonet during the American War of Independence.[14] The subsequent Caribbean campaign remained true to Grey's tenets of war, consisting of brisk raids conducted with cold steel.

From 13 November 1793 to the middle of January 1794, Grey's expedition slowly trickled across the Atlantic, eventually pooling into Carlisle Bay, Barbados. Upon arriving in Barbados, the regiments were confined to their ships, only being rowed ashore for drill between three and eight o'clock each morning. After drilling, the men were returned to Carlisle Bay and the transports before the sun rose, thus limiting the dangers of heatstroke.[15]

Grey understood that he held a very fine and delicate instrument in his hands, assuring his men that they, 'are able to fight any troops upon earth'.[16] He particularly admired the flank companies from Ireland and considered them to be, 'the pick of the Irish army' and he thought, 'it was unlikely that such excellent soldiers could ever be assembled again in the war.'[17] This final sentence shows some of Grey's concerns, as despite his praise, one false movement and the entire army would slip through his fingers like smoke. Even before the expedition left Barbados, the men were already proving susceptible to the climate, with outbreaks of sickness as early as late January. Major General Thomas Dundas, who commanded the 2nd Brigade, described, 'the grenadiers from Ireland are yet young soldiers' and while they would become 'fine soldiers',[18] their lack

11 Philip Haythornthwaite, *British Napoleonic Infantry Tactics 1792-1815* (Oxford: Osprey Publishing, 2008), p.10.
12 Duffy, *Soldiers, Sugar, and Seapower*, p.61.
13 Brown, *By Fire and Bayonet*, p.38.
14 Huw J. Davies, *The Wandering Army* (New Haven: Yale University Press, 2022), pp.245–247.
15 Davies, *The Wandering Army*, p.245.
16 Cooper Wylliams, *An Account of the Campaign in the West Indies in the Year 1794* (London: T. Bensley, 1796), Appendix.
17 Duffy, *Soldiers, Sugar, and Seapower*, p.63.
18 Brown, *By Fire and Bayonet*, p.82.

of acclimatisation and campaign experience left them vulnerable in the Caribbean theatre. Adding to Grey's woes, the expedition had departed late in the campaigning season, which meant he only had five months to come to grips with the French, before hurricanes and sickness struck from July–November.[19] With these problems already bubbling under the surface, Grey's expedition weighed anchor in late January 1794 with his first target, Martinique, in his sights.

It took two months to secure the capitulation of the island, as the indomitable *lieutenant général* Donatien-Marie-Joseph de Vimeur, vicomte de Rochambeau, organised Martinique's defences and kept the British at bay. The vicomte was eventually forced to capitulate on 22 March 1794, having significantly delayed Grey's expedition.[20] Aware that any further tardiness spelt disaster, Grey immediately set sail determined to seize the last of the French islands. In a lightning campaign, St Lucia and Guadeloupe fell by 22 April and within three months British control of the Lesser Antilles had been secured. In the west, troops from Jamaica had landed on Saint-Domingue in September 1793 and secured both the southern port of Jérémie and the great naval base at the Môle-Saint-Nicolas, in the north. The year 1794 seemed set to become another *annus mirabilis* for the British, as the landings on Saint-Domingue met little resistance amid the acclimations of French counter-revolutionary planters.[21]

With victory came the necessity to provide garrisons for the captured islands. Despite the British Army's already stretched deployments, Dundas stripped more men from Ireland's garrisons, including the centre companies of 22nd Foot.[22] Whilst reinforcements were welcome, they could not cover the men Grey had to send from his army to bolster the garrison at Saint-Domingue. The soldiers taken from Grey included the flank companies of the 22nd, and their departure left the British forces thinly spread across the Lesser Antilles.

## Pestilence and War on Saint-Domingue

When the centre companies of the 22nd Foot reached Saint-Domingue, in May 1794, the regiment found the island in the grip of a brutal civil war and slave uprising. The French colony had descended into anarchy following the outbreak of the revolution in the metropole in 1789. The *grand blancs* – the major plantation owners – were keenly aware that the enlightened principles of the revolution opened their narrow power base out to the *petit blancs* – poor white workers – and the *gens de couleur* – the few free people of colour on the island. These political and ethnic groups were a mere drop in the ocean compared to the number of enslaved people who made up 90 percent of the colony's population. The enslaved men and women had no hope of representation

19 Brown, *By Fire and Bayonet*, p.20.
20 J.W. Fortescue, *A History of the British Army* (London: Macmillan and Co., Limited, 1906), vol.4, p.365.
21 Howard, *Death Before Glory!*, p.36.
22 Brown, *By Fire and Bayonet*, p.65.

or support from either the French government or the factions on Saint-Domingue.[23] Their lives were defined by cutting sugar cane or plucking cotton under the blazing sun and the constant threat of corporal punishment and torture at the hands of plantation overseers.[24]

In this tense political climate, fighting broke out after the 'Night of Fire' on 22–23 August 1791, when the slaves of many of the northern plantations rose up and attacked the masters.[25] In the ensuing struggle, numerous factions fought for control of the island. Royalist, Republican, and armies of former slaves struggled for paramountcy, while the looming possibility of intervention from the Spanish controlled eastern two-thirds of Hispaniola, and the eventual arrival of the British from Jamaica, kept the colony in turmoil. With so many factions to contend with and limited resources, the British conquests were confined to the coast, where the army focused on garrisoning ports and surviving the numerous tropical diseases that were endemic to Saint-Domingue.

To illustrate how taxing the next two years were for the British garrisons in the West Indies, the 16th and the 22nd Foot both provide clear examples of the strain a posting in the tropics placed on the British Army. Both of these battalions were selected to study because they later formed part of the boy recruitment experiment due to their losses sustained in the Caribbean. Additionally, these battalions have the most complete monthly returns of any of the other future boy regiments.

The first of the monthly returns for the 22nd Foot was taken on 1 May 1794, just before the battalion made landfall on Saint-Domingue and records the regimental rank and file as 571 men (rank and file included privates and corporals, but not serjeants and drummers).[26] Their flank companies were reckoned at about 144 men based in Martinique who rejoined the regiment later on 8 June 1794.[27] When eventually reunited, the battalion should have numbered 715 rank and file, not including sick and men listed as recruiting for the battalion, an incomplete but still strong regiment. Aside from the flank companies, these were fresh troops plucked straight from their billets in Ireland and deposited in the sweltering heat of the tropics.

In contrast, the 16th had been posted to Halifax, Nova Scotia from August 1790, where they remained until at least July 1792, when they were subsequently dispatched to Jamaica. A regimental return taken on 1 July 1792 in Halifax, Nova Scotia counted 341 rank and file present and fit for duty with 21 in hospital.[28] Much like the 65th Foot, encountered earlier in this chapter, the 16th's peacetime tour of duty in the colonies meant they were understrength before they even embarked on active service.

In Table 1, the losses incurred by the 16th become starkly apparent, as over the course of four years (c.1792–1796) the battalion was steadily whittled down from 373 rank

23 Adam Zamoyski, *Holy Madness: Romantics, Patriots, and Revolutionaries, 1776–1871* (London: Weidenfeld & Nicholson, 1999), pp.124–125.
24 Dubois, *Avengers of the New World*, p.30.
25 Dubois, *Avengers of the New World*, pp.96–97.
26 TNA: WO 17/1986: General Returns, Jamaica, 20 May 1794.
27 TNA: WO 17/124: 22nd Foot Monthly Returns, 1 May 1794; David Patrick Geggus, *The British Occupation of Saint-Domingue 1793–98* (PhD thesis, York University, 1978), p.377.
28 TNA: WO 17/118: 16th Foot Monthly Returns, 1 July 1792.

and file to just 41, barely half the strength of a company. During their time in Jamaica, the 16th spent most of their days engaged in garrison duty, maintaining a watchful eye on the coast for a French descent or an uprising from the island's slave population. Although the monotony of garrison work was eventually broken by the outbreak of the Second Maroon War or Trelawney War in 1795.

**Table 1: 16th Foot, Rank and File Strength 1792–1796[29]**

| | Present | Sick | Recruiting/On Command |
|---|---|---|---|
| 1 July 1792, Halifax | 341 | 21 | 10 |
| 1 January 1794, Jamaica | 168 | 63 | 10 |
| 1 December 1794 | 95 | 8 | 61 |
| 1 June 1795 | 156 | 22 | 67 |
| 1 December 1795[30] | 22 | 21 | 140 |
| 1 May 1796[31] | 25 | 4 | 42 |
| 1 November 1796, Romsey | 18 | 2 | 17 |

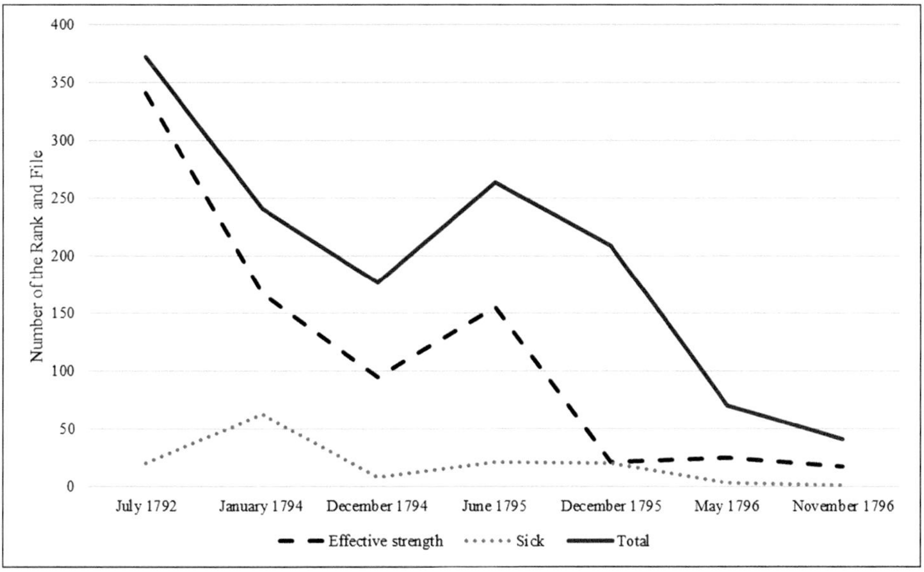


16th Foot, Regimental Strength from 1792–1796.

The Maroons were the descendants of African slaves who had fled from Spanish plantations when the English conquered Jamaica in 1655 and taken refuge in the mountains and valleys of the island's interior. The mountainous terrain the Maroons settled in was

29 TNA: WO 17/118: 16th Foot Monthly Returns; TNA: WO 17/1986: General Returns, Jamaica, 1 January 1794.
30 TNA: WO 17/1987: General Returns, Jamaica, 1 December 1795.
31 TNA: WO 17/118: 16th Foot Monthly Returns, 1 May 1796.

described by Lady Nugent, wife of the Governor, Lieutenant General George Nugent, in 1801 as 'An immense amphitheatre of mountains, irregular in their shape and various in verdure; some steep and rugged, others sloping gently, and presenting the thickest foliage.'[32] A treaty signed between Britain and the Maroons in 1738 had granted them a degree of independence and the right to several towns in the rugged interior, in return for hunting down runaway slaves from the plantations.[33] By 1795 tensions had steadily mounted between the Maroons and the Jamaican government, eventually erupting into war after two Maroons were publicly flogged for stealing pigs.[34]

In the resulting campaign, the 16th Foot, despite being woefully understrength, with just 264 men in the ranks, had to supply troops for expeditions into the heart of Jamaica. The war itself mostly consisted of ambushes in the many cockpits – narrow valleys hemmed in with rocks and mountain ridges – that marked the countryside.[35] British strategy aimed to maintain a cordon around the Maroons, containing them in the mountains and then launching counter-raids and destroying crops to starve the Maroons out.[36] By October most of the 16th Foot were deployed in the mountains. During this time, it is hard to discern any precise casualties because the Jamaica garrison return for November 1795 is missing, while the return for December 1795 records only three deaths in the regiment.[37] This was at a time when 140 men were posted 'on command' fighting the Maroons in the mountains. Although it must be noted that these three deaths are not stated to be directly caused in a raid and so may indicate deaths by disease or accident. Overall, the constant nature of raids and ambushes resulted in a slow drain on the garrison's manpower. The entire British force amounted to 2,052 sergeants, drummers and rank and file. During the early stages of the war, at least 65 men were lost by the entire garrison of Jamaica, although the exact final figure for British casualties has not been identified and may be much higher.[38]

In contrast, the 22nd Foot found themselves launched into the thick of the action upon landing in Saint-Domingue. The arrival of reinforcements from Britain in May 1794 marked a significant injection of manpower into the garrison, allowing Major General John Whyte to go on the offensive. The target was set for Port-au-Prince, the capital and main commercial port of the colony.[39] Landing to the west of the port on 31 May 1794, the 22nd saw some fighting around 1 June, losing Captain Thomas Wallace and an unstated number of private soldiers.[40] While most sources

32 Lady Nugent quoted in Sir Alan Burns, *History of the British West Indies* (London: George Allen & Unwin Ltd., 1965), p.550.
33 Howard, *Death Before Glory!*, p.24.
34 R.C. Dallas, *The History of the Maroons* (London: T.M. Longman and O. Rees, 1803), pp.144–145.
35 Howard, *Death Before Glory!*, p.25.
36 Fortescue, *A History of the British Army*, vol.4, p.463.
37 TNA: WO 17/1987: General Returns, Jamaica, 1 December 1795.
38 Michael Sivapragasam, *After the Treaties: A Social, Economic and Demographic History of Maroon Society in Jamaica, 1739–1842* (PhD Thesis, University of Southampton, 2018), p.144.
39 Duffy, *Soldiers, Sugar, and Seapower*, p.101.
40 W.H. Anderson, *History of the Twenty-Second Cheshire Regiment* (London: Hugh Rees, Limited, 1920), p.102; TNA: WO 12/3873: General Muster Books and Pay Lists, 22nd Foot 1st Battalion,

do not provide a specific figure, the regimental returns taken on 1 June and 1 July list 24 deaths over the course of the month, although this figure probably includes deaths by disease as well as combat.[41] With the capture of Port-au-Prince, the role of the 22nd Foot shifted to garrison work, which meant the unacclimatised Cheshires were left days on end sweltering in cantonments. Unfortunately for these men, they had been set ashore on an island described by the British Inspector of Hospitals as ripe with 'fever in each treacherous breeze.'[42] Topographically, Saint-Domingue was likened by some contemporary commentators to a Caribbean Switzerland, rugged and mountainous, but unlike its European counterpart, Saint-Domingue was hot, humid, and teemed with swarms of insects, particularly in the verdant lowlands of the island.

During the 1790s there were a plethora of maladies which preyed on the British expeditions. Insect-borne infections included yellow fever, malaria, and typhus, whilst unsanitary conditions in the water could also spread typhoid fever, dysentery and cholera.[43] Of all these maladies, yellow fever was considered particularly severe between 1793 and 1798, and many contemporary observers suggested that a pandemic had gripped the West Indies, devastating Grey's expedition and the British garrisons on Saint-Domingue and Jamaica.[44] While yellow fever does seem to have been the main culprit in the 1790s, historian David Geggus has observed there is also strong evidence that the rise in mortality was partly associated with the sudden influx of unseasoned outsiders entering the Caribbean, such as the 22nd Foot fresh off the boat from the wind-blown docksides of Cork.[45] Conditions were exacerbated by the need to pack these men into coastal barracks to guard the newly won towns of Saint-Domingue such as Port-au-Prince. In these cramped garrisons, the men, women, and children of the 22nd were easy pickings for *Aedes aegypti*, a species of mosquito that acted as the vector for yellow fever.[46] Once bitten and infected by the mosquito, the army surgeon Robert Jackson relayed the ordeal that a patient faced: 'The first symptoms were languor, debility and headache, together with an affection of the stomach peculiarly disagreeable.'[47] Jaundice and delirium might follow, and then vomiting up blood and later haemorrhage.[48] This disease was rendered even more terrifying by patients seemingly recovering only to be struck down within a matter of hours, as experienced by Surgeon William Fergusson whilst attending to Lieutenant Mackay, at the Môle-Saint-Nicolas: 'on the day of his death, [he] was up and dressed on the sofa, with books and papers before him at ten in the morning, passing jokes of comparison

1785–1797, 24 June 1794.

41 TNA: WO 17/124: 22nd Foot Monthly Returns, 1 June and 1 July 1794.

42 Howard, *Death Before Glory!*, p.35.

43 Roger Norman Buckley, *The British Army in the West Indies: Society and the Military in the Revolutionary Age* (Mona: University of the West Indies Press, 1988), p.272.

44 Geggus, *The British Occupation of Saint-Domingue*, p.323.

45 Geggus, *The British Occupation of Saint-Domingue*, p.327.

46 Buckley, *The British Army in the West Indies*, p.281.

47 Robert Jackson quoted in Howard, *Death Before Glory!*, p.201.

48 Geggus, *The British Occupation of Saint-Domingue*, p.323.

This painting from c.1790 provides a good idea of the type of uniform and equipment worn by an officer in the 22nd Foot. (Anne S.K. Brown Collection)

between his own dingy complexion, made so by the disease, and that of his mulatto nurse; at two he expired' in a 'torrent of black vomit'.[49]

Eighteenth-century medical practitioners had not discovered the importance of microbiology or how mosquitoes acted as the vectors for diseases like malaria and yellow fever, but there were still some preventative measures that could have been taken to limit the impact of these plagues.[50] This included stationing soldiers from Britain and Ireland on the mountain tops of Saint-Domingue and Jamaica, because *Aedes aegypti* needs a hot and humid environment to survive, which is impossible in the cooler mountain air.[51] In 1794, the 22nd were unable to avail themselves of any mountain fastness, due to strategic concerns; they were required to guard the port towns such as Port-au-Prince, which sat in the lowlands. In addition to the poor location, Geggus has also pointed out that the city's water supply had been cut off, forcing the garrison to rely on water stored in barrels. This, he argues, might have produced the perfect breeding ground for *Aedes aegypti*, which prefers standing water and consequently their populations tend to rapidly expand during water shortages.[52] These factors came together to produce the perfect environment for a surge in mortality in the 22nd Foot during the autumn of 1794.

**Table 2: 22nd Foot, Dispositions 29 June 1794.**[53]

| | Port-au-Prince | Môle-Saint-Nicolas | Saint-Marc | Jérémie | Total |
|---|---|---|---|---|---|
| NCOs and Drummers | – | 14 | 10 | 4 | 28 |
| Rank and File | – | 127 | 181 | 104 | 412 |
| Sick NCOs and Drummers | 2 | 3 | – | – | 5 |
| Sick Rank and File | 56 | 101 | – | – | 157 |

By 29 June 1794, the 22nd had been scattered across Saint-Domingue, with the battalion's principal headquarters listed in the regimental returns as the Môle-Saint-Nicolas.[54] Although the figures taken from the General Returns for Jamaica and Saint-Domingue, as listed in Table 2, show the detachments from the 22nd were stationed around the Gulf of Gonâve. Some parties of the 22nd were sent to the extreme south-west at Jérémie, and a further detachment was temporarily sent to Saint-Marc in the centre of the gulf.[55] The regiment's time away from Port-au-Prince likely helped to mitigate the rise of yellow fever, because Port-au-Prince was considered one of the unhealthiest billets in the already infamous climate of Saint-Domingue. The 22nd's inevitable pestilential destruction finally struck over the course of eight weeks between September and October 1794.

49 William Fergusson, *Notes and Recollections of a Professional Life* (London: Longman, Brown, Green, and Longmans, 1846), p.147.
50 Howard, *Death Before Glory!*, p.206.
51 Buckley, *The British Army in the West Indies*, p.310.
52 Geggus, *The British Occupation of Saint-Domingue*, p.330.
53 TNA: WO 17/1986: General Returns, Jamaica, 29 June 1794.
54 TNA: WO 17/124: 22nd Foot Monthly Returns; TNA: WO 17/1986: General Returns, Jamaica, 01 July 1794.
55 TNA: WO 17/1986: General Returns, Jamaica, 29 June and 31 August 1794.

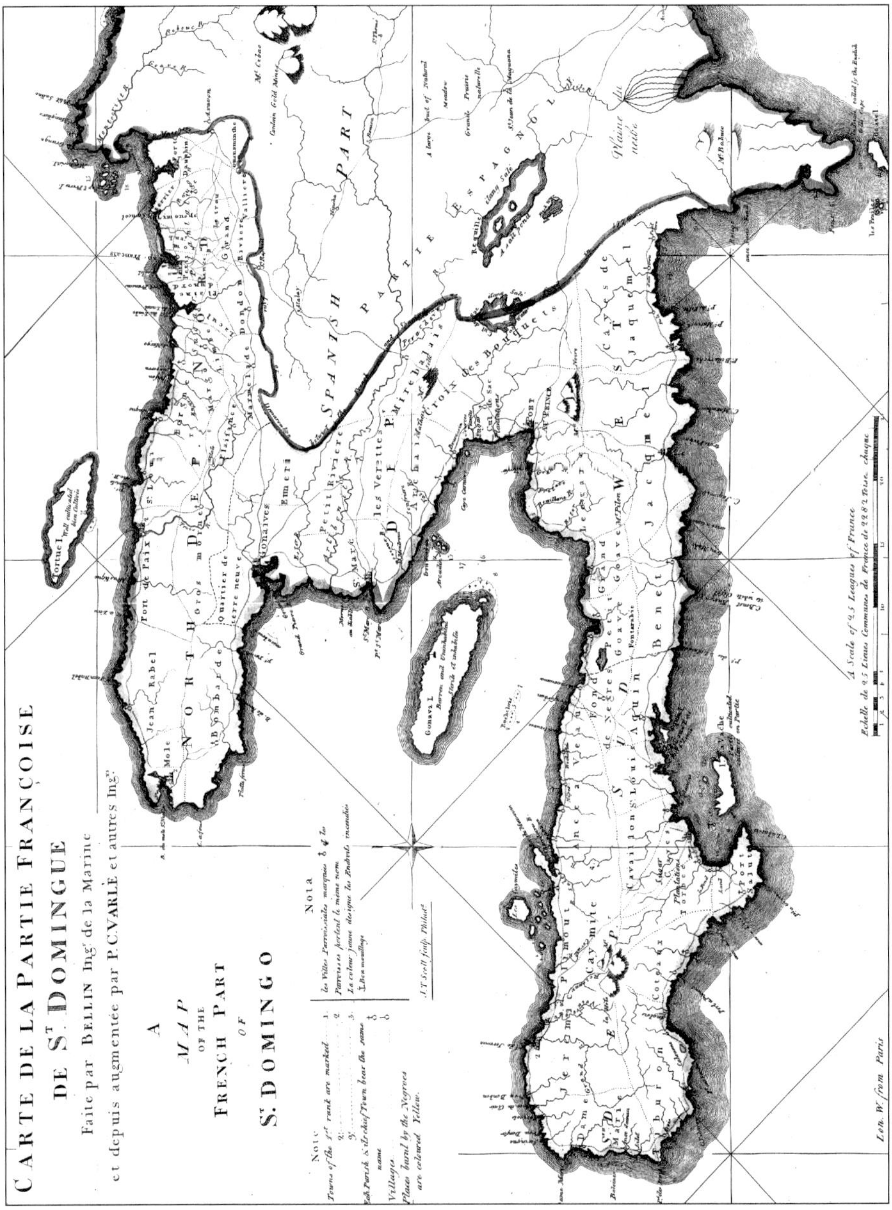


Map of Saint-Domingue in 1814. (David Rumsey Historical Map Collection)

**Table 3: 22nd Foot, Rank and File Strength 1792–1796**[56]

| | Present | Sick | On Command | Recruiting/Furlow | Total |
|---|---|---|---|---|---|
| 1 January 1794, Cork | 580 | 18 | 144 | 19 | 761 |
| 20 May 1794, On Transports | 576 | 10 | 144 | 15 | 745 |
| 29 June 1794 | 412 | 157 | Not Stated | Not Stated | 569 |
| 26 October 1794 | 24 | 134 | 0 | N/A | 158 |
| 1 January 1795 | 103 | 87 | Not Stated | Not Stated | 190 |
| 1 July 1795 | 40 | 86 | 63 | 14 | 203 |
| 1 December 1795 Jérémie | 31 | 67 | 42 | 7 | 147 |
| 1 July 1796 Port Royal, Jamaica | 42 | 14 | 25 | 7 | 88 |
| 1 November 1796 En route to Colchester Barracks | 28 | 8 | 15 | 10 | 61 |

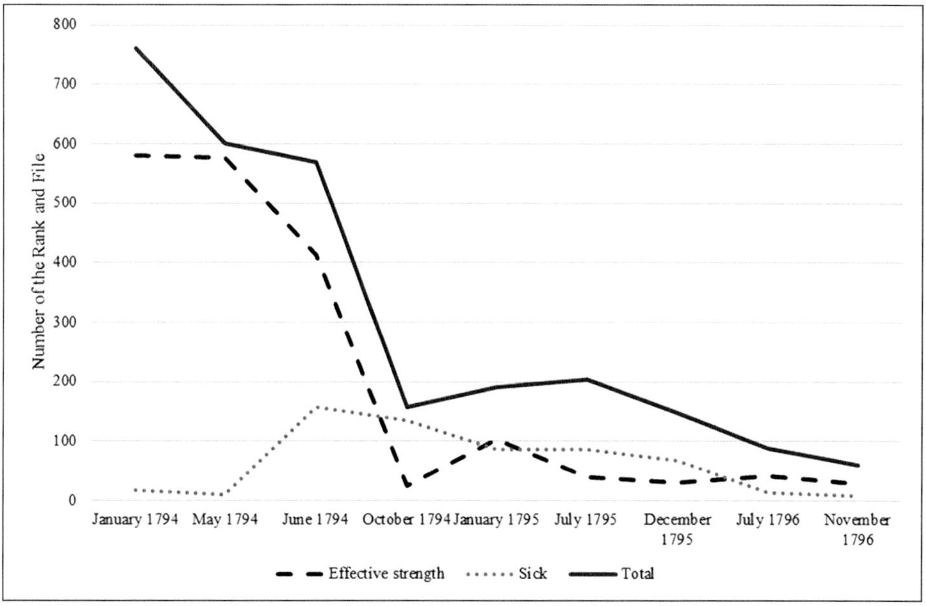


22nd Foot, Regimental Strength 1792–1796.

Like the 16th Foot, the 22nd had experienced a steady decline in their rank and file, accompanied by increasing cases of sickness. When compared, the 22nd Foot's losses were far more dramatic than the 16th, because the 22nd had no time to become seasoned to the Caribbean climate, their men were vulnerable to yellow fever, and as a

56 TNA: WO 17/124: 22nd Foot Monthly Returns ; TNA: WO 17/1986: General Returns, Jamaica, 1 January 1794.

result 60 percent of the regimental strength was lost. By 26 October, the regiment was barely able to field a company, with just 24 men fit for duty and a staggering 85 percent of rank and file sick in hospital.[57] Despite these debilitating losses, the 22nd spent nearly two years in Saint-Domingue, continually beset with various fevers and slowly whittled away until they retired to Port Royal, Jamaica and were eventually sent home during the autumn of 1796.[58]

As they longed for orders for home, the 16th was also decimated by disease, leaving just 25 rank and file fit for duty by May 1796. They eventually left Montego Bay, Jamaica, for Romsey, Hampshire, in the autumn of the same year. Four other regiments suffered the same devastating losses in the West Indies. The 9th Foot, as previously noted, had been posted to St Christopher in 1788. This long deployment in the colony potentially gave them time to acclimatise to the West Indies, but they were a small battalion amounting to just 256 men fit for duty in 1793.[59] The 9th fought in most of the major actions of Grey's expedition and were instrumental in suppressing a French colonist and slave revolt in Grenada in 1795. These actions took their toll on the regiment and by the time they had returned to Norwich in 1796, the losses from battle, disease and draftees leaving to join the 27th (Inniskilling) Regiment had reduced the 9th to 81 men.[60]

Of the other remnants of Grey's expedition, the 34th and the 55th Foot had both sent their flank companies in 1794. The centre companies of the 34th eventually followed the leading elements of the regiment to the Caribbean in February 1795. Prior to their departure, the last return taken on 1 October 1794 gave the battalion's rank and file strength as 659 with 131 men already in the West Indies.[61] Their first posting was St Lucia, but they were forced to evacuate after the island erupted in a revolt inspired by French provocateurs from Guadeloupe.[62] After fleeing the frying pan, they had to jump straight into the fire as they landed on St Vincent, which was engulfed in a war with the island's Caribs. Another major British expedition in 1796, this time led by Major General Sir Ralph Abercromby, enabled the island's garrison, including the 34th, to go on the offensive, subduing the Caribs who were later deported to Balliceaux Island in the Grenadines.[63] By the time the regiment had returned to Poole on 23 October 1796, just 60 men were available for duty.[64]

Likewise, the 55th, having sent their flank companies to the Caribbean with Grey, had the dubious honour of dispatching their centre companies to the Low Countries to serve under the Duke of York.[65] The centre companies arrived in Ostend in May 1794, where they endured the steady decline of British fortunes, including the terrible winter

57 TNA: WO 17/1986: General Returns, Jamaica, 26 October 1794.
58 TNA: WO 17/124: 22nd Foot Monthly Returns, 1 July and 1 October 1796.
59 Brown, *By Fire and Bayonet*, p.203.
60 Richard Cannon, *Historical Record of the Ninth, or the East Norfolk Regiment of Foot* (London: Parker, Furnivall & Parker, 1848), pp.36–37.
61 TNA: WO 17/143: Monthly Returns for the 34th Foot, 1 October 1794.
62 Richard Cannon, *Historical Record of the Thirty-Fourth* (London: Parker, Furnivall & Parker, 1844), pp.39–40.
63 Howard, *Death Before Glory!*, pp.103–104.
64 TNA: WO 17/143: Monthly Returns for the 34th Foot, 1 January 1797.
65 Ball, *Neither Up nor Down*, p.239

of 1794–1795 and the retreat to Bremen in the midst of snowstorms. Their time on the continent came to an end in April 1795.[66] Having taken on fresh recruits and shaken the snow from their red coats, the 798 men of the 55th were then ordered to embark again, in October 1795, to join Abercromby in the Caribbean.[67] Their task was to reduce St Lucia, for the third time during the war. After the success of the landings, the 55th were left under the command of Brigadier John Moore, fighting against the twin foes of freed slaves and yellow fever.[68] They came back to Chatham Barracks on 19 July 1797, with 196 rank and file on their strength.[69]

Finally, the 65th, who, like the 9th, had fought under Grey as a complete regiment, experienced the most dramatic demise of all. Following Grey's capture of Martinique, the 65th's centre companies remained part of the garrison, whilst the flank companies continued fighting with the rest of Grey's men.[70] This was until the summer of 1794, when following the highs of the spring, British fortunes in the West Indies were steadily slipping to their nadir. Yellow fever ripped through the Lesser Antilles and French forces were given fresh impetus by the arrival of the tough Jacobin, and civil commissioner, Victor Hughes at Guadeloupe.[71] Hughes had quickly augmented the soldiers he had brought from France with locally raised men whom he freed from slavery and rapidly set about retaking Guadeloupe's two islands, Grande and Basse Terres.[72]

The eastern island, Grande Terre, was reoccupied first, its sickly garrisons overrun by the resurgent Republicans. Grey rushed to Guadeloupe, shoring up its defences and placing the 65th at a fortified encampment at Berville, which overlooked the narrow strait between the Basse and Grande Terre. Malaria played havoc with the British forces, rapidly reducing the men at Grey's disposal. Then on the night of 26 September 1794, *général de brigade* Mathieu Pélardy slipped past the Royal Navy's blockade and landed on Basse Terre.[73] By the time the French arrived, the garrison of Berville was in a sorry state. It included elements from the 35th, 39th, 43rd and 65th Foot, and the remnants of some of the elite flank battalions, including the 34th and 55th's flank companies. This garrison should have fielded over 2,000 men, but 330 had died in August, 1,400 were sick, and just 400 men were fit enough to hold the camp.[74]

The French attacked on the morning of 30 September and were driven off five times during the day.[75] Despite this gallant defence, the disparity in numbers, poor supplies

66 George Noakes, *A Historical Account of the Services of the 34th and 55th Regiments* (Carlisle: C. Thurnam and Sons, 1875), pp.38-39.
67 Noakes, *A Historical Account*, p.42.
68 Douglas Sutherland, *Tried and Valiant: The History of the Border Regiment* (London: Leo Cooper, 1972), p.58.
69 TNA: WO 17/170: Monthly Returns for the 55th Foot, 19 July 1797.
70 E.C. Broughton, *Memoirs of the 65th Regiment* (London: William Clowes & Sons Limited, 1914), p.6.
71 Brown, *By Fire and Bayonet*, p.141.
72 Howard, *Death Before Glory!*, p.59.
73 Brown, *By Fire and Bayonet*, p.161.
74 Brown, *By Fire and Bayonet*, p.161 and p.163.
75 Fortescue, *A History of the British Army*, vol.4, p.381.

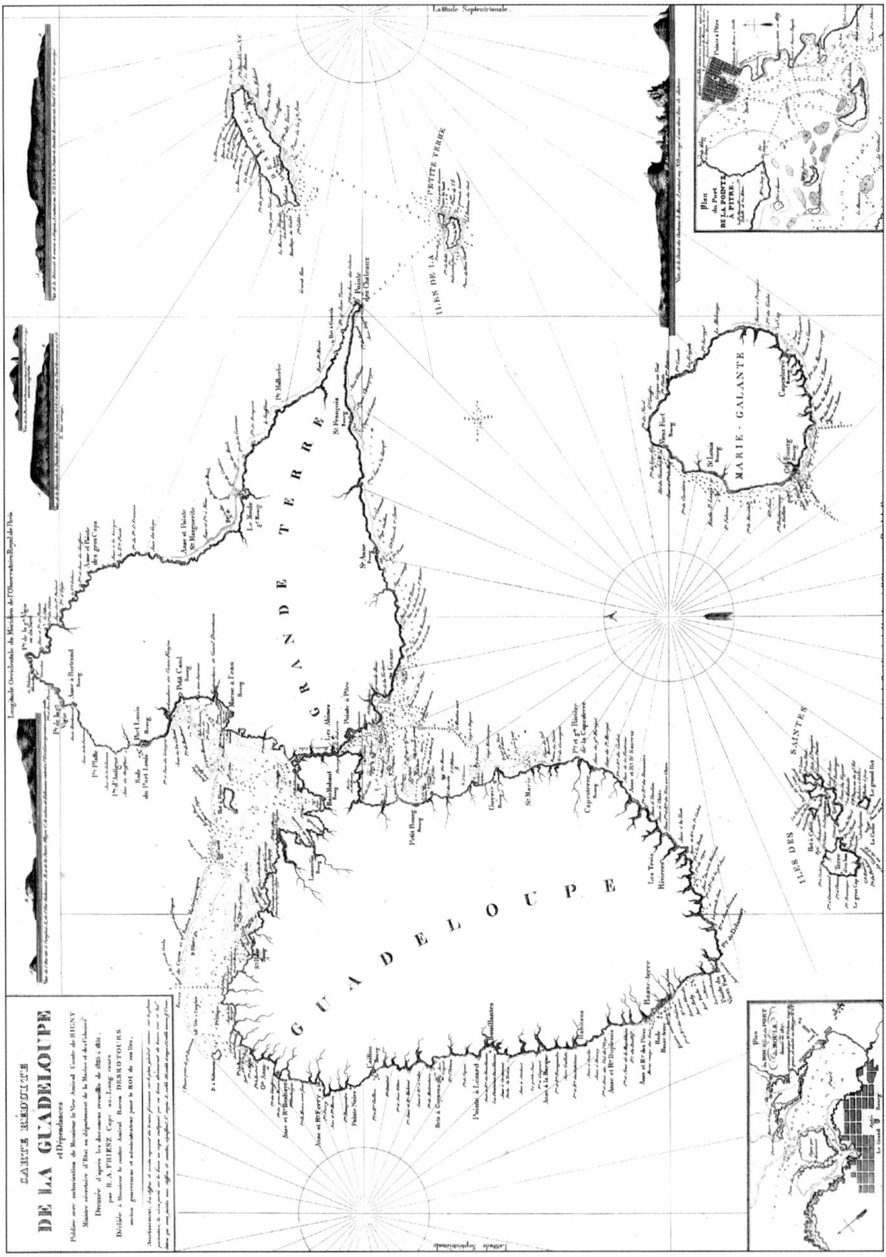


1831 Map of Guadeloupe. (David Rumsey Historical Map Collection)

and a garrison stricken with sickness eventually forced the soldiers of Berville to capitulate on 6 October. Over 1,000 sickly men marched into French captivity, where many of them later died. The terms agreed between the British and the French promised that all British troops would be given their parole and allowed to return home if they consented not to serve against France. Despite the agreed terms, Hughes reneged on the articles of capitulation and the remains of the 65th and the flank companies of the 34th and 55th were left to rot in Guadeloupe. The devastated 65th could barely muster 10 rank and file when the remnants were assembled at Winchester Barracks in September 1795.[76]

**Table 4: Rank and File Strength on Return to Great Britain**

| | Present | Sick | Recruiting/On Command | On Furlow | Total |
|---|---|---|---|---|---|
| 9th Foot[77] | 74 | 0 | 7 | 0 | 81 |
| 16th Foot[78] | 18 | 2 | 17 | 4 | 41 |
| 22nd Foot[79] | 28 | 8 | 25 | 0 | 61 |
| 34th Foot[80] | 5 | 0 | 55 | 0 | 60 |
| 55th Foot[81] | 0 | 37 | 11 | 148 | 196 |
| 65th Foot[82] | 5 | 0 | 5 | 0 | 10 |

The years spent in the Caribbean had a devastating impact on the six line regiments; between them these battalions – at a conservative estimate – had lost over 2,700 men. Although the final figure must be much higher, as this total does not account for the numerous drafts from recruiting parties in Britain, who were ferried out to the Caribbean to keep the regiments up to strength. Even if 2,700 is the low end of the scale, this would still account for nearly 6 percent of the entire losses the British suffered in the Caribbean between 1793–1801, based on the calculations conducted by the historian Michael Duffy, who estimated that 45,250 European soldiers died in this period.[83] The remaining skeletal battalions had to be rebuilt in Britain, and in this painful process lay the germ of a novel approach to recruitment.

76 TNA: WO 17/185: Monthly Returns for the 65th Foot, 1 September 1795.
77 TNA: WO 17/109: Monthly Returns for the 9th Foot, 1 October 1796.
78 TNA: WO 17/118: Monthly Returns for the 16th Foot, 1 November 1796.
79 TNA: WO 17/124: Monthly Returns for the 22nd Foot, 1 November 1796.
80 TNA: WO 17/143: Monthly Returns for the 34th Foot, 23 October 1796.
81 TNA: WO 17/170: Monthly Returns for the 55th Foot, 19 July 1797.
82 TNA: WO 17/185: Monthly Returns for the 65th Foot, 1 September 1795.
83 Buckley, *The British Army in the West Indies*, p.276.

# 2

# Between Scylla and Charybdis

By 1797 the pressure to maintain the British Army's numerous garrisons across the globe, whilst fighting a world war with Revolutionary France, placed a severe strain on the army's resources. For Europe's nations locked into the War of the First Coalition, manpower remained problematic, encouraging the exploration of radical solutions by Britain's contemporaries. In 1793 Revolutionary France's War Minister, Lazare Carnot, instituted the *levée en masse*, the mass mobilisation of France's entire male population, which resulted in the conscription of hundreds of thousands of young men into the French Army.[1] The prospect of mass conscription was anathema to the British government and public, leaving the United Kingdom's army – unlike France's – stretched to the limit to find the recruits necessary to defend the home front and the empire, whilst remaining on standby to provide an expeditionary force to either seize French colonies, or land on the continent to reinforce their Coalition partners.

With so much at stake in the war with France and the dispiriting condition in which many battalions returned from active service, the army was left with a vital question. How could the army replenish the ranks of depleted regiments such as the six battalions freshly arrived from the West Indies, whose stark losses are reproduced in Table 4.

## Filling the Ranks

Initially, the Commander in Chief's office lowered the requirement to complete a battalion from 1,050 to the peacetime establishment of 600 men, which had been the standard prior to the war in 1793.[2] Lowering the establishment only went some of the way to assuaging the manpower shortage, by simply moving the goalposts a little closer, failing to ease the task of recruiting the necessary manpower. Additionally, finding recruits was handicapped by a plethora of underlying issues inherent in British recruitment practices, ranging from competition between regiments to rampant corruption.

1 Mikaberidze, *The Napoleonic Wars*, p.50.
2 J.R. Western, 'The Recruitment of the Land Forces in Great Britain, 1793–99' (PhD Thesis, University of Edinburgh, 1953), p.42.

A depiction of a recruiting party enlisting men in 1797. A common sight at local markets and sporting events. (Anne S.K. Brown Collection)

Recruitment in the 1790s was not for the faint of heart and could be a hair-raising experience for recruiting parties. During this decade, competition for men was high; in addition to the decimated battalions mentioned above, the army had to find a steady supply of men for the remainder of the infantry, cavalry and artillery. Men were also needed to maintain the regiments of militia, the volunteer army and the fencible regiments who were formed for the defence of the United Kingdom, and drew men from the same recruiting pool as regular regiments.[3] On top of the needs of the army, the Royal Navy also required a steady supply of men to maintain the blockade against France and keep Britain's commercial routes open.

In the British Army, finding willing enlistees was undertaken through recruiting parties. These small bands of soldiers were given beating orders by their parent regiment to enlist recruits. Each party was usually led by one or two serjeants, accompanied by several private soldiers, and either a drummer or fifer. This detachment came under the supervision of an officer, although the day-to-day enlistment of recruits was usually undertaken by the non-commissioned officers (NCOs).[4] The 'beating orders', issued to recruiting parties, authorised them to raise the men they required, 'By Beat of Drum or otherwise'.[5] Keen to gather the largest crowds, recruiting parties tended to gravitate towards a principal local gathering space, market, or local sporting event, including races. Once established in a prominent location, the party attempted to draw in prospective young men by playing the regimental repertoire of drumming rhythms and marches, whilst clad in their best uniforms and garlanded with ribbons. This showmanship was accompanied by calls for 'gentlemen soldiers' to volunteer or,[6] as one poster for the 81st Regiment of Foot declared in 1793, they sought 'Those Loyal Heroes, who, ambitious of gaining Glory in the Honourable Profession of Arms'.[7] These displays of martial music and robust calls on the masculinity of young men to come forward and serve proved to be sound inducements for many during the French Revolutionary War.

The British Army has always maintained a strong regimental tradition; each regiment proudly boasts of its history, mottos, nicknames, and marches, representing an inseparable limb of the regimental organism. These regimental identities collectively produced the ecosystem that symbolised the British Army of the late eighteenth century.[8] Whilst this led to a strong *esprit de corps* in individual battalions, regimental identities tended to lend themselves to Charles Darwin's concept of 'survival of the fittest'. As in the wilderness of nature, each regiment needed to ensure its survival by securing its own recruits.

3 Linda Colley, 'The Reach of the State, the Appeal of the Nation: Mass arming and political culture in the Napoleonic Wars', in Lawrence Stone (ed.), *An Imperial State at War: Britain from 1689 to 1815* (London: Routledge, 1994), pp.168–169. The name 'fencibles' derives from defensible.

4 Philip Haythornthwaite, *Redcoats: The British Soldiers of the Napoleonic Wars* (Barnsley: Pen & Sword Military, 2012), pp.16–17.

5 Richard Holmes, *Redcoat: The British Soldier in the Age of Horse and Musket* (London: HarperCollins, 2001), p.139.

6 John Shipp, *The Extraordinary Military Career of John Shipp: The Experiences of a soldier in the Kaffir, Mahratta, Ghurka and Pindari Wars of the Early Nineteenth Century* (Driffield: Leonaur, 2010), p.11.

7 Haythornthwaite, *Redcoats*, p.19.

8 Haythornthwaite, *Redcoats*, p.7.

This resulted in intense competition, especially during 1793–1796 and the early years of the war against France. Across the country, recruiting parties competed for the strongest and ablest men for their regiments. Without a centralised body to administer recruitment and encourage cooperation, individual recruiting parties often resorted to almost any tactic to find the requisite quota of men.

Some of the more underhand practices resorted to by recruiters included slandering their rivals, or spreading rumours that recruits were about to be shipped out to dangerous postings in either the West Indies or India. These stations had a reputation for sickness, and many men chose to desert if they knew the regiment was bound for one of these destinations. These fears were used by rival recruiting parties to encourage men to join their regiment instead. Captain McLean of the 60th (Royal American) Regiment of Foot, encountered an example of these confidence tricks whilst leading his own recruiting party in Colchester in 1794. A man claiming to be a serjeant in the militia tempted the recruits McLean had just enlisted in the 60th to 'desert, by informing them, that they are certainly to be turned over to the East India Company's Service'.[9] Once the supposed militia 'serjeant' had duped and ensnared the 60th recruits, he sent them to a crimp – a term used to describe agents who used unscrupulously means to find men for either the army or the navy. Once he had received the men, the crimp 'sold' them to various regiments from his base which in this case was located in London.[10] The Office of Commander in Chief at Horse Guards attempted to mitigate against the antics of crimps and charlatan serjeants by requiring recruiting parties to prove they were attached to the regiment they were recruiting for when they entered a civil parish.[11]

In 1782, in an effort to control competition, each regiment was issued a county designation in addition to their original number in the line. For instance, the 9th Foot was assigned East Norfolk, becoming the 9th (East Norfolk) Regiment of Foot. This designation was aimed at encouraging regiments to recruit from their assigned county. Despite the designations, recruiting parties continued to flout this rule until 1796 when instructions were issued requiring regiments to operate within their county. While these initiatives mitigated the chances of conflict amongst recruiting parties in the countryside, it did little to stem the competition in the industrial cities of England and Wales, namely London, Manchester, and Swansea, which were still considered fair game as were the entirety of Scotland and Ireland.[12] In an attempt to bring some order to recruitment, the Duke of York created 24 recruiting districts across Britain and Ireland.[13] Established in 1795, the districts were overseen by an inspecting field officer who was charged with maintaining discipline amongst the regiments with beating orders in their jurisdiction. To maintain discipline, the inspecting field officers were able to convene courts martial to deal with unscrupulous recruiting practices. Although the districts did

9 TNA: WO 1/1068, War Office In-Letters, b. Series II correspondence. B, 22 July 1794, p.35.
10 TNA: WO 1/1068, War Office In-Letters, b. Series II correspondence. B, 22 July 1794, p.35.
11 TNA: WO 1/1083, War Office In-Letters, b. Series II correspondence. B, 1795, p.69.
12 Western, 'The Recruitment of the Land Forces in Great Britain', p.49.
13 Derek Winterbottom, *The Grand Old Duke of York: The Life of Prince Frederick, Duke of York and Albany 1763–1827* (Barnsley: Pen & Sword Military, 2016), p.79.

not solve the problems inherent in recruitment practices, they were an important first step towards a centralised system of recruitment for Britain.[14]

These attempts to stifle competition and bring some order to recruitment by restraining regiments to their native counties, was still far from perfect. The recruiting system was made even harder by the indifference and, at times, open hostility of the public. Never keen on recruiting parties taking away their young men for a life with the colours and the prospect of maiming or death in some foreign field, civilians could devastate a recruiting party's hard work. For instance, some regiments avoided towns like Banbury in Oxfordshire due to an infamous occasion when a regiment 'lost fifty men in two, or three days ... from the persuasion of the inhabitants.'[15] Even with open conflict against France, the populace's hostility to recruiters and soldiers could swiftly turn violent. In May 1795, for example, a recruiting party consisting of a serjeant and some privates were set upon at a local racing day near Bath. The men were 'almost beat to death' by the crowd, barely escaping from the hostile mob.[16] Occasionally, scuffles with civilians ended in tragedy, as experienced again in 1795, by two troopers of the 12th (Prince of Wales' Own) Light Dragoons, who were assaulted by a mob in Holborn. The two dragoons were attempting to bring a deserter back to barracks when a crowd formed, drawn by the shouts of the deserter who claimed he was being kidnapped and impressed into service. Tempers flared, and a brawl ensued, and amid the scuffle one of the troopers drew his sabre in defence and cut off the nose of a civilian. Sadly, one of the dragoons was so badly beaten that he later succumbed to his injuries.[17]

Public animosity was made worse by resentment of the army's dual role, as both armed force abroad and law enforcement at home.[18] Acting as keepers of the peace often led to disastrous encounters between soldiers and the public. The infamous Gordon Riots of 1780 were one such incident. Enflamed by the politician Lord George Gordon, who wished to see the repeal of the 1778 Catholic Relief Act toward Catholics, Londoners rioted and attacked the private chapels of ambassadors from Catholic nations. This was followed by attacks on the property of politicians who had supported the Catholic Relief Act and eventually to general looting in the metropolis.[19] Several regiments from London's garrison including the Guards and militia battalions from outside of the capital were deployed to conduct arrests and restore order.[20] During the pacification of the city over 300 rioters were killed.[21] Events like the Gordon Riots, and the army's role in supporting the civil power during protests and anti-smuggling patrols, produced a tense relationship between the army and public. This fraught atmosphere made the task of recruiting not only frustrating but dangerous, slowing the process of rebuilding the skeletal regiments to a crawl.

14 Western, 'The Recruitment of the Land Forces in Great Britain', p.130.
15 TNA: WO 1/1079, War Office In-Letters, b. Series II correspondence. S–T, 28 September 1794, p.233.
16 TNA: WO 1/1083: War Office In-Letters, b. Series II correspondence. B, 05 May 1795, p.55.
17 Haythornthwaite, *Redcoats*, pp.15–16.
18 Stanley H. Palmer, 'The Military, the Law, and Public Order in England, 1650-1850', *Journal of the Society for Army Historical Research*, 56:228 (Winter 1978), p.201.
19 Peter Ackroyd, *London: The Biography* (London: Vintage, 2001), pp.484–485.
20 Christopher Hibbert, *King Mob: The Story of Lord George Gordon and the London Riots of 1780* (Cleveland: The World Publishing Company, 1958), p.138.
21 Holmes, *Redcoat*, p.72.

## Charting the Turbulent Waters

Amidst this sea of troubles, how did the recruiting parties of the depleted regiments fare as they tried to fill their ranks? On their return from Saint-Domingue in late October-November 1796, the 22nd were posted to Colchester Barracks, Essex. From here they dispatched recruiting parties to their designated county, Cheshire, establishing beating orders in Chester, Congleton, Knutsford, Northwich and Macclesfield, with a single party based in Ireland.[22] The 22nd were unusual in this respect as many regiments were unable to exclusively recruit in their home county. Additionally, some regiments had not received a county designation, and even those that did sent recruiting parties to other parts of the country, often near the barracks or town they were garrisoned in. Despite the regiment's best attempts, the recruitment effort proved futile when a year later, on 1 December 1797, the 22nd had only added one extra soldier to the muster rolls, rising from 61 rank and file to 62.[23]

**Table 5: Rank and File Returns After a Year of Recruitment**

| | Present | Sick | Recruiting/On Command | On Furlow | Total |
|---|---|---|---|---|---|
| 9th Foot[24] | 69 | 14 | 19 | 7 | 109 |
| 16th Foot[25] | 35 | N/A | 27 | N/A | 35 |
| 22nd Foot[26] | 55 | 2 | 3 | 2 | 62 |
| 34th Foot[27] | 91 | 15 | 7 | 1 | 114 |
| 55th Foot[28] | 330 | 57 | 3 | 1 | 391 |
| 65th Foot[29] | 36 | N/A | 22 | N/A | 58 |

This pattern was repeated across the regiments listed in Table 5. For the 9th, 34th and 65th in the year following their return from the West Indies, they managed to raise just half a company of men in each regiment.[30] While these units struggled, one outlier was the 55th, which easily doubled their ranks after they received a draft of 109 men

22 TNA: WO 17/124: Monthly Returns for the 22nd Foot 1766–1812, 1 December 1796.
23 TNA: WO 17/124: Monthly Returns for the 22nd Foot 1766–1812, 1 November 1796 and 1 November 1797.
24 TNA: WO 17/109: Monthly Returns for the 9th Foot 1759–1802, 1 October 1797.
25 The Monthly Returns for the 16th are missing between 1 March 1797 and 13 May 1799, so the Muster Rolls have been used instead. TNA: WO 12/3321: General Muster Books and Pay Lists, 16th Foot 1st Battalion 1787–1797, 26 April 1798.
26 TNA: WO 17/124: Monthly Returns for the 22nd Foot 1766–1812, 1 December 1797.
27 TNA: WO 17/143: Monthly Returns for the 34th Foot 1759–1799, 1 October 1798.
28 TNA: WO 17/170: Monthly Returns for the 55th Foot 1785–1812, 1 July 1798.
29 TNA: WO 12/7378: General Muster Books ; Pay Lists, 65th Foot 1st Battalion, 1783–1797, 24 December 1796.
30 TNA: WO 17/109: Monthly Returns for the 9th Foot 1759–1802, 1 October 1796 and 1 October 1797; TNA: WO 17/143: Monthly Returns for the 34th Foot 1759–1799, 23 October 1796 and 1 October 1797; TNA: WO 17/185: Monthly Returns for the 65th Foot 1763–1812, 1 October 1795 and 1 October 1796.

from the 46th (South Devonshire) Regiment of Foot.[31] Despite this one success, all six of these regiments could barely be considered anywhere near full strength, let alone deployable on campaign. The lack of growth was unsustainable, particularly given the continued threat from across the Channel, as by 1797 Napoleon's sweeping victories in northern Italy had crushed the armies of Habsburg Austria and contributed to the collapse of the First Coalition. When France and Austria eventually signed the Peace of Campo Formio on 17 October, Britain's last major continental ally was removed from the war.[32] Historically, Britain had relied upon its continental allies to provide most of the manpower for campaigns in Europe. As her alliances faltered, Britain's struggle for manpower was of paramount concern to the Commander in Chief of the British Army. Amidst this bleak period, the Duke of York formulated a radical solution to tackle the low manpower crisis: the enlistment of boys to fill the ranks.

## Plans for the Experimental Regiments

The Commander in Chief's plan for overcoming, 'the difficulty of obtaining Recruits of a proper Description, for the regular Regiments', was laid out in a letter composed by York's adjutant general, Sir William Fawcett on 2 December 1797.[33] York and Fawcett's plan proposed the enlistment of boys who should be, 'Healthy Lads under Sixteen years of age, who are likely to grow, [and] may be taken as low as five Feet one Inch [154cm].'[34] With particular care to avoid any recruits who were, 'not perfectly straight, open chested and what is commonly called, long in the Fork, nor any who are small limbed'.[35] This deviated from the established enlistment regulations, which stipulated that soldiers should be at least 18 and 5ft 4in (162cm) tall.[36] York's plan involved the conversion of six of the British Army's line regiments into what would today be considered 'child soldier battalions'.

To apply the United Nations current definition, as agreed in the Paris principles of 2007, a child soldier is, 'any person below 18 years of age who is or who has been recruited or used by an armed force … in any capacity, including but not limited to children, boys, and girls used as fighters'.[37] To outfit six of the line regiments in their entirety as child soldiers was at the time highly unusual for the British Army. There had

31 Sutherland, *Tried and Valiant*, p.59.
32 Mikaberidze, *The Napoleonic Wars*, p.54.
33 TNA: WO 3/17, General letters: (series 1-1767-1800), 1797 Jan.–1798 Feb., 2 December 1797, p.321.
34 TNA: WO 3/17, General letters: (series 1-1767-1800), 1797 Jan.–1798 Feb., 2 December 1797, p.325.
35 TNA: WO 3/17, General letters: (series 1-1767-1800), 1797 Jan.–1798 Feb., 2 December 1797, p.325.
36 Kevin Barry Linch, 'The Recruitment of the British Army 1807–1815' (PhD thesis, The University of Leeds, 2001), p.162.
37 Children and Armed Conflict, 'The Paris Principles', *United Nations*, <https://childrenandarmedconflict.un.org/publications/ParisPrinciples_EN.pdf>, February 2007, accessed 15 January 2024.

As George III reviews two cavalry regiments, the Duke of York sits behind his father with his hat removed, whilst Fawcett can be seen standing in the foreground. (Anne S.K. Brown Collection)

been ad hoc recruitment of adolescents, both in the army and the Royal Navy, but these lads were predominantly sons of NCOs or other ranks in the military, either following in their father's trade or enlisting because of their parents' death on campaign. These were individual cases, not the state-sponsored mass enrolment of boys to form the regimental rank and file.

The rationale behind York's and Fawcett's advocacy for this plan is more complicated than the reasons many modern non-state actors impress underage recruits. For many non-state actors, including the Katangese in the Congo during the 1960s, the West Side Boys of Sierra Leone during the 1990s and the continued recruitment of child soldiers in Taliban controlled Afghanistan, the motivations are simple: child soldiers are cheap, easy to train and can be turned into highly motivated combatants.[38] Modern weaponry has facilitated this trend as rifles are lighter and easier to handle, enabling non-state actors to liberally issue assault rifles, including the infamous Kalashnikov, to adolescents

38 Herfried Münkler, *The New Wars* (Cambridge: Polity Press, 2005), p.18; Jo Becker, 'This is our opportunity to end the Taliban's use of child soldiers', *Human Rights Watch*, <https://www.hrw.org/news/2021/09/20/our-opportunity-end-talibans-use-child-soldiers>, 20 September 2021, accessed 15 January 2024.

and send them into combat.[39] For example, an AK-1953 held by the Royal Armouries collection is 34inches (878mm) long overall with a weight of 8lbs (3kg).[40] While this would be easier to handle for a boy of at least 5ft 1in, as York had stipulated, the same could not be said of the weaponry available in the 1790s. At the time, there were two muskets in circulation in the British Army: the Short Land Pattern Musket, which ceased manufacturing in 1797 and the India Pattern Musket, which was adopted that same year.[41] The Short Land Pattern came in at 58.5inches (1500mm) in length and weighed 10lbs 8oz (4.7kg), whereas the India Pattern was slightly smaller, measuring 55.25inches (1403mm), and weighing around 9lbs 11oz (4.4kg).[42] Both weapons were significantly longer and heavier than a modern firearm, hindering any rapid deployment of what were sometimes referred to as the 'experimental battalions', as the boys needed to become accustomed to army drill with a cumbersome firearm. These eighteenth-century weapons hindered a youthful user, rather than the relative ease with which modern child soldiers can be deployed into combat.

From the plans laid out by York and Fawcett, there is an appreciation of this problem, and unlike a modern warlord, these two eighteenth-century generals seem to have considered the recruitment of boys as an investment and not an immediate draft to fill the ranks. For example, York clearly directs that when the 'lads', 'in the course of two or three years … attain sufficient Size, and Strength to fulfil the duties of soldiers', the boys could then be deployed on active operations.[43] Additionally, York's caveat that the prospective recruits should be taller than 5ft 1in (1.54m) further supports that this initiative was not just a rush to feed drafted recruits onto the battlefield, but a long-term strategy. By placing height restrictions, York was looking for the best and healthiest youths and not just any boy under the age of 16.

Some idea of the Duke of York's reasoning for these battalions can be inferred from his own character and interests outside of Horse Guards. In addition to serving as Commander in Chief of the British Army, York was a committed philanthropist. Both York and his wife, Princess Frederica Charlotte of Prussia, were patrons of several charities for military families and other benevolent causes. An especially interesting case was York's patronage of the Philanthropic Society of St George's Fields, London, which supported youth offenders and the children of convicted criminals by providing them with an education in a trade.[44] This interest in philanthropy seems to be part of the Duke's reasoning behind raising these regiments. The boy battalions were intended not only to rebuild the shattered battalions of the British Army, but also to create a career path for young men to learn the trade of soldiering, almost like a military apprenticeship. This hypothesis is further borne out by Fawcett's instructions to the regiments

39 Münkler, *The New Wars,* p.18.
40 The AK-1953 is one variant of a family of assault rifles often inaccurately referred to as AK-47s. Royal Armouries, 'Centrefire Automatic Rifle – Kalashnikov AK-1953', *Royal Armouries*, <https://royalarmouries.org/collection/object/object-275679>, accessed 20 January 2024.
41 C.E. Franklin, *British Napoleonic Uniforms* (Stroud: Spellmount, 2010), pp.140–142.
42 Franklin, *British Napoleonic Uniforms*, pp.140–142.
43 TNA: WO 3/17: General letters, 2 December 1797, p.321.
44 Winterbottom, *The Grand Old Duke of York*, p.81.

recruiting boys, 'His Royal Highness [York] recommends in general terms the utmost Mildness, & Lenity [sic] as the best Modes of establishing Discipline, and attaching the Lads you may enlist, to His Majesty's Service'.[45]

The Duke of York and Albany, the architect behind the plan for recruiting boy soldiers in the British Army. (Anne S.K. Brown Collection)

45 TNA: WO 3/17: General letters, 2 December 1797, p.324.

Additionally, the Duke proposed that a regimental school should be established in each of these units. These schools would be 'for the instruction of such of them [the boys], as discover abilities, in the necessary Qualifications of reading and writing, with a view of their becoming hereafter useful and valuable non commiss.[sic, non-commissioned] Officers'.[46] In the 22nd Foot, the commanding officer, Lieutenant Colonel John Gustavus Crosbie, anticipated these instructions and established a regimental school, on 30 October 1797, through an order in which he 'wishes to give every soldier of the 22nd (or Cheshire) Regiment an opportunity to learn to Read and Write and has directed that a School shall be established and open to All persons who are desirous to improve themselves.'[47] This school formed part of the tradition of privately founded regimental schools, first implemented by the 1st Regiment of Foot Guards in 1762 and chimed with York's attempts to create educational establishments for the army.[48]

The success of York's initiative is illustrated by a later inspection return taken in 1812, which suggests that a version of the Duke's proposed school still survived in some form over a decade later. On 27 December 1811, York ordered all regiments in the British Army to create a regimental school. At the time, the 22nd were posted on Mauritius, which meant they did not receive the circular letter until 25 July 1812. In the same year, an inspection found that, 'a School has not been effectually established' in the 22nd Foot. However, the inspector Lieutenant Colonel Henry Keating discovered there already was one, 'kept up for the instruction of the Boys on the strength of the Corps, and for the Children (including orphans) of either Sex'.[49] The formation of York's boy battalions forms part of the story of military education and came at a time when experimentation was popular amongst British officers.

Another example of how York's boy battalions connect with wider education initiatives appears in January 1799, when Lieutenant Colonel John Gaspard Le Marchant, famed for his designs for the 1796 heavy and light cavalry sabres and authorship of the cavalry's sabre drill book, approached the Duke of York on the subject of establishing a military college for the army.[50] His plan, which became a forerunner of the Royal Military Academy Sandhurst, consisted of three departments: the First Department for the education of young men destined for the army, the Second for serving officers without military training, and the Third would be a traditional Staff College. In addition to the training for commissioned officers, the Second Department also had a branch called the Legion, intended for the education of NCOs, just like the regimental schools of the experimental battalions. The strictures for entry bear an uncanny resemblance to York's plans for the boy battalions. The boys had to be between the ages of 13 and 15, and their curriculum consisted of reading, writing and arithmetic over the course of three years. The only difference was that the boys enlisted in the Legion had to be

46 TNA: WO 3/17: General letters, 2 December 1797, p.324.
47 Bernard Rigby, *Ever Glorious: The Story of the 22nd (Cheshire) Regiment* (Chester: Cheshire Military Museum, 2010), vol.1, p.115.
48 Howard R. Clarke, *Redcoats in the Classroom* (Warwick: Helion & Company Ltd., 2021), p.30.
49 TNA: WO 27/111: Inspection Returns, To 30 Foot, 1812 2nd Half-Year, 30 September 1812.
50 Denis Le Marchant, *Le Marchant: Wellington's Scientific Cavalry General* (Driffield: Leonaur, 2014), p.50.

the sons of soldiers. Just like York, Le Marchant considered that the time was sufficient for the boys to be, 'a proper age for service; in consequence, a draft of one-third may be made annually into regiments of the line'.[51] Although Le Marchant's proposal for the Legion never became part of his college, York did pursue the idea and helped to found The Royal Military Asylum for Children of Soldiers of the Regular Army, in 1801. This school was opened for the sons of servicemen killed during the war and received its first pupils in 1803.[52] All of these efforts eventually culminated in the establishment of regimental schools across the entirety of the army in 1811, paving the way for future educational opportunities for the rank and file in the years to come.[53] While we cannot be sure if Le Marchant was aware of York's experiment with the boy regiments, his plans certainly chimed with those of the Commander in Chief.

While a modern reader might find the philanthropic ideals, which motivated these officers and in particular York, unusual. From the proposals outlined for the boy battalions by Horse Guards there is a range of strict requirements for enlistment and inducements for the regiments to promote literacy and leniency. These provisions for the experimental battalions fulfilled two roles; on a practical note, the enlistment plan provided a means for the depleted regiments to rebuild their strength and, at the same time, created a valuable training ground for the next generation of soldiers. The concepts outlined by York and Fawcett fitted into contemporary discourse about the future of soldiering, as there was an increasing appreciation of the importance of education to make soldiers more effective on the battlefield. This had been highlighted by General Henry Lloyd, a Welsh soldier of fortune, who had served in many of the armies of the *ancien régime* including France and Russia. Lloyd argued for less draconian discipline and called for simplified drills and manuals to facilitate the training of soldiers.[54] As historian Huw J. Davies has highlighted, Lloyd's work became staple reading material for many British officers following the publication of an updated version of Lloyd's history of the Seven Years War (*The History of the Late War in Germany*), which included his 'Reflections on the General Principles of War' in the early 1780s. The education and recruitment of these boys lay in the realm of the Enlightenment's experiments in encouraging recruits into the army, rather than a rush to enlist youths to fill the ranks.

Education and training were vital to ensure the regiments were ready for active service. However, the boy recruits needed more time to reach this point. This meant that for almost three years, six regiments would be in training, delaying their usefulness in the European theatre of operations. To overcome the additional time required to prepare the boys, York planned to send the boy battalions to the East Indies, as the passage to India could take anywhere between five and eight months, providing much-needed time for the boys to complete their training. York seems to have felt the scheme merited a broader audience and accordingly proposed that other British regiments serving in India should also recruit boys using the same provisions as the boy battalions.

51 Le Marchant, *Le Marchant*, p.56.
52 Winterbottom, *The Grand Old Duke of York*, p.100.
53 Rigby, *Ever Glorious*, p.115.
54 Davies, *The Wandering Army*, pp.100–101.

As the boys enlisted and began their training, York was clear that the officers of the boy battalions should mitigate the harshness of military discipline and treat their charges with a degree of leniency. Whilst the Duke's orders are laudable and demonstrated his appreciation that boy recruits should be treated appropriately to their age, his directive was frequently impeded by the reality of the often-brutal nature of army service. It is also not clear whether York had considered the impact of the climate on the young recruits once they had reached the East Indies. This region was notorious for the prevalence of tropical diseases and could devastate regiments just as effectively as the West Indies. Although York's plans for the boy battalions were not foolproof. Deciding to send the boys to India might have provided time for them to mature, but the trade-off was exposure to a myriad of tropical diseases. However, York had attempted to mitigate many of the problems the boys could face, endeavouring to overcome the zealous disciplinary procedures effected by some officers and NCOs and encouraging a more paternal approach in the hope that they would look upon the boys as their charges and value their contribution to securing the future of the regiment.

The formation of the boy battalions was an important step in the history not only of education in the military but in Great Britain as well. These first battalions of boys paved the way for the establishment of regimental schools across the British Army in 1811, which provided education to both young soldiers and the children of soldiers. The historian Howard R. Clarke noted the 'considerable achievement' of the formation of the regimental schools in 1811, as they were the first publicly funded primary schools for both adults and children in Britain, paving the way for state-funded education to take root across Britain and her army.[55]

55 Clarke, *Redcoats in the Classroom*, p.86.

# 3

# 'To go for a soldier'

The plans organised by York and Fawcett clearly outlined that the boys selected for recruitment needed to be 'Healthy Lads under Sixteen years of age, who are likely to grow'.[1] Despite this focus on fit and healthy youths, a perception has grown up around the boy regiments that they were made up of impoverished boys, who were wards of the parish and stuck in the Poor Law system. For example, the official histories of these regiments state that the lads selected were drawn from the parish system, as a means to relieve the growing cost of poor relief.[2] This perception does not tally with the official orders for enlisting boys as stipulated by York, which focused on the enlistment of boys in general rather than targeting poor or underprivileged minors. Nevertheless, this 'stigma' seems to have arisen from the recollections of one of the boys themselves.

The earliest record of this supposed connection is contained within a footnote in the memoirs of John Shipp. Shipp was both a boy soldier and a ward of the parish of Saxmundham, Suffolk. His colourful memoirs of the 22nd Foot provide an invaluable glimpse into life in the boy regiments. However, some care needs to be taken with their contents as they were written and published in 1829, long after Shipp's initial enlistment in 1797. His perception that the boy regiments were exclusively recruited from parish wards is born from his own experience, rather than official sources, but his account does suggest that York's orders could be turned to the advantage of parish officers keen to alleviate the growing economic privation in the British countryside.

## The Recruiting Pool

Since 1750, the price of food had risen substantially, whilst access to common agricultural land had diminished; this pushed out farmers with small holdings, as the enclosure of the English countryside gathered pace, creating an economic squeeze.[3] This

1 TNA: WO 3/17, General letters: (series 1-1767-1800), 1797 Jan.–1798 Feb., 2 December 1797, p.325.

2 Anderson, *History of the Twenty-Second Cheshire Regiment*, p.105; Henry Manners Chichester and George Burges-Short, *The Records and Badges of Every Regiment and Corps of the British Army* (London: Gale & Polden, Ltd., 1900), pp.349, 472, 710.

3 K.D.M. Snell, *Parish and Belonging: Community, Identity and Welfare in England and Wales 1700–1950* (Cambridge: Cambridge University Press, 2009), p.65.

situation was further exacerbated by Britain's expanding population, which since the middle of the eighteenth century had grown from around 5.9 million to 8.5 million people by 1798 and was still rising.[4] A contemporary of this population growth was the economist and cleric, Thomas Malthus, who observed this increase with dread and infamously warned in the *An Essay on the Principle of Population* published in 1798, that without restraint on the poor, there would be a population explosion. Eventually, in Malthus' view, this would result in famine and mass death to bring the population back under control.[5] In the minds of the middle and upper classes, excessive population growth fed their anxiety of the lower classes, and the possibility of revolution, an ever-present fear following the recent example of the French Revolution and the subsequent Jacobin Terror of 1793–1794.

Another serious concern for Britain's propertied class was youth violence amongst the lower classes. Many parts of the countryside were prone to aggressive outbursts, usually associated with drink and an increasing number of young men with few opportunities for advancement. Some of this violence stemmed in part from the nature of the parish system in England and Wales. Civil Parishes were a fundamental administrative body, dealing with an extensive range of issues from road and bridge repair to pauper settlement, the limits for common land, and poor rates.[6] The parish played a fundamental role in administering key aspects of their residents' lives, which meant that, in many cases, the parish was the entire world for those born within its confines. For instance, in the 1830s, the radical politician and farmer, William Cobbett encountered a 30-year-old woman, for whom, 'the utmost extent of her voyages had been about two and a half miles!'[7]

Localisation was so ingrained that any person from outside of the parish, even if they came from the next village, was regarded and referred to as a 'foreigner', a view that remained prevalent in some areas into the 1940s.[8] Inter-parish relations could almost be described as akin to stepping into a 'foreign' country. These interparish 'Cold Wars' aimed at neighbours who lived just a mile down the road, created an air of hostility and suspicion, which also encompassed any wanderers, including pedlars, knife-grinders and recruiting parties. This othering of outsiders could very quickly turn hostile, as strangers were in danger of being assaulted when passing through a parish and youths often crossed county lines to cause trouble with their neighbours. One example from the district of Rhuthun (Ruthin) in Wales, in the 1780s illustrates the type of violence that marked the relationship between neighbouring villages when, even in the solemn midst of a wake,

> …young men of the surrounding parishes would assemble all their force and visit the wake; and towards the evening, when the liquours had begun to operate upon

4 'Population of England over history', *Our World in Data*, <https://ourworldindata.org/grapher/population-of-england-millennium?time=1748…1798>, accessed 20 August 2023.
5 Ben Wilson, *Decency & Disorder: The Age of Cant 1789–1837* (London: Faber and Faber Limited, 2007), p.18.
6 Snell, *Parish and Belonging*, p.37.
7 Cobbett quoted in Snell, *Parish and Belonging*, pp.34-35.
8 Snell, *Parish and Belonging*, p.28.

> their senses, the men of one parish would be easily provoked to quarrel with those of another, and both would turn out, and the encounter would commence with clubs, sticks and stones, in a most furious manner.[9]

While this example comes from Wales, it remained true for much of England as well.

Prejudices were passed down to young men and boys who routinely attacked not only passersby but also rival youths from neighbouring parishes because they were courting a local girl, and so infringing on their neighbourhood.[10] The role of these gangs of youths in stirring up trouble became an increasing source of concern, particularly amongst the growing Methodist and non-conformist congregations of the middle classes.[11] Local occasions including sporting events like racing and bullbaiting were particularly feared as hotbeds for insurrection, especially when excessive drinking led to fights and rowdiness.[12]

In the minds of the parish administrators, many of these issues coalesced into the spectre identified by Malthus, the growing lower-class population, and the increased number of young people seeking poor relief through the Poor Law. The law stipulated that each parish had a duty to look after any members of the community who were too young, old, or ill to work. Their upkeep was paid for through a tax levied on the property of the wealthier members of the parish.[13] This naturally made the middle and upper classes particularly concerned about the potential for corruption in the Poor Law rates and the distribution of funds to 'undeserving' members of the community. Writing in 1788, Edward Parry a local guardian in Gressenhall in Norfolk summed up the views of some ratepayers who disapproved of 'profligate men who through idleness and debauchery [had] reduced their families to depend on the establishment for their support'.[14] The growing numbers seeking poor relief were seen as a sign of a corrupting influence, which in the mind of ratepayers, robbed the poor of their independence, producing a lackadaisical working class, who it was thought lived off the poor rates and the hard labour of the rest of society. It was also feared that much of the money given to the poor was being spent on drink with the potential to contribute to alcohol fuelled violence in the parish.[15] With more of the working population relying on support through the Poor Law, including growing numbers of young boys, it was feared that parish poor rates were being abused to pay for the debauchery of people seeking poor relief.

In addition to the costs associated with a rising population, growing inflation stoked by the war with France had also pushed up prices in England and Wales, resulting in

9 Snell, *Parish and Belonging*, p.59.
10 Joseph Lawson, *Letters to the Young on Progress in Pudsey during the Last Sixty Years* (Firle: Caliban Books, 1978), p.30
11 Snell, *Parish and Belonging*, p.59
12 Wilson, *Decency & Disorder*, pp.52–53.
13 J.D. Marshall, *The Old Poor Law, 1795–1834* (Basingstoke: Macmillan Publishers Ltd., 1985), p.10.
14 Edward Parry quoted in, Simon Fowler, *The Workhouse: The People, The Places, The Life Behind Doors* (Barnsley: Pen and Sword History, 2014), p.30.
15 Fowler, *The Workhouse*, p.20.

increased expenditure on the poor rate to cover the costs of supporting impoverished families and individuals. By 1797, English and Welsh parishes were caught in a maelstrom of rocketing poor rates, rising from an annual expenditure of £2,000,000 in 1784 to £6,000,000 by the end of the Napoleonic Wars in 1815.[16] The drastic inflation of the poor rates required equally radical solutions, with many parishes resorting to the construction of workhouses, where the poor could be housed and put to work as labourers.[17] The simplest option was to reduce the number of individuals seeking poor relief. Emigration to the United States of America, or one of Britain's colonies, namely what is now Canada, was an option, but the parishes did not have an official role in managing and facilitating the emigration of their poorest and adolescent parishioners until the New Poor Law of 1834.[18] Some of the first government programmes for resettlement abroad only started after the war when ex-soldiers were encouraged to settle in Canada. Without a formal resettlement programme, parishes needed a way to lower the poor rates, and they focused on the adolescent boys seeking poor relief.

Shipp recounts the role of the parish in encouraging enlistment in his memoirs. By his own account, the young Shipp was a prankster and tearaway, who was frequently beaten by his master – a local farmer. To escape this violent and prosaic life, Shipp had tried to run away in c.1793 and claims he attempted to enlist in the Royal Horse Artillery at the tender age of nine. A potential stretch, as the regiment was only formed that year, and so he may be referring to the Royal Artillery. During his spare time, Shipp often played at being a soldier in the farmyard.[19] His desire to take the King's shilling had been noted by the parish officer who approached Shipp in early 1797, 'I have frequently heard of, and observed your great wish to go for a soldier',[20] he is reported to have said. In his hand the parish officer had a paper, possibly the *Ipswich Journal*, which had published an advertisement from the 22nd Foot on 17 December 1796:

> TWENTY-SECOND, or CHESHIRE REGIMENT of FOOT.
> WANTED, A number of Boys, from 12 to 14 years of age, who will answer for Drummers or Music. The Commanding Officer assures their friends that the greatest care and attention will be paid to them. Any person bringing a boy of the above description, to Lieut.-Col. Mercer, commanding the regiment at Colchester Barracks shall receive ONE GUINEA, if approved of.[21]

While this advertisement was placed before the official recruitment of boy soldiers in December 1797, it gives a good idea of how the parishes could view the recruitment of boy soldiers as a means to remove troublesome youths from the poor relief system. In addition to running away, Shipp seems to have constantly aggravated his master; his

16 Marshall, *The Old Poor Law*, p.24.
17 Fowler, *The Workhouse*, pp.22–23.
18 Eric Richards, *Britannia's Children: Emigration from England, Scotland, Wales and Ireland since 1600* (London: Hambledon and London, 2004), p.118.
19 Shipp, *The Extraordinary Military Career*, pp.13–14.
20 Shipp, *The Extraordinary Military Career*, p.20.
21 *Ipswich Journal*, 17 December 1796.

dispatch to the army would thus remove an irritant and an extra mouth to be paid for by the parish. In this rather dispassionate calculation, the departure of poor boys also had less emotional impact on the community, because boys like Shipp, whose mother was dead and his father serving abroad as a Marine, did not have a familial network to protest their enlistment. In contrast to their fellow parishioners, whose families were reluctant to see their sons don the red coat and, as previously mentioned, would protest.

Additionally, many parishes had already been involved in recruiting men for the army during the brief introduction of the Quota Act by Pitt's government in 1796. The act required parishes to enlist a quota of recruits for the army; failure to do so resulted in a fine being issued to the parish. The act was designed to replenish the depleted regiments returning from the Caribbean, but unlike the boy regiments, the quota system did not produce the manpower required.[22] Interestingly, subsequent amendments to the Quota Act authorised the rejection of boys under 18, and 5ft 3in, highlighting that the reason for the act's failure lay in the parish viewing it as an opportunity to offload their superfluous mouths.[23] Further supporting the notion that prior to the official sanction of recruiting boys, the parishes had already attempted to offload their youths onto the army. The 1797 recruitment drive then gave parishes the impetus to encourage youths into the army, through a legitimate channel of recruitment.

While it is difficult to establish how many of these boys were wards of the parish, the discharge papers taken by the Royal Hospital, Chelsea give a clue to the social strata of these young men. Many of them were listed as labourers prior to enlistment, such as Alex Cooper, from Bury St Edmunds, who served in the 34th Foot.[24] Furthermore, the 1806 Statements of Periods of Service, taken for all NCOs and men, sometimes list the former careers of some boys prior to enlistment. This information is, however, sparse because careers were only listed when two soldiers shared the same name. For instance, the survey taken by the 22nd Foot records 13 former labourers, three shoemakers, two weavers, a baker, a wool comber, a brush maker, a nailor and an anchor smith who had enlisted as boys.[25] This incomplete survey gives a glimpse into the lives of some of these young men and does hint that the majority of these youths came from unskilled labouring backgrounds, possibly suggesting that the boys enlisted were already employed and not part of the parish poor relief. A possible exception may be the wool comber, as during the late eighteenth century, brushing out wool was a task undertaken by workhouse inmates. This is a potential clue that some of the boys may have been wards of the parish, like Shipp, who enlisted and may have preferred to give an occupation rather than reveal they were parish wards.

Following the official order in 1797, the 22nd, 34th and 65th Foot managed to recruit a selection of boys mostly from unskilled or working-class backgrounds, but not exclusively from poor houses. The official orders for enlistment from the Commander in

22 Linch, *The British Army*, pp.134–135.
23 Richard Glover, *Peninsular Preparation: The Reform of the British Army 1795–1809* (Cambridge: Cambridge University Press, 1963), pp.215–216.
24 TNA: WO 121: Royal Hospital, Chelsea: Discharge Documents of Pensioners, Piece 45, 1802, p.113.
25 TNA: WO 25/944: 22 Foot, Statements of the Periods of Service, 24 June 1806.

Chief were not concerned with relieving the cost of the poor rates, as Shipp claims, but there was an avenue for the unofficial encouragement of boys to enlist through the machinations of zealous parish officers. The subsequent misconception that the boy regiments were used by the government to cut costs was fed by Shipp's account, as he is the only child soldier to publish a memoir from the boy regiments. Certainly, many youths saw an opportunity to enlist and escape from the pressures of the parish system, but this was not the Commander in Chief's *raison d'être* for these battalions. York's focus remained on rebuilding the shattered regiments returning from the Caribbean. The enrolment of the 'spare mouths' from the parish was a welcome outcome for the parish officers, but it was not an officially sanctioned practice.

## The Results

The results of the boy recruitment drive proved to be particularly dramatic for three of the six regiments chosen to join the programme. In *Sons of the Brave*, A.W. Cockerill goes so far as to claim 6,000 boys enlisted under the auspices of York's programme, citing 4,000 as conservative.[26] The only source Cockerill provides is Shipp, who quotes 1,000 boys in the 22nd alone.[27] Whilst this sounds impressive, a further examination indicates that whilst the recovery was effective, the results were not quite as dramatic as Cockerill envisaged. Charts 3–5 provide the increase in regimental rank and file for the years 1798 and 1799 for the 22nd, 34th and 65th Foot after they had received the order to recruit boys. The charts show effective strengths of the battalions, their sick and the total size of the rank and file, which includes men posted on command or recruiting duties across the country.

By 1800 the 22nd had raised 557 boys to fill the ranks, whilst the 34th raised 681, and the 65th – whose returns are patchy for 1798 – managed to find 522. Within two years these regiments had gone from skeletal to over half strength and, in the case of the 34th, almost a full battalion. Unlike previous recruitment drives, the returns show that these regiments had spread their efforts outside of their counties. For example, the 22nd were based in Colchester Barracks, and whilst their recruiting parties initially returned to Cheshire, by May 1798 they had spread across the country, taking boys from nearby Norwich, as well as London, Manchester, Exeter, Leeds, Edinburgh, and Dumfries, to name just a few.[28] The demographics for the battalion taken during a general review in 1799 reinforce the English focus of their recruitment drive. The review noted that out of the 696 other ranks, 460 were English (this also includes Wales), 25 were Scottish, 203 were Irish, and eight were considered foreigners born outside of Great Britain.[29] With 66 percent of the regiment being English/Welsh, it reveals the primary focus of the boy battalion's recruitment drives was centred around the regions they were stationed

26 A.W. Cockerill, *Sons of the Brave* (London: Leo Cooper, 1984), p.71.
27 Cockerill, *Sons of the Brave*, p.220.
28 TNA: WO 17/124: Monthly Returns for the 22nd Foot 1766–1812, November 1797–December 1799.
29 TNA: WO 27/82: Inspection Returns, Pt. 1 General, 1799, 26 November 1799

in, such as Essex and East Anglia for the 22nd, with offshoots in the cities of Britain. Most of the recruits from Ireland were not part of the 22nd's recruitment efforts, and instead were a draft from the 4th (The King's Own) Regiment of Foot, who sent some of their underage recruits to the 22nd. Sadly, only the 22nd has any details on these demographics, but those that are available suggest that the recruitment efforts for the three battalions were local in character, with the occasional draft from other regiments.

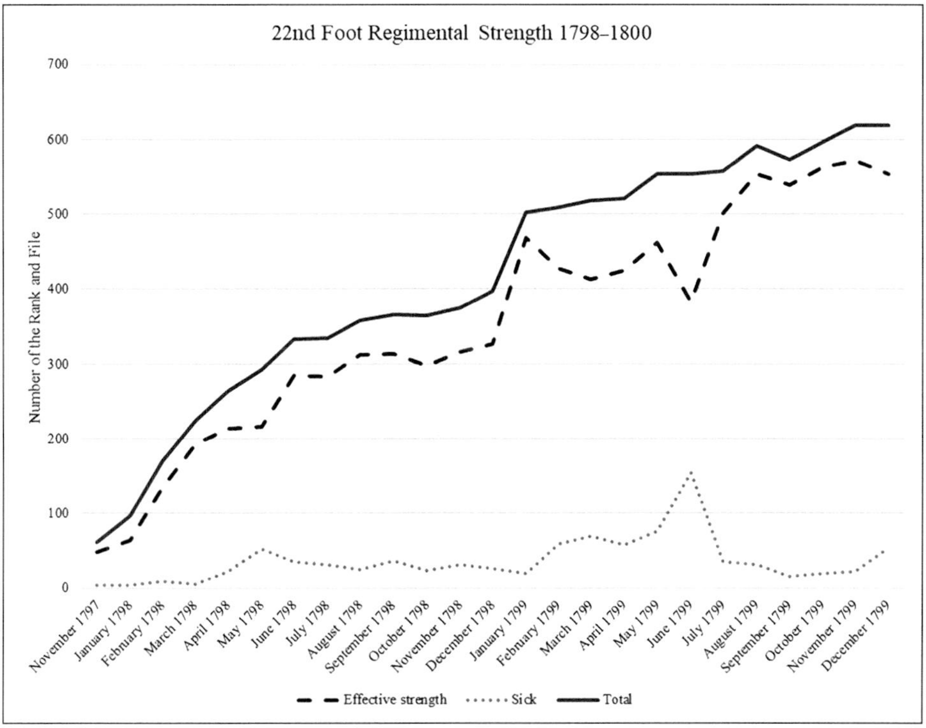


Regimental Strength of the 22nd Foot 1798–1800.[30]

In contrast, the 34th and 65th's monthly returns were remarkably reticent about where their recruiting parties were based, although some evidence can be gleaned from the marching orders in their muster rolls. These indicate that, like the 22nd, these regiments primarily recruited locally in addition to sending parties to their respective counties. For instance, in March 1798, the 65th – then based in Dunbar – sent men in groups of three to Manchester, Barnard Castle, Kendal, Penrith and Sheffield. The 65th's posting on the Scottish Borders and later to Berwick-Upon-Tweed from 1799, meant they also sent recruiting parties into Scotland, as evidenced in a letter from

30 TNA: WO 17/124: Monthly Returns for the 22nd Foot 1766–1812, November 1797–December 1799

Peebles sent by Captain William Stopford to Major William Augustus Bygrave on 29 November 1797, 'I have taken the liberty of sending by private Greenaway a very fine boy that I enlisted in this place, he has an exceeding good character'.[31] This suggests that at least some of the boys raised for this battalion came from Scotland as well as northern England.

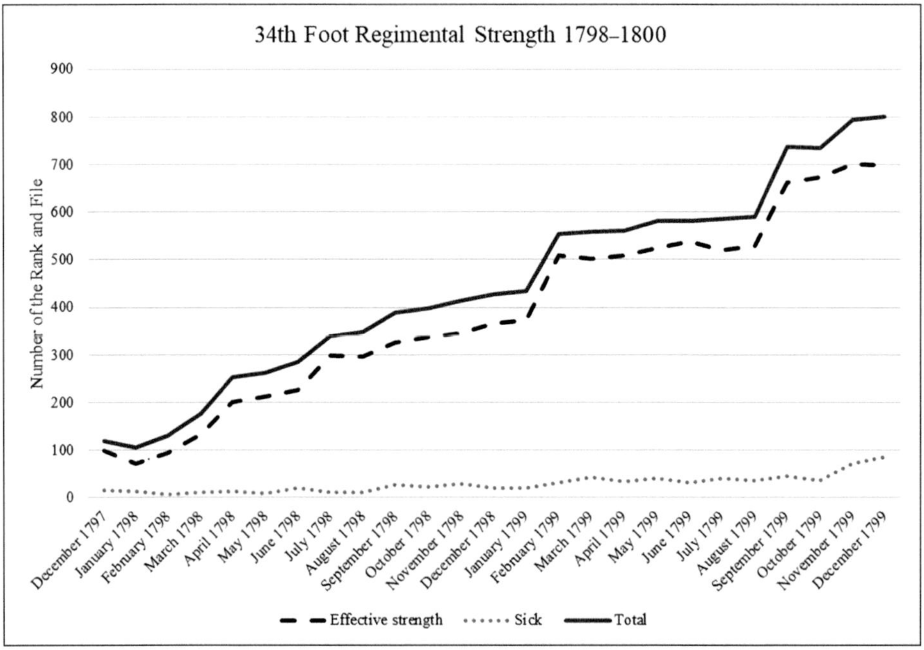


Regimental strength of the 34th Foot 1798–1800.[32]

The 34th were quartered in Lincoln, and like the 22nd and 65th, their recruitment efforts were predominantly based in their local area, with a party recorded as far as Norwich in September 1798.[33] In June of that year, pairs of soldiers were also sent to Hull, Doncaster, King's Lynn and the commanding officer had even trekked as far as Marlborough in Wiltshire in pursuit of a deserter.[34] The recruitment drives produced effective results for these regiments, drawing on the youthful thirst for adventure and lack of concern for mortality. However, this success was not repeated across the board.

31 York & Lancaster Regiment Museum: 578-K/2/5/1: Administrative and financial records of Major William Augustus Bygrave, 29 November 1797.
32 TNA: WO 17/143: Monthly Returns for the 34th Foot, December 1797–December 1799.
33 TNA: WO 17/143: Monthly Returns for the 34th Foot, 1 September 1798.
34 TNA: WO 12/4868: General Muster Books and Pay Lists, 34th Foot, 24 June 1798.

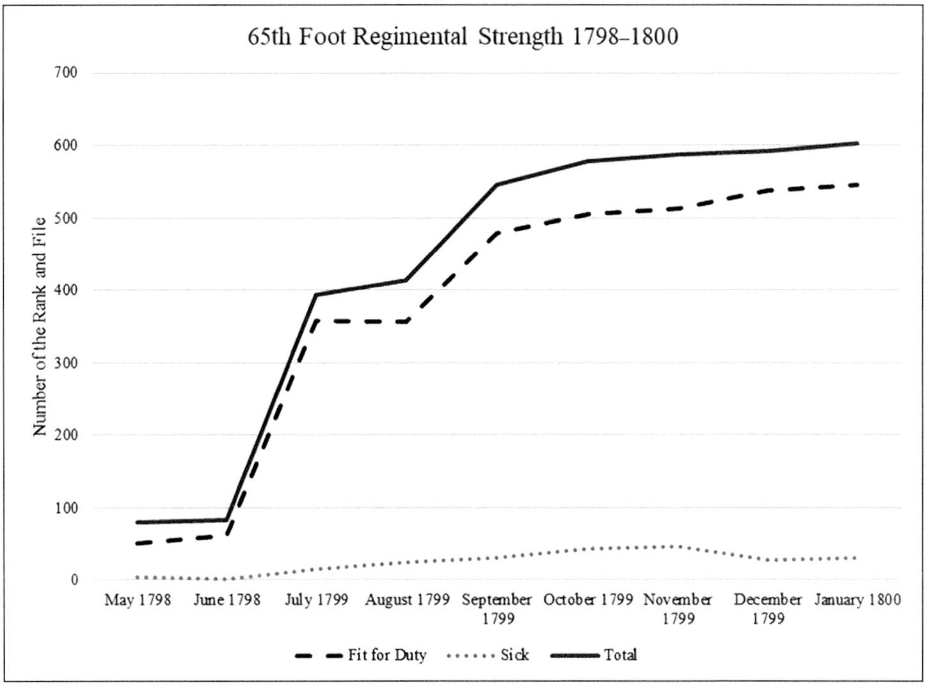


Regimental strength of the 65th Foot 1798–1800.[35]

While these three battalions prospered under the influx of youths, their brothers in the 9th, 16th, and 55th found a different well to tap for recruits. In the early days of the recruitment drive, the 9th were drafting boys out to the 22nd, with 48 sent in January and February 1798, while the 16th sent drafts to the 34th and 65th Foot.[36] Instead of finding boy recruits, these regiments were able to take advantage of the Supplementary Militia, which had been raised in England in 1797 to bolster the militia and provide more men for the defence of Britain. Additional legislation passed in early 1798 allowed men who had been enrolled in the Supplementary Militia, but not joined a regiment, to enlist in a battalion in the British Army. Eleven regiments were permitted to draw on recruits this way, including the 9th and 55th. The 16th was later allowed to recruit from the militia by an order dated 26 July 1799.[37] The 9th were particularly successful in their recruitment efforts from their base in Sudbury, where they managed to raise 152 men from the militias of Norfolk, Suffolk, Essex, and Cambridge in May 1798.[38] Finding a ready supply of able-bodied men keen for active service meant the 9th could dispense

35 TNA: WO 17/185: Monthly Returns for the 65th Foot, May 1798–January 1800.

36 TNA: WO 17/109: Monthly Returns for the 9th Foot, January–February 1798; Chichester and Burges-Short, *The Records and Badges of Every Regiment*, p.304.

37 TNA: WO 3/18: General letters: (series 1-1767-1800), 1798 Feb. – 1798 Sep., 14 April 1798, pp.150–151; TNA: WO 3/20: General letters: (series 1-1767-1800), 1799 July –1799 Nov., p.21.

38 TNA: WO 17/109: Monthly Returns for the 9th Foot, June 1798.

with the need to find boys. Additionally, the 9th was quartered near the 22nd, with only 12 miles (20km) between them. Potentially to forestall competition, the 9th sent their boys to the 22nd and focused on militia recruits instead.

The success that the 9th, 16th, and 55th found during their efforts recruiting from the militia meant that by December 1799 they had mostly dispensed with recruiting boy soldiers. At this time, the 16th boasted an effective strength of 950 private soldiers.[39] Whilst the 9th and the 55th could muster 697 and 442 rank and file, respectively. With men swelling the ranks, these regiments eventually ceased recruiting boys and sent any they had to the other regiments, just as the 16th Foot did when they ceased enlisting boys on 22 August 1799 and then sent their youths to the 34th on 3 October.[40]

This was repeated for several other regiments that briefly received orders to recruit boys, the 4th, 32nd (Cornwall), 45th (1st Nottinghamshire), and the 52nd (Oxfordshire) Regiments of Foot, all at one point received orders to recruit boys between 1798–1799, many of whom were later drafted out. For example, following significant success in raising men from the militia – resulting in the regiment being augmented to three battalions – the 4th sent over 100 boys to the 22nd Foot in December 1798.[41] For the regiments who could draw men from the militia, their ability to quickly raise men meant they could be rapidly deployed into the main conflict with France in Europe. In contrast, the 22nd, 34th, and 65th Foot needed time, both to train their young charges and to allow them to become old enough for active service. Time was on their side as the Commander in Chief had already earmarked them for the East Indies, giving these regiments the opportunity to come up to strength. This was a luxury that would have been hard to justify if all 10 of the proposed line regiments, totalling a potential establishment of 10,500 bayonets, had been kept out of the line to recruit and train boys. This would have been particularly hard to defend given that in 1798–1799, the British Army were preparing to launch an amphibious assault on Holland alongside their Russian allies, whilst faced with Napoleon's invasion of Egypt and a rebellion in Ireland supported by French troops.

39 TNA: WO 12/3322: General Muster Books and Pay Lists, 16th Foot 1st Battalion 1798–1799, 25 December 1799.
40 TNA: WO 3/20: General letters: (series 1-1767-1800), 1799 July – 1799 Nov., p.154 and p.313.
41 TNA: WO 12/3874: General Muster Books and Pay Lists, 22nd Foot 1798, December 1798.

# 4

# Discipline and Pranks

As the ranks of each battalion swelled, the regimental staff set about the laborious task of bringing the boy recruits up to fighting standards. For some of the regiments it was not an easy journey. The British Army at the turn of the nineteenth century was a tough environment. For some of the boy recruits, including Shipp and Roger Burns, who had both enlisted at just 13 years old, they were thrust into a world where violence, corporal punishment, and alcohol were part and parcel of daily life. In the brief references gleaned from the few surviving memoirs, the boys grew from youths to manhood in a strange blend of military discipline and *Tom Brown's School Days*, mixing corporal punishment and youthful hijinks.

## Training

Basic training, as outlined by the historian J.A. Houlding, centred on methodical and regular drilling through each of the motions required by the recruit.[1] Boys were trained to become a 'master of his person', including posture, turning on the spot and the correct pace for marching. York and Fawcett reinforced this stipulation in their orders stating, 'In regard to Drill, it is His Royal Highness' wish, that Arms should not be put into the hands of these Lads, until they have attained some Knowledge of the different modes of Marching, Wheeling, and of the formations which occur in the ordinary Field Exercise'.[2] Most recruits were drilled alone before progressing to group exercises, commencing in files and then gradually growing in numbers as the boys mastered their feet and bearing. By the 1770s, music was mostly used for training, so young fifers such as Shipp spent their time on the parade ground keeping time for their fellow recruits as they progressed through their evolutions.[3]

1 J.A. Houlding, *Fit for Service: The Training of the British Army, 1715–1795* (Oxford: Clarendon Press, 1981), p.257.
2 TNA: WO 3/17: General letters: (series 1-1767-1800), 1797 Jan.–1798 Feb., 2 December 1797, p.323.
3 TNA: WO 3/17: General letters: (series 1-1767-1800), 1797 Jan.–1798 Feb., 2 December 1797, pp.259–261.

Training the boys with standard firelocks, familiarly called a Brown Bess, proved challenging because the standard firelock was too long and unwieldy for boys. York and Fawcett had anticipated this challenge and were aware that the boys' 'strength will not at first be adequate to the management of the Firelock'.[4] They ordered the boy regiments to apply to the Board of Ordnance for 100 fusils as these were much shorter and lighter than the standard musket.[5] The boy battalions were only to retain regulation muskets, 'for the Corporals, and those Private Men whom you [regimental officers] recommend to be kept in the Regiment'.[6] This cadre of NCOs and private soldiers formed the training nucleus for the boys, as they passed on their experience to the recruits. York and Fawcett stipulated these selected men should exhibit 'the utmost Mildness, & Lenity as the best Modes of establishing Discipline, and attaching the Lads you may enlist, to His Majesty's Service'.[7] Despite York's and Fawcett's best efforts, these suggestions struggled to take root in some of the regiments, where the hard realities of life in the army left little room for 'mildness'.

Despite the calls for leniency, barrack room discipline was relentless. Some first offenders might receive a verbal warning administered by an officer. One example of this type of admonishment occurred in late 1798, when the 22nd Foot marched from Colchester to Portsmouth. During their stay at an inn, the boys felt their rations from the innkeeper were inadequate, so they decided to steal a goose and hide it in a regimental drum. On the march the next day, the innkeeper caught up with the column and persuaded Lieutenant Colonel James Mercer to help him search for his missing property. The hunt proved futile, and the boys almost got away with their prize, until the bird expired in the drum and in its death throes let out a terrible wail, to which the landlord exclaimed, 'Dang my buttons, if my goose bean't in that there drum!'[8] Mercer ordered the bird to be returned to the publican and promised the boys involved would be 'severely punished', Shipp recalls anticipating his chastisement and felt 'sure of as many stripes on our backs as there were feathers on the goose's'.[9] Fortunately for them, the innkeeper was just as shocked at the punishment, 'Get a child flogged for a tarnation old goose? no, no!'[10] So he denied it was his goose and on this occasion Shipp and his comrades were let off with a stern admonishment due to their age and what Mercer considered was their first offence. Although Shipp emphasises it was the first misdemeanour that Mercer knew about.

'Stripes' or whipping with the lash frequently crops up in Shipp's memoirs as they were meted out to the boys for various infringements. For example, three boys were beaten for wandering the woods during the nutting season – when autumnal nuts such as hazelnuts were ripe for picking – as the regiment feared the boys may have been taken for deserters. Indeed, Shipp states he was demoted from fife-major back to fifer for the

4 TNA: WO 3/17: General letters: (series 1-1767-1800), 1797 Jan.–1798 Feb., 2 December 1797, pp.259–261.
5 David Gates, *The British Light Infantry Arm c.1790-1815* (London: B.T. Batsford Ltd., 1987), p.91.
6 TNA: WO 3/17: General letters: (series 1-1767-1800), 1797 Jan.–1798 Feb., 2 December 1797, p.323.
7 TNA: WO 3/17: General letters: (series 1-1767-1800), 1797 Jan.–1798 Feb., 2 December 1797, p.323.
8 Shipp, *The Extraordinary Military Career*, p.30.
9 Shipp, *The Extraordinary Military Career*, p.30.
10 Shipp, *The Extraordinary Military Career*, p.31.

same offence.[11] Further punishments included confinement to barracks, or imprisonment in a black hole. This last confinement seems to have only been available in the larger barracks such as Hilsea Barracks, as Shipp only mentions the black hole whilst the regiment were at Portsmouth, in 1798.[12] A particularly humiliating punishment was forcing offenders to drill three times a day, with their jacket reversed, literally marking them as a turncoat. This sentence was awarded to Shipp for the misdemeanour of removing his name from the list of boys confined to barracks. Some of the more vicious punishments in the 22nd Foot appear to have cropped up due to a clash between the boys and many of their NCOs, an issue which steadily came to light during the regiment's posting to Guernsey.

In an inspection of the 22nd Foot conducted by Major General Sir Hew Whitefoord Dalrymple on 31 July 1799, the Major General included a list of 'Old Serjeants' that Lieutenant Colonel John Gustavus Crosbie 'wishes to Discharge & recommend for Chelsea'.[13] Dalrymple comments that these men were singled out due to 'some difficulties to encounter particularly those resulting from bad N.C. Officers, & a regiment of Boys, from which others to replace them [the NCOs] could not be obtained.'[14] Whilst the 22nd Foot's NCOs seemed to have been overly keen to hand out lashings and brutalise their charges, the officers, including Mercer and Crosbie, were equally intent on leniency and putting a stop to their NCOs' excesses. Perhaps these old redcoats felt frustrated that they were required to train boys and so resorted to a heavy-handed approach rather than York's humanitarian principles. Indeed, many of these men had been in the army a long time and might have served through the horrors of Saint-Domingue and perhaps even the American War of Independence. One of the men on Crosbie's list, Serjeant Richard Wood, who was 55 years old, had served since 1769, and certainly would have been old enough for both conflicts. Wood was earmarked for retirement alongside two other serjeants, a corporal and a private soldier, all of whom were aged from 35 to 55 years old and all, with the exception of Private James Taylor, had served over 20 years with the colours.[15]

A subsequent inspection at Portsmouth on 27 November 1799 conducted by Major General John Whitelocke confirms that, 'The Officers are well instructed. Amongst the noncommissioned officers there are some very good but it is evident from the length of service, of many of the Serjeants, and who are at the same time *Old West India Soldiers* that they want the kind of Conduct so essentially necessary in a Regiment of Boys.'[16] Whitelocke, like Dalrymple, recommended more of the old West Indian veterans should be discharged, adding that, 'The Boys themselves make good Corporals but are not sufficiently steady for the higher station[serjeant]',[17] and every effort should be made to find experienced serjeants from other regiments to replace the more brutal veterans.

11 Shipp, *The Extraordinary Military Career*, p.28.
12 Shipp, *The Extraordinary Military Career*, pp.32–33, 37–38.
13 TNA: WO 27/82: Inspection Returns, Pt. 1 General, 1799, 31 July 1799.
14 TNA: WO 27/82: Inspection Returns, Pt. 1 General, 1799, 31 July 1799.
15 TNA: WO 27/82: Inspection Returns, Pt. 1 General, 1799, 31 July 1799.
16 TNA: WO 27/82: Inspection Returns, Pt. 1 General, 1799, 27 November 1799.
17 TNA: WO 27/82: Inspection Returns, Pt. 1 General, 1799, 27 November 1799.

Whitelocke particularly lamented that the 'severity of Punishment has been in some instances resorted to, though not beyond the Rules of the Service in Regiments formed of Men.'[18] Far from being a host of ramrod disciplinarians, Crosbie, Dalrymple, and Whitelocke were concerned about the welfare of the boy soldiers. Working within the army's procedures, they attempted to reduce the worst excesses against the boy recruits and conform to the programme devised by York. They may well have understood that constant brutality could lead to jaded and truculent soldiers, something Shipp reflected upon, 'Had I been a depraved and callous-hearted youth, this method of disgracing me would have only served to harden me in vice'.[19]

## 'My youthful tricks'

Whilst damning the NCOs' inappropriate conduct, Dalrymple also obliquely mentions the 'difficulties to encounter particularly those resulting from … a regiment of Boys'.[20] These problems were numerous, and some have been mentioned: the lack of physical strength and stature, and the issuing of smaller firearms. Additionally, the boys were prone to indulge in childish pranks. Shipp frequently mentions he was partial to pranks even before he enlisted in the army, and once he had signed up, these became far more elaborate and at times dangerous.

Some of Shipp's more harmless pursuits included, blacking a comrade's hands with soot and then tickling them so they scratched their heads, pulling stools away, or sewing their shirts to their beds whilst they were asleep. These were comparatively mild compared to tying a comrade's legs together and then shouting fire, placing a lit candle in a sleeping bunkmate's hand or adding gunpowder to another soldier's pipe.[21] Pranks like these and teasing frequently resulted in fights in the barracks room, creating what must have been very intense conditions where the boys jostled, jeered and bullied each other, to establish their pecking order. This boisterous posturing coupled with the ever-present expectation of violent or humiliating punishment – meted out by the NCOs – produced a high-octane environment where tragedy could easily strike. William Mansfield, a boy soldier from Essex who had enlisted into the 22nd Foot at 16, recalled a game of handball inside Fort George, Guernsey. Whilst the boys were tossing the ball, it hit the mantelpiece and, 'struck a Bayonet that was lying [there]'. This then fell onto a soldier's head and apparently killed him.[22] This sorry story concluded with the boy who had thrown the ball being convicted and transported back to England.

Further examples occasionally appear in other battalions; for example, Alex Cooper, from Bury St Edmunds, who had enlisted at 16, was discharged after four years in

18 TNA: WO 27/82: Inspection Returns, Pt. 1 General, 1799, 27 November 1799.
19 Shipp, *The Extraordinary Military Career*, p.39.
20 TNA: WO 27/82: Inspection Returns, Pt. 1 General, 1799, 31 July 1799.
21 Shipp, *The Extraordinary Military Career*, p.27.
22 Cheshire Military Museum (CMM): 0003.01/16: Personal reminisces of QM William Mansfield, 1798–1834, pp.2–3.

1801 because of a 'bad scalded leg.'[23] While the circumstances are not elaborated on in the Royal Hospital Chelsea discharge records, they hint at a range of accidents and scuffles that seem to have broken out amongst the boys, which caused some of them to be discharged due to injuries sustained or worse die before they had even left Britain's shores.

## The Final Article

Despite these day-to-day scuffles, Dalrymple found much to commend the 22nd Foot. He singled out Crosbie and the temporary commander Captain Effingham Lindsay and praised, 'The Boys of which it is composed, have grown considerably since they came here, but the improvement in Discipline is still more remarkable, which I attribute to the Zeal & attention of Lt. Col. Crosbie.' Dalrymple noted, 'that the 400 rank and file actually in the Ranks, were unusually well drilled and that the movements performed were done with very considerable precision and exactness.'[24] Despite strictures and difficult NCOs, the 22nd had come out of the recruitment dearth of 1797 with a robust rank and file that, despite 'the points (few and trifling) in which I thought improvements might be made', Dalrymple had, 'no doubt that in a short time it would be difficult to suggest any amendment'.[25] Praise indeed for a regiment that two years ago was barely able to field a company. While Whitelocke adds his own commendations, lauding that 'I have only further to add that there does not exist a Doubt, but that the 22nd Regiment will in a short time exemplify everything that could be wished in a British Regiment.' Again singling out Crosbie as he 'appears to have clearly understood the management of a system which promises such advantages to his majesty's service.'[26] Praise indeed, as Crosbie had been absent in Ireland on the Staff for most of 1798 until January 1799, but within a year his efforts at reform had borne fruit.[27]

Shipp also comments on Crosbie's innovative atmosphere; he recalled that whilst the 22nd were stationed at Fort George, Guernsey, Shipp had been entrusted as drum-major to lead a party of boys into town. They had been given tickets – possibly paid for by Crosbie – to watch a play at the local theatre.[28] This commitment to providing an opportunity for the boys to experience culture and receive an education continued, even though Crosbie did not accompany the 22nd to India and eventually left the regiment in 1803. His legacy appears again in 1803 when Shipp was stationed in India and recounts how his company commander, Captain Effingham Lindsay, 'generously undertook to improve me in reading and writing'.[29] This openness to encourage men to engage with education not only helped to mitigate the worst excesses of the old West

23 TNA: WO 121: Piece 45, Discharge Papers, 1801, p.113
24 TNA: WO 27/82: Inspection Returns, Pt. 1 General, 1799, 31 July 1799.
25 TNA: WO 27/82: Inspection Returns, Pt. 1 General, 1799, 31 July 1799.
26 TNA: WO 27/82: Inspection Returns, Pt. 1 General, 1799, 27 November 1799.
27 TNA: WO 17/124: Monthly Returns for the 22nd Foot 1766–1812, January 1799.
28 Shipp, *The Extraordinary Military Career*, p.37.
29 Shipp, *The Extraordinary Military Career*, p.58.

India veterans, but also fostered the very spirit of leniency and encouragement, which York had been at pains to emphasise was required to inspire the boys to improve and adhere to the rigours of military life.

For the other regiments, their inspecting officers were just as fulsome. On 15 November 1798, Lieutenant General Sir Ralph Abercromby inspected the 65th Foot at Dumbarton Castle and found, 'This Regiment is composed of very fine Boys, Colonel Johnston and the other Officers pay them great attention & they are getting very forward in their discipline.'[30] Two years later the commander of the Northern District, the Duke of Gloucester and Edinburgh, had 'much satisfaction, in doing justice to the great attention and zeal of Lieutenant Colonel Rudsdell and the other officers ... in following up closely and successfully the plan of His Royal Highness the Duke of York', and that he was confident, 'that the 65th will very soon be an excellent battalion'.[31] Unlike the 22nd Foot, the 65th seem to have had an easier task of training their boys and may also have exhibited the leniency that York had hoped for, in contrast to the harsher conditions that Dalrymple discovered amongst the 22nd. Indeed, Gloucester could not praise Rudsdell enough, adding that during the 14 months he had been in command, 'great care ... has been taken of the health and behaviour of the Boys, and the judicious manner in which the whole has been conducted'.[32]

While both the 22nd and 65th proved to be very disciplined and effective soldiers, the path trod by the 34th was not as easily followed. On 17 September 1799, whilst stationed in Lincoln, a letter arrived at the desk of Lieutenant Colonel Richard Mark Dickens – commanding officer of the 34th – from William Day of Horse Guards. Day informed Dickens that orders and a route would soon arrive directing the 34th to Poole Barracks. The decision came from Fawcett, who had, 'been made acquainted with some circumstances in the general conduct of a part of the 34th Regt'. Those circumstances consisted of 'some very recent irregularity of conduct in Lincoln which is represented ... in so serious a light as to cause the removal of the Regiment'.[33] What had caused Fawcett so much disquiet was not included in the letter, although he hoped that once the regiment had reached Poole Barracks, 'a System of regularity can be pursued'.[34] Whilst it is hard to pin down what these 'irregularities' could have been, the local newspapers give some clues to what incidents might have caused the 34th's ejection from Lincoln.

According to local reports, compiled from 1798, the 34th had created a troublesome reputation for themselves. In July 1798 at Fundenhall, Norfolk, two soldiers were arrested for the rape and assault of a 12-year-old girl, Rebecca Beighton, who subsequently died because of their heinous crime. Both men, Samuel Windham and James Fleming, were convicted and executed in March 1799.[35] A month after the conviction, the *Stamford Mercury* reported that another 34th soldier, William Richardson,

30 TNA: WO 27/81: Inspection Returns, 1798, 15 November 1798.
31 TNA: WO 27/83: Inspection Returns, 1800, 5 October 1800.
32 TNA: WO 27/83: Inspection Returns, 1800, 5 October 1800.
33 TNA: WO 3/20: General letters: (series 1-1767-1800), 1799 July–1799 Nov., p.259.
34 TNA: WO 3/20: General letters: (series 1-1767-1800), 1799 July–1799 Nov., p.259.
35 *Stamford Mercury*, 22 March 1799.

had shot himself in the head. He had positioned himself in such a way that his body fell into a waterlogged ditch. At the time, it was thought that Richardson's debts caused his suicide.[36] All of these incidents certainly would not have endeared the 34th Foot to their neighbours in Lincoln, but the case Day may be referring to seems to have occurred in late August or early September 1799, a fortnight before the 34th received their marching orders.

A report in the *Stamford Mercury*, dated 2 September and published on the 6th, states that Joseph Audis, an apprentice described as being '14 Years of Age, about five Feet three Inches high, has light coloured Hair and a Scar across his Forehead',[37] had broken his contract with Mr Thomas Teesdale of Boston, Lincolnshire. Teesdale obtained a warrant from the Mayor of Boston to apprehend Audis, who by this time had enlisted with the other boys of the 34th. The Mayor of Lincoln and the local magistrate, Henry Hutton, had received the warrant from Boston and authorised the constables of Lincoln to find Audis and return him to his master. As the arm of the law reached out to the 34th, an unidentified officer caught wind of the constables' approach and had Audis whisked out of Lincoln before he could be caught. Naturally incensed by this clear act of military disobedience, a notice was placed in the *Stamford Mercury* requesting any information or help to lay hands on the errant apprentice and haul him before a magistrate would be 'handsomely rewarded'.[38] Such an incident may well have been the cause of Fawcett's disquiet regarding the 34th and their subsequent removal. Enlisting an apprentice in the army was illegal as it flouted their contract, and the officer's deliberate obstruction of the Lincoln constables only made matters worse. It can well be imagined that Fawcett, keen to protect the reputation of the army and the boy enlistment project, was eager to remove the 34th from Lincolnshire as soon as possible to avoid further trouble.

Despite their previous infamy, by the time the 34th were reviewed a couple of months later on 21 November 1799, all sins seemed to have been forgotten, and Lieutenant General Edmund Stevens found the regiment 'exercised, fired well, and performed Evolutions, presented by His Majesty's regulations, with great readiness and exactness'.[39] Again, this success was placed at the commanding officer's door, in this case Dickens. Stevens' greatest concern was that the boys were still too young to undertake active duties, although he did consider them 'a stout description of Boys, particularly those which have been received from the 16th or [possibly 52nd] Regiments, and in some instances from Chatham [Depot].'[40]

Alongside the written reports provided by reviewing generals, these inspection reviews were also an opportunity to take relevant statistics for the regiments. These records were not always assiduously done as in the case of the 65th, whose inspection returns for 1798–1800 only list the number of boys in the ranks. In contrast, both the 22nd and the 34th provide fascinating statistics detailing the composition of their regiments.

36 *Stamford Mercury*, 19 April 1799.
37 *Stamford Mercury*, 6 September 1799.
38 *Stamford Mercury*, 6 September 1799.
39 TNA: WO 27/82: Inspection Returns, Pt. 1 General, 1799, 28 November 1799.
40 TNA: WO 27/82: Inspection Returns, Pt. 1 General, 1799, 28 November 1799.

When Whitelocke conducted his review in November 1799, the 22nd consisted of 696 serjeants, drummers and rank and file. He took details of their age and the country where they were born, which is reproduced in Table 6. The ages taken of the other ranks varied from 50–54 down to 14 years old. From these statistics, it is possible to gauge an approximate average age for the regiment, which at the time was around 19 years old, far below the typical averages in line regiments identified by Professor Kevin Linch, which tended to be around 28 years old between 1807–1815.[41]

**Table 6. Ages of the 22nd Foot.**[42]

| Age | Number of Soldiers |
|---|---|
| 55 | |
| 50 | 3 |
| 45 | 6 |
| 40 | 10 |
| 35 | 33 |
| 30 | 24 |
| 25 | 45 |
| 20 | 64 |
| 18 | 250 |
| 14 | 261 |

Whilst reviewing the 34th, Stevens separated the serjeants and corporals from the privates, providing tables for each of their age ranges. At the time, there were 762 private soldiers ranging in age from 25 all the way down to the mere stripling 14-year-olds. Like the 22nd, the average age of the privates in the 34th was below average, at 18 years old. Using the definition of child soldiers established by the UN, the percentage of the regiment's rank and file who could be considered 'child soldiers' was 63 percent of the privates in the 34th. Whilst the 34th only counted privates, the 22nd also included serjeants, corporals and drummers. Nearly three-quarters, or 73 percent of the 22nd's NCOs, drummers and rank and file were underage. With such overwhelming numbers of lads enlisted in the ranks, it is a testament both to the regimental staffs and the boys' own fortitude that generals such as Abercromby, Dalrymple, and Whitelocke, were ready to give such glowing reviews of the boys and their ability to adapt to life in the army.

41 Kevin Barry Linch, 'The Recruitment of the British Army 1807-1815', p.194.
42 TNA: WO 27/82: Inspection Returns, Pt. 1 General, 1799, 26 November 1799.

**Table 7. Ages of the 34th[43]**

| Age | Number of Soldiers |
|---|---|
| 21–25 | 14 |
| 20–21 | 33 |
| 19–20 | 91 |
| 18–19 | 141 |
| 17–18 | 153 |
| 16–17 | 174 |
| 15–16 | 104 |
| 14–15 | 52 |

With their credentials as flourishing soldiers, the boys did not have long before their training was put to the test. By 1799 all three regiments were posted along the British coast. In December of that year, the pranksters of the 22nd, were garrisoned in Portsea Barracks, at Portsmouth harbour. By January 1800, the troublesome boys of the 34th were stationed just up the road at Hilsea Barracks, whilst in Berwick, the boys of the 65th felt the chill wind of the North Sea whip their faces. For many of these boys, these were their last billets in Britain, as they were about to embark on an adventure across the face of the globe, to the southern hemisphere.

43 TNA: WO 27/82: Inspection Returns, Pt. 1 General, 1799, 23 November 1799.

# 5

# To the Cape

In late January 1800, the 22nd and 34th began to embark for Britain's colonies in the East Indies. They boarded one of the regular convoys of East Indiamen – the popular name for HEIC trading vessels – that sailed between Britain and India. The regularity of HEIC sailings allowed the British Army to use the departure of the Indiamen as an opportunity to dispatch their regiments across the world. The same was true of the boy regiments who sailed with the 1800 convoy. Initially only the 22nd and the 34th embarked for service in the east, whilst the 65th remained at home. The 22nd's headquarters was established aboard the *Surat Castle*, whilst an estimated 600 boys from the 34th were berthed on the *Scaleby Castle*.[1] Problems started to surface before the boys had even begun to find their berths.

Aboard the *Surat Castle*, Shipp found the East Indiaman 'was most dreadfully crowded; men literally slept upon one another'.[2] Packed in like sardines, tempers were fraught and the air ripe for the terrible spectre of disease to haunt the decks of the vessel. Shipp recalled a 'pestilential smell between decks was beyond the power of description'.[3] Many of the crew already showed signs of sickness, particularly the lascars – usually sailors from India – who served aboard the HEIC's convoys.

According to Shipp, many of the lascars had been previously employed aboard earlier convoys but had remained in England after their first voyage. Electing to return to the sea, it was claimed the crew had 'been picked up in every sink of poverty'.[4] With many of the sailors already ill, they became the scapegoats for subsequent outbreaks during the voyage. *The Oxford Journal* later reported on 13 December 1800 that the lascars were the source of an epidemic. Although not all contemporary accounts agree with this simple narrative, for example in her private diary, Lady Anne Barnard challenges the assertion that the crew were solely to blame. After encountering the boys' officers at the Cape, Barnard claims that in addition to the sickly sailors, too many boys had been stowed aboard.[5] Barnard asserts that the *Surat Castle's* captain was concerned about

1 *Hampshire Chronicle*, 20 January 1800 and *Sherborne Mercury*, 17 March 1800.
2 Shipp, *The Extraordinary Military Career*, p.39.
3 Shipp, *The Extraordinary Military Career*, p.39.
4 Shipp, *The Extraordinary Military Career*, p.39.
5 *The Oxford Journal*, 13 December 1800; Lady Anne Barnard, Margaret Lenta and Basil Le Cordeur (eds), *The Cape Diaries of Lady Anne Barnard, 1799–1800* (Cape Town: Van Riebeeck

the crowding, but the agent for transports, 'pronounced that they were better accommodated than most troops in similar situations'.[6] Despite the agent's assertions, the overcrowding on the *Surat Castle* meant that as the 1800 convoy packed the boys in below decks, they were vulnerable to outbreaks of disease.

The convoy sailed in late January 1800, and as the night stole across the *Surat Castle*'s decks, the captain decided to strike out and sail on alone. This may have been due to a storm which hit the convoy, although Shipp suggests the captain was keen to sail by himself. Shipp's suspicions were seemingly validated as the captain avoided rejoining the convoy, despite sighting some of the ships in the distance.[7] Whilst the 22nd raced southwards, the *Scaleby Castle* lost the convoy during the storm and returned to Falmouth on 27 February. If conditions for the 34th were anything like as cramped as those for the 22nd, then it is little wonder that a fight broke out between the boys and the sailors on 28 February.[8] We can only guess what the flashpoint of the fight was, as the *Sherborne Mercury*'s report provides no clue to the cause. Additionally, the journals for the *Scaleby Castle* can offer no further insights as they are missing, hindering a definitive answer. Losing the convoy forced the *Scaleby Castle* to remain in Falmouth, while the rest of the Indiamen made for the deep waters of the Atlantic, delaying the 34th's departure until March.

Meanwhile, the 22nd were now in the heart of the ocean, despite another storm, which buffeted the *Surat Castle* and tore off the main mast. Below decks, barrels of paint had broken loose, turning the gun deck into 'one mass of colours, in which lay the dead and the dying'.[9] In the lurid mess of paint-splattered woodwork, scurvy – a disease caused by a lack of Vitamin C – afflicted the boys, leaving them in a terrible condition. Shipp describes his own symptoms during the ordeal, relating, 'My poor legs were as big as drums; my gums swollen to an enormous size; my tongue too big for my mouth; and all I could eat was raw potatoes and vinegar'.[10] As he sat there with the wind and water lapping at the ship, his body swollen and in pain, the young Drummer Shipp had just turned 16.

Despite the best efforts of the 22nd's officers, who gave up their own fresh meat and offered tea and coffee to the afflicted, the disease ran rampant. A grizzly reminder of the fate that awaited those who expired on the *Surat Castle* was all too easily glimpsed from the deck. Prowling in the wake of the East Indiaman was a shiver of sharks, lazily picking off the bodies of the boys who had been committed to the deep.[11] In total, 89 boys and men were lost at sea during that fateful voyage.[12]

Finally, in May 1800, on a 'foggy and dreary day' the *Surat Castle* sighted shore at Simon's Bay, an anchorage south of Cape Town.[13] Hot on their heels came the 34th,

Society, 1999), vol.2, p.129.

6 Barnard, *The Cape Diaries*, vol.2, p.129.

7 Shipp, *The Extraordinary Military Career*, pp.40–41.

8 *Sherborne Mercury*, 3 March 1800.

9 Shipp, *The Extraordinary Military Career*, p.41.

10 Shipp, *The Extraordinary Military Career*, p.42.

11 Shipp, *The Extraordinary Military Career*, pp.41–42.

12 TNA: WO 12/4870: General Muster Books and Pay Lists, 34th Foot 1st Battalion, 1800, 25 March–25 May 1800.

13 Shipp, *The Extraordinary Military Career*, p.42.

who managed to arrive at the Cape by June 1800 despite their delayed departure.[14] The 34th had also suffered as they crossed the equator, losing 70 boys during the passage.[15] The loss was significant enough to be commented on by both the *Sherborne Mercury* and *The Oxford Journal*, who, 'lament to learn, that the 22nd and 34th of foot, regiments whose privates were composed of boys, became sickly on their voyage to the Cape and suffered much.'[16]

Both regiments were placed in quarantine by the Cape authorities, and whilst they remained ensconced aboard their ships, the boys were provided with an ample supply of fresh produce to aid recovery. This treatment worked well enough for the regiments to be ordered ashore. The boys had barely stepped onto *terra firma* when a fight broke out between the governor, Sir George Yonge, and the commander of the Cape garrison, Major General Francis Dundas. The Major General appears to have been an irascible character and frequently feuded with both his officers and the colonial administrators. When Yonge ordered the regiments ashore, Dundas, resentful of the governor's interference in military affairs, ordered the re-embarkation of the boys who had already been put ashore. Fortunately for the boys, as Lady Anne Barnard observed, 'that woud [sic] have been carrying the jest too far with sick men', and Dundas' command was rescinded.[17] Having unwittingly exacerbated the already frayed relations between Yonge and Dundas, the 22nd finally landed at Simon's Town, later moving to Muizenberg. Whilst the 34th were posted first to Cape Town and then later to Wynberg, which, like Muizenberg, was situated to the south of Cape Town.[18] Eventually the two boy regiments were united when the 22nd were posted to Wynberg in September 1800.[19]

## The 65th Sets Sail

Meanwhile, the 65th had remained in garrison at Berwick until November 1800 when they boarded the frigate HMS *Sensible* (formerly the French *La Sensible*) and set sail for the Downs.[20] Their rendezvous was with the inveterate adventurer Commodore Sir Home Popham, then commanding HMS *Romney*. Popham was under orders to escort the 65th to the Cape and then continue onto a 'secret expedition', picking up an additional regiment from the colony *en route*.[21] Popham's squadron set sail on 5 December 1800, leaving behind a speculative public to debate the final destination of the Commodore's escapade.

14 TNA: WO 17/1586: Cape of Good Hope Monthly Returns, 1800, 1 June 1800.
15 TNA: WO 12/3876: General Muster Books and Pay Lists, 22nd Foot 1st Battalion, 1800, 25 May 1800
16 *The Oxford Journal*, 13 December 1800.
17 Barnard, *The Cape Diaries*, vol.2, pp.129–130.
18 Shipp, *The Extraordinary Military Career*, p.44; TNA: WO 12/4870: General Muster Books and Pay Lists, 34th Foot 1st Battalion, 1800, 25 June 1800.
19 TNA: WO 17/1586: Cape of Good Hope Monthly Returns, 1800, 1 September 1800.
20 TNA: WO 17/185: Monthly Returns for the 65th Foot, 1 November 1800.
21 Jacqueline Reiter, *Quicksilver Captain: The Improbable Life of Sir Home Popham* (Warwick: Helion & Company, 2024), pp.94–95.

By 27 December 1800, just south of the Canary Islands, the two frigates *Romney* and *Sensible* raced ahead of the slower troop transports. On 9 January 1801, the 65th were safely south of the equator and celebrated the traditional crossing the line ceremony in fine style with Popham's jack tars.[22] On 12 February their passage came to an end when *Sensible* put into Table Bay and offloaded the 744 boys of the 65th at the foot of Africa, following a relatively quiet passage compared to their brothers in arms in the 22nd and 34th.

As the 65th made landfall, Popham set about selecting which regiments he needed for his secret expedition. The Commodore initially chose the 22nd and the 61st (South Gloucester) Regiment of Foot and had embarked both of these regiments in preparation to sail on 28 February, to assist the British and HEIC forces landing in the Red Sea as part of the campaign against Napoleon Bonaparte's *Armée d'Orient*.[23] Ultimately, Popham changed his mind and the boys of the 22nd were put ashore after 28 February and remained in South Africa.

## At the Ends of the Earth

At the time of Britain's conquest, the Cape of Good Hope had been an important stopping point on the passage from Europe to India for centuries. To facilitate and control the flow of goods from the East Indies, the *Vereenigde Oostindische Compagnie* (VOC), the Dutch equivalent to Britain's HEIC, had established the port at Cape Town in 1652.[24] The Cape had remained firmly under the sway of the VOC, until the defeat of Britain and her Coalition allies in the Low Countries in 1795 and Revolutionary France's occupation of the Netherlands. France's victory transferred administration of the VOC and the Cape to the new republican administration in The Hague, now styled the Batavian Republic.[25] In response to the establishment of this French puppet government, Henry Dundas, Secretary of State for Home and the Colonies, orchestrated an expedition to capture Cape Town in 1795 and secure the route to India. In a relatively swift operation, the colony was captured, denying France a base from which privateers could raid British commerce.[26]

After the conquest, the Cape reverted to supplying the annual convoys of East Indiamen, bearing their cargoes of luxury items including fine silks, tea, dyes, and spices, from the factories of Calcutta, Madras and Bombay to the high streets of Britain. The mild climate meant Cape Town was also a valuable stopping point for British soldiers sailing to and from the east. Stopping in South Africa allowed regiments to become 'salted' or acclimatised to the harsher tropical climates and diseases of the East

22 Reiter, *Quicksilver Captain*, p.96.
23 Reiter, *Quicksilver Captain*, p.93.
24 George McCall Theal, *History of South Africa* (London: Swan Sonnenschein, Lowrey & Co., 1888), vol.1, p.40.
25 Nöel Mostert, *Frontiers: The Epic of South Africa's Creation and the Tragedy of the Xhosa People* (London: Jonathan Cape, 1992), p.258.
26 Fortescue, *A History of the British Army*, vol.4, pp.392–393.

Indies.[27] Although physicians and surgeons at the time had no concept of germ theory – the discovery of which took another half-century – they did understand that regiments who had spent time in mild tropical climates fared better when faced with more extreme environments, such as the West Indies or India.[28] In 1796, for example, Abercromby had requested several regiments from Gibraltar for his expedition to the Caribbean, as they were less prone to sickness, having been already exposed to malaria and yellow fever in Gibraltar.[29]

The proof was in the climatic pudding as both the 22nd and the 34th started to recover from their oceanic ordeal. On 1 June 1800, 72 percent of the 22nd were sick, whilst the 34th seemed to have escaped the worst of the maladies aboard ship with just 25 percent of their strength on the sick list.[30] Similarly, the 65th appears to have come off comparatively lightly, with only 22 percent of its ranks in hospital on 1 March 1801.[31] Whilst the climate and fresh provisions proved to be beneficial, the treatment the boys received was variable at best. The 22nd Foot, posted in Simon's Town, fared better than most, receiving treatment from Doctor William Pattison, the Chief Surgeon at the naval hospital. Barnard describes Pattison's charges as 'doing well, he [Pattison] throws in plenty of port wine, the only thing that will stay on the stomachs of the invalids'.[32] In stark contrast, the Physician and Director of the General Hospital for the Forces, Doctor Edmund Somers, barely visited his patients. Barnard acidly remarked that he was too busy putting on a production of the farce *Taste* at his home, a production Somers' wife hoped would introduce 'theatricals into Africa', seemingly in blissful ignorance of the hundreds of boys crowding the hospitals.[33] Even when Somers belatedly prescribed port for his charges, he received instead 'bad Cape [wine] – pernicious to men newly arrived'.[34] Despite Somers' poor record, physicians such as Pattison, combined with the mild Cape climate, made up for his shortcomings and helped to bring the sick rate under control as it steadily fell over the next three months, reaching just 7 percent in the 22nd and 11 percent in the 34th.[35] Whilst the officers of the 22nd and 34th had cause to complain about some of the medical treatment meted out to their charges, they reserved their particular ire for Francis Dundas.

The Major General had already shown a callous regard for his soldiers. Even after his attempt to order the re-embarkation of the sick boys onto their ships, Dundas continued to treat the boys as if they were up to strength. In late May 1800 barely a couple of weeks after the two regiments reached the Cape, Captain Lorenzo Moore of the 34th, described by Barnard as a 'very pretty young man … told us one day with tears

27 Sir Neil Cantlie, *A History of the Army Medical Department* (Edinburgh: Churchill Livingstone, 1974), vol.1, p.231.
28 Cantlie, *A History of the Army Medical Department*, p.231.
29 Carole Divall, *General Sir Ralph Abercromby and the French Revolutionary Wars 1792–1801* (Barnsley: Pen and Sword Military, 2018), p.74.
30 TNA: WO 17/1586: Cape of Good Hope Monthly Returns, 1800, 1 June 1800.
31 TNA: WO 17/1587: Cape of Good Hope Monthly Returns, 1801, 1 March 1801.
32 Barnard, *The Cape Diaries*, vol.2, p.135.
33 Barnard, *The Cape Diaries*, vol.2, p.146.
34 Barnard, *The Cape Diaries*, vol.2, p.135.
35 TNA: WO 17/1586: Cape of Good Hope Monthly Returns, 1800, 1 September 1800.

in his eyes, how his company weak & enfeebled by illness' were ordered to wait near Muizenberg until Dundas had met them. The Major General 'neither thought nor cared whether they stood in cloaths [sic] wet or not'.[36] Moore's 74 boys were left standing and shivering in the damp for an hour and a half, before they were ordered to march, only for it to be countermanded as Dundas was on his way. It had been a rough introduction to service overseas for the boys, but despite these trials and tribulations, the boys slowly seemed to have become accustomed to life in Africa.

Passing through Wynberg, Barnard noted that the 34th Foot were 'chiefly composed of boys, Infants under the Musquet'. Some of them were so young that when they were found in the wine houses, the boys did not ask for drink; instead, a local Dutch woman told Barnard they usually asked for 'brot [bread] & butter ... & they put raisins between the slices'.[37] Whilst some of the boys sought the simple pleasures in life, they could be difficult if not given a steady hand. The 'gentle' Major Robert Kelso of the 22nd, was ordered to accompany a detachment of his regiment *en route* from Muizenberg to Cape Town, as Barnard claims that if they were commanded by an inexperienced subaltern, the boys could 'behave ill'.[38] Suggesting that their penchant for tricks and roughhousing had not abandoned them.

As the regiments found their feet, the 22nd Foot also faced their first trial by combat. Posted at Muizenberg, the Cheshires found the beaches protected by a small battery, whilst the hinterland was marked with 'craggy hills, covered with masses of stone, which have the appearance of being merely suspended in the air'.[39] Amongst these crags and crevices often found bathing in the southern sun were a congress of Chacma Baboons. These primates were notorious throughout Cape Town for launching raids on vineyards and orchards, plundering all that lay in their way. The baboons' privations even forced the boy regiments to place armed guards around their camps to stop clothing and equipment from being purloined.[40] At Muizenberg, the nearest congress was led by an old grey-haired baboon, who was nicknamed Father Murphy by the 22nd's boys.[41]

During one infamous encounter, a soldier's wife hung a blanket out to dry, and a baboon raced off with it into the hills. This was the final straw and a strong party of boys set off in pursuit, armed with sticks and stones. Amongst their ranks, Shipp, alongside 20 other boys, attempted to get between the baboons and the rocks where they sheltered, but they were forestalled as 50 primates rushed to block the route. Shipp returned to the main party and watched as Father Murphy marched about distributing 'his orders, and planning the attack, with the judgement of one of our best generals.'[42] As the boys advanced, Father Murphy barked in response, and the baboons counter-attacked, knocking over rocks and sending them tumbling amongst the 22nd. Fearing for their

36 Barnard, *The Cape Diaries*, vol.2, p.135.
37 Barnard, *The Cape Diaries*, vol.2, p.139.
38 Barnard, *The Cape Diaries*, vol.2, p.142.
39 Shipp, *The Extraordinary Military Career*, p.44.
40 Samuel Plummer, Revered John Riles (ed.), *The Journal of Samuel Plummer* (London: T. Cordeux, 1821), p.6.
41 Shipp, *The Extraordinary Military Career*, p.45.
42 Shipp, *The Extraordinary Military Career*, p.45.

lives, the boys fled and were pursued to the doors of their barracks, where they passed an uncomfortable evening listening to the baboons screaming at the doors as they tore up the stolen blanket. Incidents like this and the continued depredations of the primates meant that the boys could only travel in groups of five or six in case of an ambush.[43]

Revenge is a dish best served cold, and so it proved for the boys when Father Murphy later boldly walked into the grenadier company's barracks. Caught in the act of stealing a serjeant's coat, Father Murphy was muzzled and restrained by a party of boys. Despite capturing the congress leader, the young men were reluctant to kill him so instead decided to shave his head as punishment. Shipp found that after his treatment 'he was really an exceedingly good-looking fellow', adding that there are many 'a "blood" in Bond Street' not half as good looking. Sadly, the rest of the congress did not recognise Father Murphy and drove him back to the 22nd, where he became a part of daily life at Muizenberg.[44]

Chacma Baboons were a common sight amongst the British encampments at Muizenberg. (K.D.)

Over 6,000miles (9,600km) from their homes in East Anglia and Lincolnshire, inured in a world of discipline, disease, and death, for many of these boys it must have been a bewildering experience. Barnard was sympathetic to their plight, commenting 'poor things! Yet these are our defences, our bullwarks, [sic] & two or three years will make them grow up into Heroes.'[45] Unfortunately for the boys, they did not have two or three years.

## Fires on the Frontier

Cape Town had remained relatively quiet since the British descent on the coast and subsequent occupation, however, to the east the British were faced with the thorny issue

43 Shipp, *The Extraordinary Military Career*, p.45.
44 Shipp, *The Extraordinary Military Career*, pp.45–46.
45 Barnard, *The Cape Diaries*, vol.2, p.139.

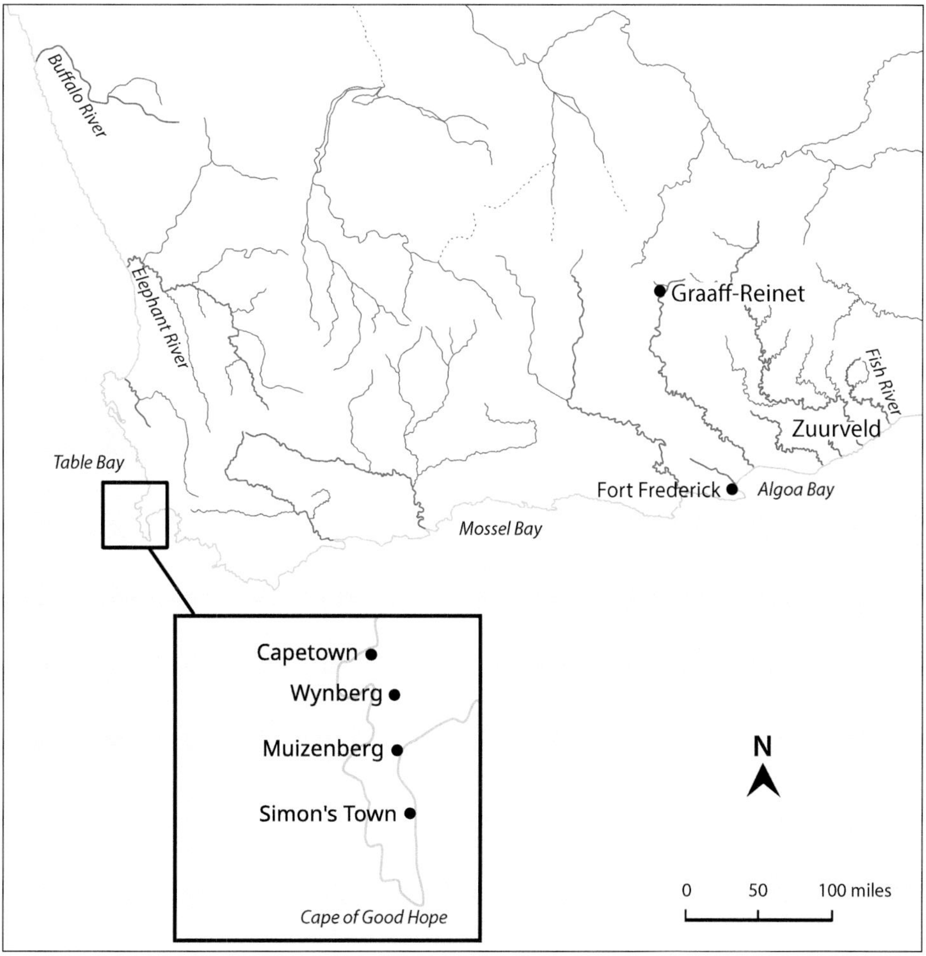


The Cape Colony in 1801.

of a fluid frontier. Since the colony's inception, some Dutch adventurers had decided to strike out on their own. These trekboers slowly pushed the frontiers of the Cape Colony ever further eastwards, where these solitary parties encountered groups of the Cape's indigenous inhabitants the Khoikhoi and the !Kung or San. When referring to these peoples the Dutch used the racially charged names of Hottentots – this name has obscure origins and may refer to the click consonants used in Khoikhoi languages – whilst the !Kung were simply called Bushmen.[46] Since the founding of the colony, relations between the colonists and the Khoikhoi had oscillated between conflict and accommodation. Slavery was a common feature of the relationship between these two

46 Willem Steenkamp, *Assegais, Drums & Dragoons: A Military & Social History of the Cape* (Johannesburg: Jonathan Ball Publishers, 2012), pp.32–34.

groups, with many of the Khoikhoi being enslaved by the Dutch. This often led to sexual liaisons and sometimes marriages between the Dutch and some of the Khoikhoi. The children of these sexual encounters, both non-consensual and consensual, were called Bastaards, a name that in time was given to the communities they formed on the frontier. They were either born as slaves in their father's houses or lived alongside the trekboer settlements, as they probed the interior of Africa.[47]

To this mix of various ethnic identities must be added the Xhosa, a Bantu-speaking people, who had been on their own migration westwards as the Dutch advanced towards them. The first encounter between these two nations was in 1702 when some Dutch elephant hunters met a party of Xhosa near the Great Fish River, nearly 500 miles (800km) from Cape Town.[48] The Dutch had their own name for the Xhosa, calling them Caffres or Kaffirs, from the Arabic term for 'heathen' or 'unbeliever' and a general term Arab slave traders used for sub-Saharan Africans.[49] Xhosa society and economy were based on their extensive cattle herds, with a man's status associated with the number of livestock at his kraal – an enclosure for bovines. This reliance on cattle placed the Xhosa clans on a collision course with the trekboer ranchers coming from the west, and by the 1800s the battlefield between these peoples had become the Zuurveld.

Enclosed by the Great Fish River to the east and the Bushman River to the west, the Zuurveld, later renamed Albany, was a site of prime cattle pasture. Described by many British observers as an area reminiscent of 'English parkland', the Zuurveld, was usually grazed by the Xhosa's herds during the summer. As the winter set in, the Xhosa removed their cattle to better pastures in the sweet veldt.[50] This lifestyle required a porous frontier across the Great Fish River, enabling the Xhosa to come and go with their cattle. From the latter half of the eighteenth century, the border started to close as the VOC attempted to curb the progress of the trekboers and their contact with the Xhosa. In 1774, the VOC managed to broker agreements with some of the clans who accepted the Great Fish River as the frontier, but the Dutch thought this agreement extended to all of the Xhosa, as they were unaware that the Xhosa were not a single polity but collections of various clans.[51] This misunderstanding resulted in the First Frontier War in 1779 between the Dutch and the Gqunukhwebe, a mixed clan of Xhosa and Khoikhoi heritage. The Gqunukhwebe had been forced to settle in the Zuurveld due to ongoing wars amongst the Xhosa clans to the east. During the First (1779–1781) and Second (1789–1793) Frontier Wars, the VOC repeatedly attempted to establish the Great Fish River as the border between the trekboers and the Gqunukhwebe, by expelling them east and keeping the trekboers to the west of the river.[52] These wars were often indecisive, with some of the Xhosa scattered, before regrouping and reestablishing themselves in the Zuurveld again.

47 Mostert, *Frontiers*, p.175.
48 Mostert, *Frontiers*, p.153.
49 John Milton, *The Edges of War: A History of Frontier Wars (1702–1878)* (Cape Town: Juta & Co. Ltd., 1983), p.xi.
50 Mostert, *Frontiers*, pp.235–236.
51 Milton, *The Edges of War*, pp.27–28.
52 Mostert, *Frontiers*, p.243.

Most Xhosa warriors in the early nineteenth century were armed with assegais and an array of throwing spears. (Yale Center for British Art, Paul Mellon Collection)

The arrival of the British added further complications to this veritable mosaic of political factions. The nearest village to the frontier, Graaff-Reinet, was founded in 1786 as a link between the Cape and the interior. The village had always had more of the flavour of the trekboer settlements, filled with fiercely independent frontiersmen and their slaves.[53] In 1799 a former frontier commandant, Adriaan van Jaarsveld was arrested for forgery on the orders of a former VOC magistrate. In response, a faction of Patriots rose up to expel the British garrison.[54] To end this revolt, Dundas dispatched a force commanded by Lieutenant Colonel Thomas Pakenham Vandeleur to Algoa Bay, where the present-day port town of Gqeberha, formerly Port Elizabeth, is situated. Vandeleur marched rapidly into the interior and pacified Graaff-Reinet. Despite successfully bringing the Boers under Britain's sway, the Zuurveld was about to break out into open warfare.

In February 1799, a civil war amongst the Xhosa spilled over the Great Fish River, forcing many of the Xhosa settlers in the Cape Colony to pick a side.[55] As the Xhosas fought in the Zuurveld, Vandeleur, keen to avoid becoming embroiled in the conflict, gathered his men and marched for the coast. *En route* to the sea, the British encountered parties of the multi-racial descendants of the Boers and Khoikhoi, the Bastaards, led

53 Milton, *The Edges of War*, p.41.
54 Theal, *History of South Africa*, pp.36–37.
55 A.J. Smithers, *The Kaffir Wars 1779–1877* (London: Leo Cooper, 1973), pp.60–61.

by Klaas Stuurman, who, after suffering oppression from the Boers, had revolted and plundered the Dutch homesteads in lieu of payment and to hunt for muskets.[56] Many Bastaards were brought under British protection and subsequently disarmed.

The spark that lit a general conflagration finally came whilst Vandeleur was encamped and waiting for a patrol from the 81st Regiment of Foot. Accounts differ as to the subsequent course of events; the historians George McCall Theal and A.J. Smithers both follow John Barrow's description, because Barrow had accompanied Vandeleur's expedition. Barrow states that the Xhosa chief, Chungwa of the Gqunukhwebe, feared his clan would be forced east over the Great Fish River and launched an unprovoked assault on the British.[57] In contrast, the writer John Milton suggests Vandeleur was attempting to provoke the Gqunukhwebe and create a pretext for expelling them from the Zuurveld.[58] The resulting battle saw the Xhosa launch several assaults with shortened assegais against the British, only to be driven off time and again by volleys of musketry.[59] After this first combat, the situation continued to deteriorate over the course of the year.

Vandeleur's attempts to disarm Stuurman resulted in many of the Bastaards and some of the Khoikhoi fleeing and joining the Xhosa. The ensuing conflict devolved into a series of cattle raids, skirmishes, and ambushes. During the 1800s, the Xhosas fought in a style reminiscent of the Zulus, utilising spears to soften up a target before rushing on them with assegais, knobkerries, and shields.[60] With the addition of the Khoikhoi and the Bastaards, many of whom had served in Boer commandoes, the Xhosa now had access to their expertise with muskets.

Faced with this dire situation, Vandeleur called out several Boer commandoes, but this did little to bring the Zuurveld under control. Eventually Dundas took to the field and managed to negotiate a truce with the Gqunukhwebe on 16 October 1799. During the armistice, Dundas started construction on a fort at Algoa Bay, named Fort Frederick in honour of the Duke of York.[61] This fort housed a British garrison and was tasked with keeping the route between Graaff-Reinet and the coast open, whilst forestalling any attempts at a Franco-Dutch landing at the Eastern Cape. Fort Frederick became the next garrison for the boy soldiers.

## Bush Warfare

Despite the truce, the frontier remained volatile, so in October 1801, Dundas ordered the formation of a composite company drawn from the 8th (The King's Royal Irish)

56 Milton, *The Edges of War*, p.43.
57 Theal, *History of South Africa*, p.43; Smithers, *The Kaffir Wars*, p.61.
58 Milton, *The Edges of War*, p.44.
59 Theal, *History of South Africa*, p.43.
60 Roger S. Levine, '"African Warfare in All its Ferocity": Changing Military Landscapes and Precolonial and Colonial Conflict in Southern Africa', in Richard P. Tucker and Edmund Russell (eds.), *Natural Enemy, Natural Ally: Toward an Environmental History of Warfare* (Corvallis: Oregon State University Press, 2012), p.80.
61 Milton, *The Edges of War*, p.48.

Light Dragoons, 22nd, 34th, 65th, 81st, and 91st Regiments of Foot, to be sent to the Eastern Cape. This was not the first time that some of the boys had been dispatched to Algoa Bay. The muster rolls for the 22nd show that a detachment had been posted on command at Algoa in August 1801, whilst the 34th sent a handful of boys in July.[62] Due to Britain's command of the seas, the bay was selected as a convenient landing place for British troops to reach Graaff-Reinet and the frontier, which was faster than the overland route from Cape Town.

One of 22nd Foot's detachments sent during the peace included, 19-year-old William Mansfield, who had been promoted to corporal in September 1801. Mansfield recalled being sent with a party to the bay to look for bullocks for the regiment. The night after their arrival, some Xhosas came to their encampment asking for beef, which the 22nd assented to, giving them some cattle and sheep. The next day the Xhosas' chief came, and Lieutenant Hatton Smith proposed a competition. He nailed a card onto a nearby tree and paced out 100 yards. Smith then ordered one of his boys to fire at the target and in a flash the ball found its mark. In return, the Xhosa chief directed one of his men to throw his assegai and then a 'large stick' possibly a knobkerrie, both of which hit the mark.[63] This short contest built a rapport between the two groups and the Xhosa spent some time with the 22nd, until they had 'sold all their spears and sticks to the Soldiers for Rum and Bread'.[64] Whilst these small detachments provided the boys with the opportunity to discover more about the men they might have to fight against, it did not prepare them for the ruggedness of the interior, where the thorny bush was common and thick foliage obscured the rivers.

Some attempts were made to equip the boys for the rugged frontier country by outfitting the composite battalion in green jackets and issuing muskets with browned barrels to provide some camouflage in the bush. Shipp refers to the composite battalion as riflemen, but the battalion was not armed with rifles and would more accurately be described as light infantry.[65] Whilst the selection of the equipment reflected contemporary theories on light infantry tactics, the decision-making process for selecting the rank and file remains harder to discover. It could be assumed that the composite battalion would have been formed principally from the light companies of the preceding regiments; however, the muster rolls indicate that far from sending the 'light bobs', the boys were selected piecemeal from across the battalion and not sent out as complete companies. This seemingly random selection might be due to the officers selecting the most intelligent boys in their ranks. If this were the case, it would certainly chime with contemporary opinions, including those expressed by General John Money, who considered Scottish Highlanders 'make the best irregulars' because they are naturally 'an intelligent people.'[66] This might suggest that the officers of the 22nd, 34th, and 65th

62 TNA: WO 12/3876: General Muster Books and Pay Lists, 22nd Foot 1st Battalion, 1800–1801, 25 September 1801. TNA: WO 12/4871: General Muster Books and Pay Lists, 34th Foot 1st Battalion, 1801, 24 July 1801.

63 CMM: 0003.01/16: Personal reminisces of QM William Mansfield, 1798–1834, pp.3–4.

64 CMM: 0003.01/16: Personal reminisces of QM William Mansfield, 1798–1834, p.4.

65 Shipp, *The Extraordinary Military Career*, p.46.

66 John Money quoted in, Gates, *The British Light Infantry Arm*, p.26

This painting depicts an ambush during the Eighth Frontier War (1850–1853). Although from a later conflict, it provides a good example of the type of fighting experienced by British soldiers in the South African bush in 1800s. (Anne S.K. Brown Collection)

chose the boys they considered naturally attuned to serving as light infantry, rather than selecting by the entire light company.

Some historians have also suggested that the composite light infantry company was one of the first examples of mounted infantry adopted by the British Army in South Africa. Henry Manners Chichester and George Burges-Short claim the 91st Foot had a mounted company whilst posted at the Cape.[67] Whilst G. Tylden asserts the composite light infantry company were also mounted during their deployment to the Zuurveld.[68] Although these authors state the presence of mounted infantry as fact, there seems to be little contemporary evidence to back this up. The Cape regimental returns, for example, list the horses used by the 8th Light Dragoons but fail to mention any purchased for the infantry.[69] Similarly, Mansfield does not refer to any special detachments of mounted infantry, despite serving at Algoa Bay. The closest piece of evidence, which potentially suggests the light infantry were mounted, comes from Shipp, who describes escorting an officer's baggage back to the coast, as 'we commenced our march in regular battle array.'[70] This raiment consisted of a 'rifle [sic] slung over my back, always loaded, and

67 Chichester and Burges-Short, *The Records and Badges of Every Regiment*, p.815.
68 G. Tylden, 'The Third Kaffir War, 1799-1802', *Journal of the Society for Army Historical Research*, vol.37, no.150 (June 1959), p.79.
69 TNA: WO 17/1587: Cape of Good Hope Monthly Returns, 1801, 1 October–December 1801.
70 Shipp, *The Extraordinary Military Career*, p.49.

a pistol in my holster-pipe'. Shipp was also 'mounted on a horse'.[71] Whilst this lends some credence to mounted infantry, Shipp never elaborates on whether this was his usual battle array, or an exception due to his position as part of an escort. Furthermore, Shipp contradicts himself in an earlier passage lamenting having to 'march nearly fifteen hundred miles through Africa'.[72] A word of caution must be reiterated, as Shipp's memoirs were written over 20 years after serving in South Africa. Potentially the boys may be the first building block for the subsequent generations of British mounted infantry, but the evidence remains sparse at best and may only represent the occasional ad hoc mounted boy rather than an entire company.

As plans were underway to send the boys to the frontier, not all the officers were pleased with the decision to send their charges to the Eastern Cape. Whilst out riding with Dundas, Lieutenant Colonel Mark Dickens of the 34th appealed to the Major General 'if they [the boys] woud [sic] not perform the business very well, young as they were'.[73] Dundas attempted to brush the matter aside, but Dickens persisted, 'it will be the ruin of a Regt of Boys such as these to disperse on such a service as a Caffre war before they have learnt the service'. As usual the irascible Dundas had short shrift for such a fair suggestion, 'Hold your peace Sir Hold your peace … I never desire to see your face within my doors Sir.'[74] Whilst Dickens fumed, it is harder to discern if the other regiments may have felt the same. Lady Barnard does not mention an objection from Majors George Maddison or Richard Stewart of the 65th, since these two officers do not seem to have been part of her social circle at the Cape, whereas Dickens had been a childhood friend. While Mercer of the 22nd appears not to have been able to object, as he had been suffering a series of fits or strokes since June 1801 that were so severe that one episode caused him to grind out some of his front teeth.[75] Laudable as Dickens' objections were, he seems to have had to face Dundas' ire alone. His fight with the Major General further illustrates the contrast between the nineteenth-century conception of the boy regiments and their modern counterparts. In modern warfare, many child soldiers are often given rudimentary training and then thrust into the heart of the battle. In contrast, by 1801 some of these boys had been serving with the colours for almost four years, and yet Dickens still felt they needed further time to mature and remained keen to continue their training and avoid unnecessary loss of life.

Despite Dickens' attempts to forestall their deployment, the composite light infantry company set sail for Algoa Bay, commanded by Captain Effingham Lindsay of the 22nd Foot. Described by Shipp as, 'one of the bravest officers in his majesty's army',[76] Lindsay had an extensive history of campaigning – including commanding detachments when he acted as adjutant at the Môle-Saint-Nicolas, on Saint-Domingue in 1795.[77]

71 Shipp, *The Extraordinary Military Career*, p.49.
72 Shipp, *The Extraordinary Military Career*, p.48.
73 Barnard, *The Cape Diaries*, vol.2 p.262.
74 Barnard, *The Cape Diaries*, vol.2, p.262.
75 Barnard, *The Cape Diaries*, vol.2, p.183.
76 Shipp, *The Extraordinary Military Career*, p.46.
77 TNA: WO 17/124: 22nd Foot Monthly Returns, 1 July 1795.

Lindsay and his company arrived at Algoa Bay after a short voyage, and Shipp describes the scene that awaited them, as they marched across the veldt to Graaff-Reinet: 'At every farmer's house on our line march, we found sad vestiges of murder and desolation ... Not a living creature was to be seen, unless, perchance, a poor dog might be discovered howling over the dead body of his master'.[78] The composite light infantry company were tasked with maintaining the link between Fort Frederick and Graaff-Reinet; it was on these patrols that Shipp racked up the 1,500 miles that he claims to have marched. By the time the light infantry company arrived in 1801 most of the fighting had descended into skirmishes in the bush, Shipp describes a typical action as consisting of firing on the Xhosa who 'will throw themselves flat upon their faces, and thus avoid the ball', they then would race forward, throwing their assegais, which, 'when in the air it looks like a shuttlecock violently struck.'[79]

With most of their time spent struggling through the bush, the boys' green uniforms 'were soon in a terribly ragged condition.' Their shoes had to be replaced with makeshift buffalo rawhide sewn together, whilst their trousers were ragged and patched, which at a distance looked like 'spotted leopards.' To add to this unsoldierly appearance, whilst at the Cape, Shipp gained six inches and found that his jacket was too tight for him to salute and his pantaloons were turning into shorts, later writing 'we might well have been compared to Falstaff's ragged recruits.'[80]

While Lindsay and his ragged comrades in the light infantry struggled through the bush and the conflict in the Zuurveld continued to smoulder, the situation in Europe was beginning to cool. By now France was ruled by the First Consul Napoleon Bonaparte, who, in concert with the British representative, the Marquess Cornwallis, negotiated and signed the Peace of Amiens on 27 March 1802. One of the provisions of the treaty agreed by both parties as early as 1 October 1801 – just as Dundas sent the boys to Algoa Bay – was the return of the Cape to the Batavian Republic.[81] Official confirmation arrived on 12 August 1802, and Dundas quickly set about the task of withdrawing the British garrison.

The boys were destined to continue their journey east, whilst the men of 81st and 91st Foot were given the option of drafting out and taking up service with the 22nd, 34th, and 65th.[82] This augmented the three battalions, with the result that in the space of five years they had gone from the smallest battalions in the British Army to some of the largest. Collectively these three boy battalions could now field 3,027 other ranks, a far cry from the deplorable state of only being able to make up a company in 1797.[83] With this fresh intake of men, the three regiments prepared for the next leg of their journey to the Presidencies of the Honourable East India Company.

78 Shipp, *The Extraordinary Military Career*, p.47.
79 Shipp, *The Extraordinary Military Career*, p.48.
80 Shipp, *The Extraordinary Military Career*, p.48.
81 Theal, *History of South Africa*, pp.75–76.
82 TNA: WO 25/944: 22 Foot. Statements of the Periods of service of all NCOs and Men, 24 June 1806; TNA: WO 25/964: 34th Foot, 1st Battalion. Statements of the Periods of service of all NCOs and Men, 24 June 1806; TNA: WO 25/1017: 65 Foot. Statements of the Periods of service of all NCOs and Men, 24 June 1806.
83 TNA: WO 17/1749: East Indies, August 1803.

# 6

# The Parting of the Ways

The Cape was the only time in the history of all three boy regiments where they served together. In the latter half of 1802, Major General Dundas slowly wound down the British garrisons across the foot of Africa. The first elements of the garrison he dispatched to India were two companies of boys from the 65th Foot, the lieutenant colonel's and the grenadier companies, commanded by Lieutenant William Ollenranshaw and Captain Edward Bullock, respectively. The 65th commenced their passage to India on 12 September 1802 aboard the East Indiaman *Travers*. Sadly, there is very little information about what transpired during their passage, aside from their arrival at Colombo, one of the major cities of the island of Ceylon (Sri Lanka) on 2 November 1802, after a relatively rapid transit across the Indian Ocean.[1]

## 'Retaliation and Reprisal'

Ceylon was another recent acquisition for the British Crown captured during the French Revolutionary Wars. Since 1658, the island had been politically divided; the coasts were ruled by the VOC, who used them as a base for the spice trade, whilst in the interior, nestled amongst the central highlands of Ceylon, was the Kingdom of Kandy, where during the 1800s, Sri Vikrama Rajasinha ruled from his secluded capital, also called Kandy.

Just like the Cape Colony, the British secured Ceylon in 1796 after news of the formation of the Batavian Republic and the subsequent war with the metropole reached the HEIC Presidency at Madras.[2] When the two companies of the 65th arrived on the island, the British appeared to have simply replaced the Dutch on the coast and, like their predecessors, avoided interfering in Kandyan affairs. Irrespective of these attempts at non-intervention, tension was already brewing between the new British administration and the Kandyans.

1 TNA: WO 12/7382: General Muster Books and Pay Lists, 65th Foot, 24 September 1802; *Sun (London)*, 20 April 1803.

2 William Knighton, *The History of Ceylon from the Earliest Period to the Present Time* (London: Longman, Brown, Green & Longmans, 1845), p.305.

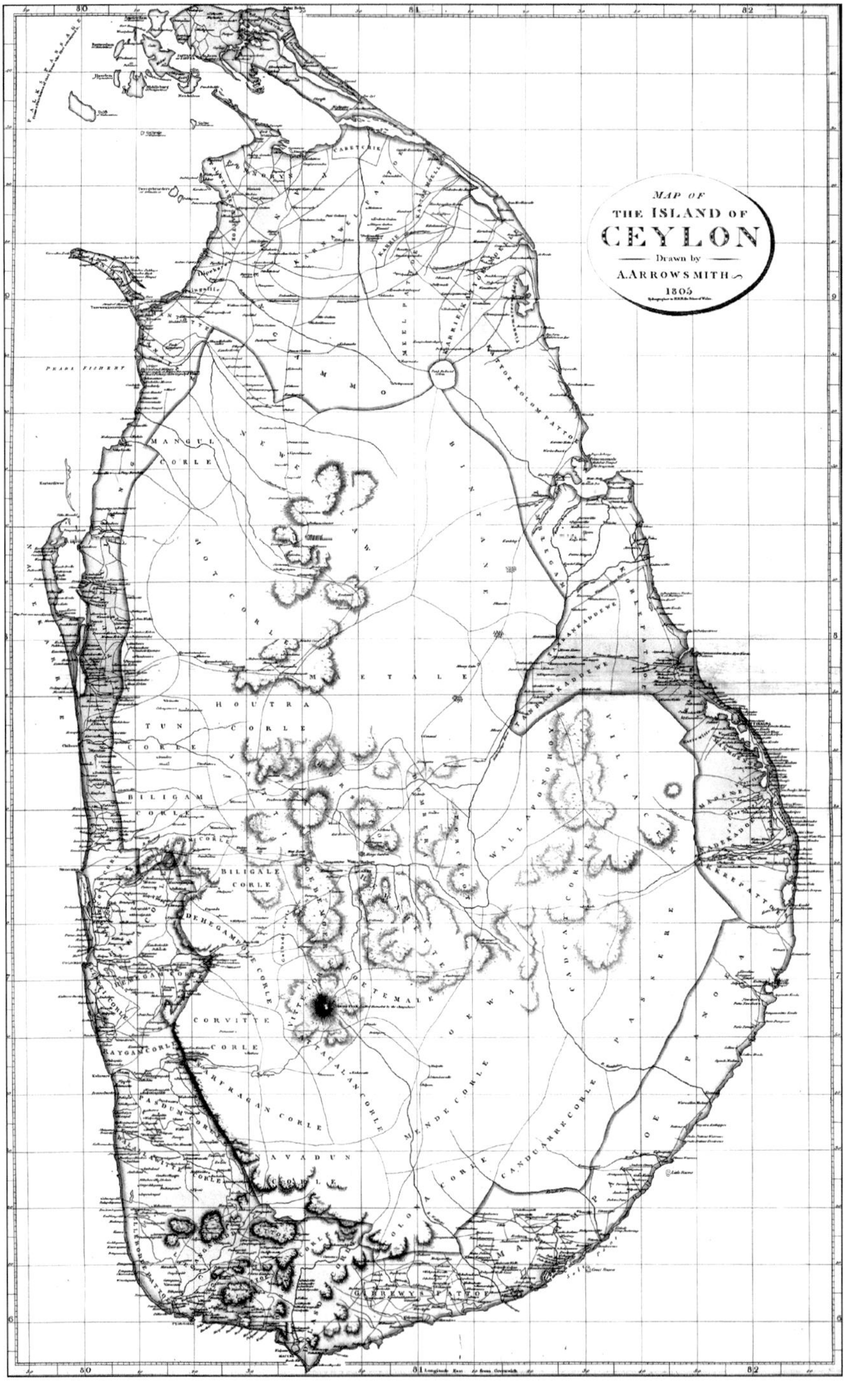


Map of Ceylon. Whilst the British held the coasts, the interior of Ceylon was ruled by the Kingdom of Kandy. (David Rumsey Historical Map Collection)

Matters came to a head in April 1802, when a party of Kandyans robbed some Muslim merchants, stealing their cargo of areca nuts, also known as betel nut – an intoxicant popular in South Asia. The merchants were operating under the protection of the British government, whose local representative, the Governor, the Honourable Frederick North, demanded restitution for the theft, which Vikrama and his *Adigar* (Prime Minister), initially consented to pay. As the year wore on, the Kandyans prevaricated, leading North to resort to force as the only means to secure repayment.[3]

The Kandyan War began on 31 January 1803 when Major General Hay MacDowell departed from Colombo with several British and Malay *sepoy* regiments and marched into the interior towards the town of Kandy. The subsequent conflict proved to be both arduous and bitterly fought as British columns struggled to move within the interior of Ceylon. The writer William Knighton described the difficult approach to Kandy experienced by an embassy sent in 1782, 'Occasionally a tolerable pathway was to be met with, but generally they [the diplomatic party] had to force their way through an almost impervious forest, inaccessible even to the light of heaven'.[4] The Kandyans were particularly adroit at allowing their enemies to advance into this difficult terrain and then harass them through persistent raids and cutting off supply routes. Travel was further hindered by the plethora of diseases that attacked unwary travellers as they attempted to penetrate the highlands and proved a particular bane of the British forces whilst they fought in Ceylon.

Whilst MacDowell struggled through the jungle, the two companies of the 65th Foot, commanded by Lieutenant Colonel George Maddison, were left behind to form the principal part of the garrison of Colombo, alongside 300 *sepoys* of the Ceylon Regiment.[5] Their time in garrison was brief, and soon the boys of the 65th were sent up country to face the Kandyans. The catalyst came on 11 March 1803, when Lieutenant Patrick Campbell of the 51st (2nd Yorkshire, West Riding) Regiment of Foot became too sick to continue in command of Fort Frederic. Consequently, Lieutenant Ollenranshaw was sent alone to take Campbell's place. The fort was situated near the village of Kotadeniyawa, about 30 miles north-east of Colombo and was a depot for MacDowell's army. Ollenranshaw's role was to superintend the transfer of supplies – through Fort Frederic – to the army in Kandy.[6]

On 13 March, barely two days after Ollenranshaw received his independent command, reports reached Colombo that a force of 6,000 Kandyans were on the march to Fort Frederic. In response, Captain Bullock was sent to the fort with his grenadiers and 50 *sepoys* of the Ceylon Regiment. Fortunately for Bullock and his boys, they did not encounter the advancing Kandyans. Bullock arrived on 17 March, and soon afterwards his small garrison was augmented by the arrival of another 25 boys of the 65th, who had been detached with a party to drive the Kandyans from British territory.[7] Prior

3 Knighton, *The History of Ceylon*, p.311.
4 Knighton, *The History of Ceylon*, p.304.
5 James Cordiner, *A Description of Ceylon*, vol.2 (London, Hurst, Rees, and Orme, 1807), p.185.
6 J. Penry Lewis, *List of Inscriptions on Tombstones and Monuments in Ceylon* (Colombo: H.C. Cottle, 1913), p.81.
7 Cordiner, *A Description of Ceylon*, p.193.

to joining Bullock, this small detachment may have been involved in a minor skirmish on 20 March 1803, which provides a good idea of the type of fighting the 65th had to endure on Ceylon.

On 19 March the commandant of the coastal town of Negombo, Captain Herbert Beaver of the 19th (1st Yorkshire, North Riding) Regiment of Foot, learnt that a force of Kandyans had advanced into British territory and occupied a strong position. Beaver managed to collect a detachment consisting of one serjeant and 12 boys of the 65th's grenadiers, alongside a *havildar* – a native officer, roughly equivalent to a serjeant – and 12 *sepoys*. Beaver and his band reached the Kandyans around 1:00 a.m. on 20 March and immediately attacked the Kandyan position. Beaver's dispatch describes the action as commencing when, 'We passed a piquet of the enemy, which fled at our approach, and then proceeded to attack. Not a shot was fired at us.' They could hear drums beating as they approached and expected some serious resistance, instead they were challenged by a single sentry, who raised the alarm and the Kandyans disappeared into the jungle.[8] These small actions – including storming forts and feints – formed much of the fighting that the 65th experienced.

## Sicken and So Die

According to James Cordiner's *A Description of Ceylon*, the grenadiers of Bullock's company were 'all picked men, about six feet high, and from eighteen to twenty-three years of age'.[9] Slowly, these soldiers who had sprouted from the boys recruited in the Borders and Lowlands of Scotland succumbed to a fever that was reminiscent of 'the common bilious remittent fever, to which the European constitution is so remarkably subject in India, when exposed to a hot sun during the day, and a highly vitiated atmosphere in the night.'[10] This medical report undertaken in April 1803 further elaborates, 'The mortality attending it however has been much greater than in any former instance'.[11]

Because of this fever, the grenadier company of the 65th was quietly destroyed within the walls of Fort Frederic during the month of March 1803. The sickness that carried away so many of these lads was most likely malaria. Evidence for the disease's identity appears in the medical report, which mentions the landscape surrounding the fort was low-lying and covered with marshes, the perfect breeding ground for mosquitoes. All 83 boys in the garrison succumbed to malaria, their condition rendered worse by a lack of medical assistance, as the nearest hospitals were situated in Colombo and could only be reached by boat. By 5 April, Ollenranshaw was dead, and Bullock was the only European left in the garrison, as it appears the remaining members of the 65th had been stricken with malaria and evacuated to Colombo. Bullock was ordered to remove any of the materials in Fort Frederic to the coastal town of Negombo and destroy the

8 *Exeter Flying Post*, 6 October 1803.
9 Cordiner, *A Description of Ceylon*, p.193.
10 Cordiner, *A Description of Ceylon*, pp.270–271.
11 Cordiner, *A Description of Ceylon*, pp.270–271.

fort as it was deemed too sickly. Despite his efforts, Bullock also fell victim to the fever and died on 5 May, alongside 81 out of the original 83 grenadiers. According to Cordiner, the only survivors were Lieutenant Thomas Hutchins and two boys of the grenadier company.[12]

## Massacre and Miasma

Meanwhile, MacDowell and the main British force had reached Kandy on 20 February and found the town completely emptied. At this time North accepted a proposal to dethrone Vikrama and replace him with Prince Muttusamy. To secure this regime change, a mixed force of 300 Europeans, 700 Malay *sepoys* and some Indian artillerymen were left to garrison Kandy.[13] Just like Bullock's detachment, the garrison of Kandy suffered severely from sickness, whilst also facing the added disaster of mounting desertion as the Kandyans attempted to entice the Malays to turn their coats. By June, the garrison had been cut off from relief from the coast. Weakened and sickly, the commander, Major Adam Davie, was forced to capitulate.

Despite agreeing to terms, including the withdrawal of the garrison to the port at Trincomalee, the Kandyans reneged on the terms of capitulation. In the resulting debacle, on 26 June, much of the garrison was massacred, falling under the knives, swords, and clubs of the Kandyans. As a result of the massacre, the British had been forced out of Kandy and the highlands. When the news reached Colombo 'it was like a clap of thunder … followed by an awful and overpowering calm.'[14]

The lull which descended on the island lasted for several weeks, as the British were unable to mount any offensive operations. The stillness was eventually broken by the Kandyans who began to encroach on British territory, threatening all the British frontier garrisons simultaneously. Knighton described this phase of the war as a 'mass of petty actions'.[15] This swarm of small skirmishes – many similar to the previously described assault on a fort by Beaver with a small party of grenadiers – became routine for the 65th whilst they were posted on Ceylon. By August, 'all parties of Europeans employed … proportions of men … from the 51st and 65th regiments', as despite their losses at Fort Frederic, the 65th still had soldiers available for firefighting the encroaching Kandyans.[16] The boys had become the main strike force for the British government on Ceylon.

At some point in the latter half of 1803, Maddison and the headquarters of the 65th moved from Colombo to Point de Galle, at the southern tip of the island. The date of the relocation is difficult to pinpoint because the regiment's monthly returns are missing from 1801–1807, whilst the muster rolls taken on Ceylon were recorded every 183 days.

12 Cordiner, *A Description of Ceylon*, p.193.
13 David Howell, 'The British Conquest of Ceylon and the Massacre at Kandy 1803', *The Napoleon Series*, <https://www.napoleon-series.org/military-information/battles-and-campaigns/the-british-conquest-of-ceylon-and-the-massacre-at-kandy-1803/>, accessed 17 March 2025.
14 Cordiner, *A Description of Ceylon*, p.213.
15 Knighton, *The History of Ceylon*, p.318.
16 Cordiner, *A Description of Ceylon*, p.226.

It is possible the move might have taken place during the summer. This tallies with Beaver's movements, as he was ordered to take over the town of Matura, situated about 20 miles east of Point de Galle. Many of the detachments he led, whilst in command at Matura, included boys from the 65th, suggesting the regimental headquarters might have moved in August 1803, at the same time Beaver relocated.

After taking up command in the south, Beaver spent several nights launching raids into the surrounding country, before assembling a force to retake Tangalle, a coastal town 20 miles east of Matura. The force set out on 27 August and on their march encountered a strong body of Kandyans holding a low wall. Their fire caused two casualties amongst the British, one of which was Corporal Thomas Maitland of the 65th, who was wounded. Beaver cleared the wall and reached Tangalle the next day, where he found the fort deserted.[17]

Meanwhile, in the north, there was considerable alarm amongst the many European families in Colombo as the town was menaced by an advancing Kandyan army. The agitation in Colombo increased when the Kandyans captured a small fort at Hanwella, barely 15 miles from the capital. In response, Lieutenant Charles Wilkinson Mercer of the 51st Foot organised a detachment of 30 Europeans – including an unknown number from the 65th – and 25 Malay *sepoys* to retake Hanwella. This detachment later rendezvoused with another 25 *sepoys* and 50 armed *lascarins*, a term used to describe indigenous Sri Lankans fighting for the British.

During the evening of 21 August, Mercer encountered a force of Kandyans marching on Colombo and dispersed them. On the 22nd, as the detachment neared Hanwella, they cleared a battery which had been placed to guard a bridge. The Kandyans faked their withdrawal from the battery in the hope they could ambush Mercer's detachment. The ruse failed, and Mercer was able to continue his advance and retake Hanwella.[18] For two weeks the garrison held a dilapidated fort, until Mercer withdrew the detachment to a nearby house, which was enclosed by a 'slight wall'.[19] Here, his detachment held against three successive attacks by the Kandyans, and during these assaults, the garrison had to watch anxiously as the number of wounded grew. Some relief came on 5 September, when Captain William Pollock of the 51st Foot arrived with a small party to take command of Hanwella. His arrival proved fortuitous as King Vikrama himself appeared on the 6th, hoping to clear the route to Colombo. The King planned to use several 6-pounder guns, manned by lascars from the British army who had been impressed into service after being captured by the Kandyans.

The Kandyan attack began with a deluge of grapeshot peppering the walls of the house occupied by the British detachment. Under this fire, the Kandyans advanced to within 200 yards and halted, seemingly hesitant to close the distance. Pollock took this opportunity to order Mercer and a part of his detachment to use an unseen pathway to come upon the Kandyan's left flank. Arriving on the Kandyan flank, Mercer's party poured fire into their ranks, whilst Pollock sallied forth, striking the Kandyans in the

17 Cordiner, *A Description of Ceylon*, p.223.
18 Cordiner, *A Description of Ceylon*, p.226.
19 Cordiner, *A Description of Ceylon*, p.231.

front. The firefight continued for two hours, during which several Malays who had deserted to the Kandyan army advanced and fought hand-to-hand with the British. One Malay speared a boy of the 65th through his thigh, but the unnamed private was able to overcome his foe. The battle ended when a shot fell near Vikrama, and he decided to withdraw from the battlefield, his army trailing in his wake.

Pollock suffered two casualties, but managed to capture the royal Kandyan standard, 80 prisoners, two lost British 6-pounders and a 3-pounder, alongside hundreds of stolen Brown Bess muskets, Singhalese muskets, and ammunition. Additionally, Pollock freed 150 Bengali and Madras lascars and 26 Malays who had been forced to work the Kandyan guns. Despite his success, Pollock was unable to complete his victory as many of his men continued to suffer from the aftermath of the ever-pervasive fever, which left them with a weakness in their knees and so unable to mount a pursuit.[20] Only after the arrival of fresh infantry from Colombo could Pollock strike out, leaving Hanwella on 9 September. The British detachment managed to march six miles, *en route* driving out a force of Kandyans blocking the path. By 12 September, Pollock had advanced into Kandyan territory and reached Ruwunwella, where Vikrama had gathered a force to oppose the British column.

As he pressed ever deeper into the highlands Pollock had to clear several batteries erected by the Kandyans to slow his progress. On reaching Ruwunwella, Pollock found the Kandyans had constructed a score of batteries mounted with cannon behind a river. Under fire, the British discovered a ford and crossed, seizing a battery before the bulk of the Kandyan army fled with Pollock in hot pursuit. Another British detachment under Captain Buchan also arrived on the right flank of the Kandyan army, causing a great deal of confusion and the loss of several pieces of artillery. Pollock, now united with Buchan, captured the village of Ruwanwella, occupying one of Vikrama's royal residences. The next day Pollock could find no trace of the Kandyan army, so he decided to burn the palace and several houses which contained provisions assembled by the Kandyans before retreating to Hanwella. This is only one of the major examples of British columns – including boys of the 65th – sent to engage the Kandyans, as the British continued to mount a plethora of similar, smaller expeditions into the jungles and hills to disperse the Kandyans from their ambushes or fortified posts.

With the countryside in turmoil, local inhabitants could not be relied on to provide food, which led to a breakdown in logistics. In response, British forces were given carte blanche to live off the land and could 'kill plenty of beef and veal, and to cut down cocoa-nut-trees, the tops of which ... afford a rich white vegetable, equal in flavour to the finest cabbage',[21] often washed down with a liberal supply of the local spirit, arrack.

While columns on the march were relatively well fed, they remained susceptible to disease, and some very unpleasant marching companions. In addition to the fatal mosquitoes, whose bite caused the dreaded fevers which could decimate entire garrisons, British soldiers were plagued with small leeches. These blood-sucking worms fastened themselves to the advancing soldiers, further adding to their discomfort.[22]

20 Cordiner, *A Description of Ceylon*, p.235.
21 Cordiner, *A Description of Ceylon*, p.231.
22 Cordiner, *A Description of Ceylon*, pp.254–255.

Amid this increasingly brutal conflict, two companies of the 34th Foot were detached from the main regiment in Madras to join the garrison of Ceylon. The companies consisted of Major George Dodsworth's and Captain John Matthias Everard's companies, who were posted on command at Trincomalee, on the east of Ceylon, in August 1803.[23] Like the 65th, they were tasked with responding to the constant Kandyan raids, and as soon as the 34th Foot landed they were deployed to Jaffna in the north of the island. On 25 August, a party of Kandyans had attacked the province of Jaffna, reaching the coast at Chundikulam. At the nearby town of Jaffnapatnam, a small party of the 34th commanded by Lieutenant Adam Downing were sent to dislodge this band of Kandyans. Downing and his boys managed to destroy several Kandyan magazines by setting them ablaze, before they returned to Jaffnapatnam.[24]

The detachments from the 34th and 65th Foot spent another year in this cycle of fighting. Both the 34th and 65th were retained on Ceylon until October 1804 when they left the island and rejoined their parent regiments in Madras and Bombay, respectively.[25] The war had been conducted 'with great cruelty on both sides. It was, in fact a system of retaliation and reprisal which no country could long endure.'[26] The constant raids and destruction continued even after the 34th and 65th had left the island, only coming to an end when Vikrama eventually called for an armistice in 1805. Whilst no formal treaty was agreed upon, the conflict did not start again until 1814, when another group of merchants under British protection were maltreated, and a force was prepared to seek retribution against the Kandyans.[27] This conflict did not concern the boys, they had far more pressing matters to attend to in Ceylon's gargantuan neighbour, the Indian subcontinent.

23 TNA: WO 12/4873: General Muster Books and Pay Lists, 34th Foot 1st Battalion, 1801, 24 August 1803.
24 Cordiner, *A Description of Ceylon*, p.244.
25 TNA: WO 17/1647: Ceylon Monthly Returns, 1804, 1 October 1804.
26 Knighton, *The History of Ceylon*, p.318.
27 Knighton, *The History of Ceylon*, p.323.

# 7

# The Coming Tempest

Having anticipated events by following the ebb and flow of the Ceylon campaign, this chapter returns to 16 October 1802 as the 22nd Foot set sail from the Cape. The boys of the 22nd had boarded a small American ship, the *Manhattan*, which had been stopped at the Cape for some time. Shipp describes both the ship and her captain as 'cranky' adding, 'She took in water in large quantities – he grog; she would not go steady – neither would he; she was often sea-sick – so was he: in fact, they were a cranky pair.'[1] Moreover, the *Manhattan*'s stay at the Cape had not improved her overall condition as her hull had become fouled with barnacles and so the vessel could only sail at a sluggish pace.

The voyage got off to a poor start; Private Samuel Plummer, the son of a 'respectable' tradesman from Dereham, Norfolk, recalled that two days out from Cape Town, 'The vessel on board, to cook the provision for the soldiers, being cased with wood, took fire when the bricks in the flue got hot'.[2] The *Manhattan* was forced to return to Table Bay for repairs, with the boys spending the following months crossing the Indian Ocean anxiously watching the cooking vessel in case it caught fire again.

The slow pace of the *Manhattan* considerably lengthened the journey time and meant that the water supply started to run low. The ship also appears to have been sailing far off course, as Shipp claims that they sighted the island of Sumatra, which lies at the eastern limit of the Bay of Bengal. As the *Manhattan* limped along the coast, the crew spotted a town and hove to, dispatching a small party, including Shipp, to purchase wood and water from the locals. Negotiations were managed by the captain's Sri Lankan servant, who could speak several languages. However, their first forays were rebuffed as the local king ordered the ship to leave. The desperate crew of the *Manhattan* were left with no option and planned to take what they needed. The morning after the failed negotiations, a small party of soldiers landed alongside the sailors of the *Manhattan* and immediately set about collecting wood and water. As they worked, a hostile crowd formed and threatened the American sailors and British boys in an attempt to force them back onto the ship. When threats proved unsatisfactory, the locals followed through by firing arrows at the working party. The officer charged with defending the sailors ordered a volley fired above the heads of the locals, which dispersed the crowd. Eventually tempers

1 Shipp, *The Extraordinary Military Career*, p.53.
2 Plummer, *The Journal of Samuel Plummer*, p.8

cooled, and the *Manhattan* was allowed to purchase supplies.[3] Soon the ship was at sea again and making for the Bay of Bengal.

Eventually, in January 1803, the *Manhattan* sighted land again, the delta of one of the great rivers of India, the mighty Ganges. The ship entered the mouth of the river at the Saugar Roads and was piloted upstream along the Hooghly River to Fort William, the main fort and principal defence for Calcutta (Kolkata).

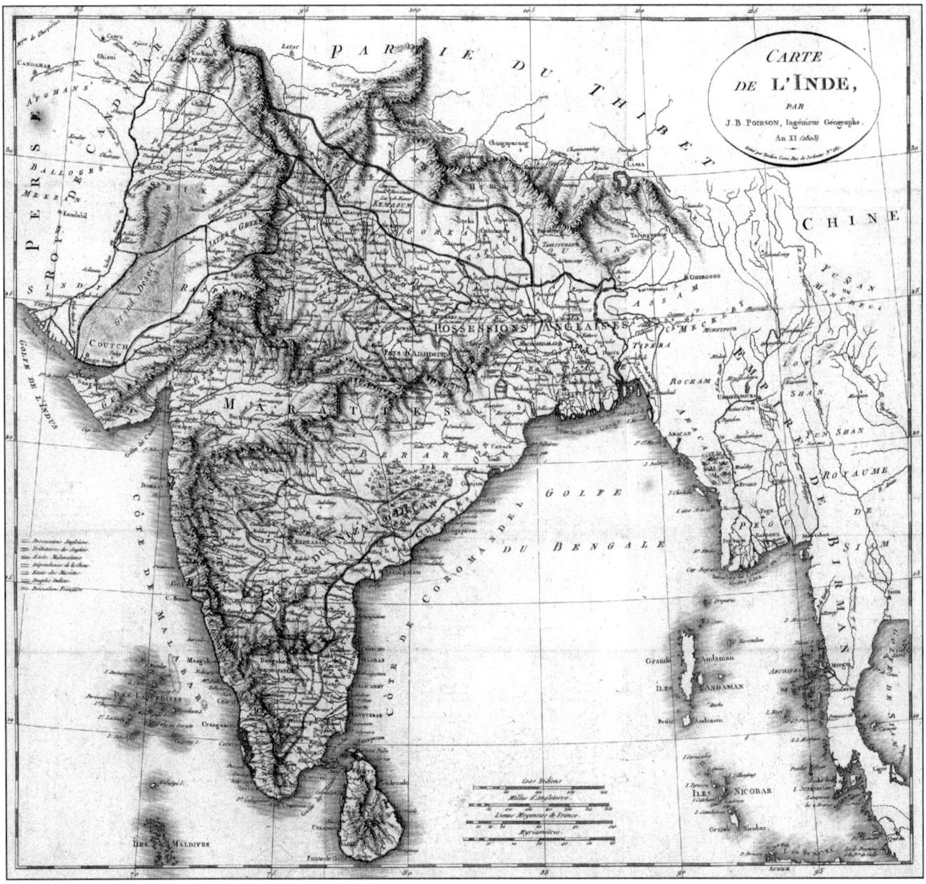


Map of India 1803. (David Rumsey Historical Map Collection)

Following in the wake of the 22nd Foot, in December 1802, the 34th began to embark their lads for service in the East Indies. The muster rolls indicate that the majority of the regiment embarked aboard the Indiaman *United Kingdom*, in February 1803.[4] Unusually, the ship's log does not include a passenger list or mention taking on

3 Shipp, *The Extraordinary Military Career*, pp.54–55.
4 TNA: WO 12/4873: General Muster Books and Pay Lists, 34th Foot, 16 April 1803.

board the 34th Foot, calling into question which ship the regiment sailed upon. It is only possible to confirm that the 34th Foot crossed the Indian Ocean in two months, eventually making landfall at Madras (Chennai) in April 1803.

Returning to the 65th Foot, as noted earlier, the regiment set sail in detachments from the Cape commencing in September 1802. The remaining eight companies set sail much later, finally quitting Cape Town in February 1803.[5] Most of the 65th, including 441 all ranks, 14 women, and 15 children, boarded the East Indiaman, *Henry Addington*, on 20 February.[6] The 65th also embarked an unrecorded number of men upon the Indiaman *Ocean* at the same time. By 25 February the convoy was ready to sail, with *Ocean* displaying the signal to weigh anchor to the *Henry Addington*.[7]

The journey proved to be relatively uneventful, marked by one major gale which caused the *Henry Addington* to take on water and split the topsail on 28 February. While *Ocean* does not mention much in the way of day-to-day details, a good impression of the life the boys led below decks can be gleaned from Captain James Kirkpatrick of the *Henry Addington*. Kirkpatrick had the 65th 'picking oakum' for most of their time aboard his ship; this painstaking task involved pulling apart old pieces of rope to be used in caulking the decks of the ship. This tedious existence was only occasionally relieved by brief moments of action, such as when a false alarm was raised on 30 March that a man had fallen overboard.[8] On the same day aboard *Ocean*, Seaman John Riddle was handed 84 lashes for drunkenness and insulting Major Richard Stewart of the 65th. Apart from these isolated instances, life within this wooden realm remained prosaic, with time slowly ticking by to the ever-present rhythmic lap of the sea and constrained by the humdrum of nautical routine.

As the days ticked by aboard these wooden islands, tragedy struck twice amidst the regiment. First on the *Henry Addington*, where one of the soldiers' children, Thomas Blair, passed away and was laid to rest in the Indian Ocean. Later, on 5 May at 4:00 p.m., Private John Allen expired aboard *Ocean*, cause of death unknown, and was subsequently committed to the deep at eight that night.[9] His passing was particularly poignant as the *Ocean* was only two days from making landfall at Bombay (Mumbai), where the 65th were brought ashore on 7 May 1803.

## The Lull

Life in a barracks in India was not for the faint-hearted, and at times just reaching the shore was a trial. When the 34th Foot reached Madras, they had to contend with

5 The British Library (BL): IOR/L/MAR/B/170C, Journals, Ledgers and Pay Books of the *Henry Addington*, 25 February 1803.
6 BL: IOR/L/MAR/B/170C, Journals, Ledgers and Pay Books of the *Henry Addington*, Passenger List.
7 BL: IOR/L/MAR/B/170C, Journals, Ledgers and Pay Books of the *Henry Addington*, 25 February 1803.
8 BL: IOR/L/MAR/B/170C, Journals, Ledgers and Pay Books of the *Henry Addington*, February–March 1803.
9 BL: IOR/L/MAR/B/222-I, Journals, Ledgers and Pay Books of the *Ocean*, 30 March and 7 May 1803.

Fort St George was the principal barracks and defence for Madras during the eighteenth and early-nineteenth centuries. (Anne S.K. Brown Collection)

the notorious surf along the Coromandel Coast, as Madras infamously did not have a natural harbour. This meant that any troops or passengers arriving in the presidency had to be rowed close to shore and then wade to the beach.[10] Despite the dangers, the sight must have been breathtaking. A prospective HEIC cadet, Valentine Blacker, testified on his arrival in 1798 that the skies above were 'interspersed with tints that I as an inhabitant of England has no idea of' whilst the shores promised, 'A flat country thickly planted but here and there diversified with dark blue mountains.'[11]

In contrast, Calcutta and Bombay were easier to alight from as both towns were low-lying. Calcutta had been constructed in the midst of a swamp, while Bombay was founded upon an island off the western coast of India. The route to Calcutta was eulogised by the memoirist and lawyer William Hickey who found Calcutta to be, 'beautiful beyond imagination, the whole of the landscape being more luxuriant than I had any expectation of seeing in the burning climate of Bengal'.[12] As Hickey noted the burning heat was a key feature of life in Bengal and whilst the low-lying land offered bountiful views for the eye, the muggy climate also raised the ever-present spectre of tropical diseases, the invisible thorns beneath Bengal's beautiful visage.

10 Richard Holmes, *Sahib: The British Soldier in India* (London: HarperCollins, 2005), pp.115–116.
11 Valentine Blacker, David C.J. Howell (ed.), *War Without Pity* (Warwick: Helion & Company Limited, 2018), p.56.
12 William Hickey, Peter Quennell (ed.), *Memoirs of William Hickey* (London: Purnell Book Services Limited, 1975), p.224.

Once the 22nd, 34th, and 65th Foot, were established in their respective barracks, life quickly settled into the routines of military discipline. The 34th Foot were posted to Fort St George, the main defence for Madras, and seemed to have passed their time relatively quietly, rarely leaving the fort, aside from a detachment sent to Ceylon. Very little of note appears to have been recorded about their time in Madras aside from a regimental review conducted on 4 January 1804 by Madras' Governor Lord William Cavendish-Bentick. The Governor 'was much pleased with the appearance of the 34th Regiment … [and] the Corps performed the Manoeuvres in a manner which reflects great credit on Colonel Dickens and the Officers.'[13]

A common feature of these early months was confinement to barracks, Plummer describes the regimen the 22nd Foot were placed under, upon disembarking at Fort William, Calcutta, 'Being a newly arrived regiment, very strict orders were given that we should be closely confined in the barracks during the day … We were allowed the privilege of walking round the inside of the fort from six till eight o'clock in the evening; and from five in the morning till nine', but Calcutta remained off limits.[14] To avoid the dangers of heatstroke, the boys' confinement lasted for the hottest parts of the day, which effectively rendered the boys to a sedentary existence as most of the day-to-day barrack work, including cooking and cleaning was undertaken by Indian workers. Whilst the HEIC's native soldiers – *sepoys* – took the watches during the day. All of this free time almost inevitably led to terrible results. Within hours of the 22nd Foot's landing at Fort William, the boys were presented with bottles of rum by another regiment and 'a scene ensued that was beyond description; drinking, singing, dancing, shouting, fighting and bottles flying in all directions.'[15] Still a teenager, the now 18-year-old Shipp recounts that he had not touched spirits and so chose to quit the barracks when this debauchery started, and often slept outside to avoid the sound of rowing and smell of drink.

While many of the boys passed their time brawling and drinking, others found alternative pursuits. Encouraged by Captain Effingham Lindsay, Shipp set time aside to learn how to read and write. Some of Shipp's comrades turned their focus toward theological concerns; Plummer, for example, found God and was encouraged to join the local prayer meeting. This process of religious instruction first appeared in Africa, where Plummer recalled some of the boys had met John Edmonds of the London Missionary Society.[16] At the time Edmonds had been preaching to the Khoikhoi, however having had a major falling out with the head of the mission, Edmonds left to continue his missionary work in India, where his congregation often included boys from the 22nd Foot.

Even the sanctity of the prayer group could not escape the violence of barrack-room life. Plummer claims he was faced with persecution from some Roman Catholic soldiers in the barracks. During one prayer meeting, an alarm was raised when several soldiers appeared with clubs, 'crying out, "Where are the Methodists?"'[17] In the ensuing fight,

13 *Madras Courier*, 11 January 1804.
14 Plummer, *The Journal of Samuel Plummer*, p.10.
15 Shipp, *The Extraordinary Military Career*, p.58.
16 Plummer, *The Journal of Samuel Plummer*, p.12.
17 Plummer, *The Journal of Samuel Plummer*, p.12.

Built amidst a swamp and known for its rowdiness, Fort William was a rough introduction to India for the boys. (Yale Center for British Art, Paul Mellon Collection)

two men were badly injured and taken to the hospital. Lieutenant Colonel Mercer ordered a hunt for the perpetrators and promised his protection to the prayer group. Despite Mercer's orders, only one man could be identified and disciplined, whilst most of the assailants escaped punishment. Although he failed to capture most of the miscreants, the Lieutenant Colonel's swift response, for the moment, seemed to have an effect and the prayer group was liberated from further molestation. Mercer also extended his protection to the 'Methodists' and encouraged them to form a prayer group of 20 boys, which according to Plummer, brought the violence to an end. Subsequently, the worst the prayer group suffered was the 'scoffs of drunkards'.[18] These petty barrack-room squabbles proved to be brief distractions, as the boys' time in a garrison was destined to be short; the Indian subcontinent was primed to erupt into a general conflagration.

## Bold Undertakings

The boys had reached India, just as the region was on the cusp of monumental change. The subcontinent was divided between two great powers, Britain's Honourable East India Company and the Maratha Confederacy. The HEIC dominated most of the coasts through its three presidencies, Calcutta, Madras, and Bombay. Each presidency was administered by its own government and fielded its own armies, but these separate governments were ultimately overseen by the Governor General of Bengal. Most regiments fielded by the

18 Plummer, *The Journal of Samuel Plummer*, p.13.

HEIC presidencies were composed of *sepoys*, native Indians drilled like the British army and wearing the famous red coat but raised and paid for by the HEIC. In addition to the native infantry and cavalry, the Company also fielded several European battalions.[19] The boy battalions were not directly administered by the HEIC, as they were King's Regiments – British Army battalions whose upkeep was paid for by the HEIC once they reached the Subcontinent.[20] Put together, the resources available to the HEIC were truly formidable, and if the King's Regiments are included in their muster, the Company had the capability to field over 100,000 men during the early nineteenth century.[21]

While John Company – as the HEIC was informally called – dominated the coast, they were not alone on the political stage. Stretching from Gujarat in the west, across the great Gangetic Plain and the Deccan plateau, until it met the sea again at Orissa and the Bay of Bengal in the east, lay the dominion of the Maratha Confederacy. A collection of maharajahs who nominally owed their allegiance to the Peshwa of the confederacy, Bajirao II. The Marathas were a Hindu empire that had displaced the Muslim Mughal emperors over the course of the eighteenth century, culminating in 1771 when they became the protectors of Emperor Shah Alam II.[22] The Marathas had proven to be adept horsemen and were skilled at swarming across the countryside, raiding and exacting tribute. The rajas of the Confederacy were also keen adaptors; for example, Mahadaji Scindia of Gwalior had amassed his own European-style regiments to dominate both his Indian and European rivals alike. Indeed, Scindia's European-trained battalions gave him the ability to control the Gangetic Plain, known as Hindustan at the time.[23]

At the beginning of the nineteenth century, there were four principal players in the Confederacy. Daulat Rao Scindia, the son of Mahadaji, had inherited his father's powerful armies and was a clear favourite to become the main power behind the Peshwa. Scindia's ascendancy did not go unchallenged, and he faced bitter competition from Yashwantrao Holkar, ruler of the Central Indian principality of Indore. Unlike Scindia, Holkar's army retained a strong tradition for freebooting cavalry raids, which had been the mainstay of Maratha tactics. Beyond Scindia's and Holkar's kingdoms and marking the eastern edge of the Maratha Confederacy was the domain of Ragoji II Bhonsle of Nagpur, who ruled a vast swath of territory that bordered both the Madras and Bengal presidencies. At the other extreme in the west in Gujarat, Anand Rao Gaekwad ruled from Beroda.[24] Unlike the other three Maratha strongmen, Gaekwad was on friendly terms with the HEIC and ultimately signed a treaty with the British, assisting them against his rival rajas.

19 Joshua Provan, *Bullocks, Grain and Good Madeira* (Warwick: Helion & Company Ltd., 2021), p.17.
20 Linch, *The British Army*, pp.57–58.
21 Stuart Reid, *Armies of the East India Company 1750–1850* (Oxford: Osprey Publishing, 2014), pp.5–8.
22 James Grant Duff, *A History of the Mahrattas* (Calcutta: R. Cambray & Co., 1912), vol.2, pp.224–225.
23 Andy Copestake, *'Their Infantry and Guns Will Astonish You'* (Warwick: Helion & Company Ltd. 2021), p.46.
24 Lawrence James, *Raj: The Making of British India* (London: Abacus, 1997), pp.69–70.

For much of the eighteenth century the HEIC had expanded in fits and starts, using treaties signed with local rulers like the Gaekwad, to extend the Company's influence and forestall French encroachment. This steady expansion was about to receive an adrenaline rush with the arrival of Governor General Richard, Marquess Wellesley in 1798. Despite the near-fatal blow delivered to the French Empire in India during the Seven Years War (1756–1763), Wellesley remained concerned about Gallic influence with local rulers. These fears initially found their form in the HEIC's nemesis, Tipu Sultan of Mysore, who had been an active correspondent with Paris until his death in 1799.[25] Tipu's removal from the political scene and the subsequent Peace of Amiens, which ended the war with France in 1802, did not allay Wellesley's apprehensions; instead, it increased them. Wellesley recognised that the Peace of Amiens removed the Royal Navy blockade and gave France breathing space to attempt to reassert herself in the east, potentially through the French adventurers serving as officers in Scindia's army.[26] In June 1803, Wellesley's worst fears materialised when a small expedition arrived at the last French enclave, Pondicherry. The force was commanded by *général de division* Charles-Mathieu-Isidore Decaen, who had been named *capitaine général des établissements français dans l'Inde* and dispatched with several battalions of infantry to try and reassert France's diminished influence.[27]

All of this served as a spur for Wellesley to push for more decisive action and bring the Marathas into an alliance. His opportunity came when a civil war broke out in 1802 between Holkar and Scindia over who would be the power behind Peshwa Bajirao's throne. When Holkar trounced Scindia's army outside the Maratha capital Pune, on 25 October 1802, Bajirao fled and sought help from the British. The aid Bajirao received was a subsidiary alliance, formalised with the Treaty of Bassein, which at a stroke brought the Marathas under the HEIC's sway. Wellesley had won permission from the Peshwa to permanently garrison 6,000 Company troops in the Maratha empire to protect Bajirao, and at the same time block any French adventurers from enlisting in the Maratha armies.[28]

Whilst this secured the Peshwa, the treaty did not include any of the other rajas. Over the course of 1803 Wellesley attempted to bring them into a subsidiary alliance, however by the end of the summer, Scindia and Bhonsle were still reluctant to come under Britain's dominion. Consequently, the HEIC began to raise one of the largest hosts the British had ever assembled in the East Indies, until war was inevitably declared against Scindia and Bhonsle in August 1803.

## John Company Goes to War

Due to the sheer size of the Maratha dominions, two armies were needed to tackle the Confederacy in the north and south, whilst smaller expeditions were launched upon the

25 Mikaberidze, *The Napoleonic Wars*, p.87.
26 BL: IOR/H/622, War with Sindhia, 5 November 1802, pp.56–57.
27 René Chartrand, *Napoleon's Overseas Army* (London: Osprey, 1989), pp.34–35.
28 Provan, *Bullocks, Grain and Good Madeira*, p.17.

western and eastern extremities. The southern thrust was led by Major General Arthur Wellesley, the future Duke of Wellington, and this much-studied campaign resulted in the close-run battle of Assaye. Meanwhile in the north, the Commander in Chief of India, General Gerard Lake, led the Grand Army across the Gangetic Plain with the aim of crushing Scindia's Army of Hindustan and its European-trained battalions.[29] The boys were not involved in these major undertakings; instead, they were ordered to join two smaller operations on the periphery, fighting in Gujarat in the west and Orissa in the east.

## The 65th at Bombay

Starting with the 65th Foot, this battalion came under Arthur Wellesley's command. In addition to acting offensively against Scindia and Bhonsle, Wellesley was also charged with the defence of Gujarat and the Gaekwad's domains. Whilst Wellesley focused on bringing the main Maratha armies to battle, he delegated the defence of Gujarat to Colonel John Murray of the 84th Regiment of Foot. Murray's command consisted of two parts; his main strike force had been posted to Beroda and operated above the Nerbudda river, whilst the 65th formed part of the defensive forces, deployed south of the river. Murray's defensive detachment was tasked with warding off raids conducted by the Marathas. To facilitate this organisation, Wellesley ordered Murray to divide his force into two brigades, the First Brigade was composed of His Majesty's (HM) 65th alongside the Bombay Grenadiers and 2/1st Bombay Native Infantry (ByNI).[30]

The first movements of the 65th saw them posted to the port of Surat, where they bolstered the defences and helped to allay the fears of the inhabitants. Their presence was intended to deter roving bands of Marathas, who had been ravaging the countryside of Britain's ally, the Nizam of Hyderabad, and it was feared they were turning their attention towards the port.[31]

Whilst Wellesley advanced into Maratha territory and captured the fortress of Ahmednagar, Murray, in contrast, proved to be extremely cautious and dilatory with his movements. One of his able subordinates, Lieutenant Colonel Woodington of the Bombay Army, managed to take Scindia's main port, Baroach, on 29 August 1803. Meanwhile, Murray complained he could not undertake active operations because of a dearth of cavalry, despite having 266 Maratha auxiliaries from the Gaekwad. Whilst it is true that these auxiliaries were tiny compared to Wellesley's or Lake's cavalry brigades, Murray compounded his lack of cavalry by placing little, if any, faith in their loyalty. This meant that he failed to deploy the Gaekwad's horsemen adequately, resulting in a lack of timely intelligence. Consequently, the Colonel's operations remained cautious and indecisive, his column moving at a snail's pace, as Murray dug in his heels and tried to remain on the defensive.[32]

29 Roderick Cavaliero, *Strangers in the Land* (London: I.B. Tauris, 2002), pp.98–99.
30 George Brenton Laurie, *History of the Royal Irish Rifles* (London: Gale & Polden, 1914), p.58.
31 *Sun (London)*, 2 November 1803.
32 Laurie, *History of the Royal Irish Rifles*, pp.63-64.

Bombay 1800. (Yale Center for British Art, Paul Mellon Collection)

By 24 September 1803, the day after Wellesley's most trying test at Assaye, Murray wrote to the Major General bemoaning, 'To defend my position is all I can expect, and I am not sanguine that I shall succeed in this.'[33] By this point the Colonel's force had become stricken with sickness and he found the 65th to be so badly affected that he ordered them to retire and recuperate in Bombay.

Wellesley, naturally not one to suffer such inaction and with the scent of victory in his nostrils, ordered Murray to complete a composite battalion by combining 100 boys of the 65th with men from the 61st, 75th (Highland) and 88th (Connaught Rangers) Regiments of Foot.[34] Once the reorganisation of his force had been completed, Murray was ordered to advance north-eastwards beyond the Nerbudda river, toward Dahod.

Complying with these orders, Murray set forth on 9th October, heading towards Godhra, where he set up magazines for his army. The Colonel's departure coincided with the 65th Foot's worst month for sickness. A regimental return taken on 1 October 1803 shows 721 rank and file present with the regiment; out of this total, only 271 boys were fit for duty. The overwhelming majority, 450 boys, were sick in quarters, which meant 62 percent of the regiment were *hors de combat*.[35] Murray's sickly army endured another month at Godhra before he pushed northward and occupied Lunavada, where he tarried again, this time to organise a troop of cavalry because he still distrusted the Gaekwad's horsemen. Eventually, on 17 December the Colonel occupied Dahod. Despite these operations taking place during some of the healthiest months in India, by December the regimental returns list 598 boys, of whom 269 were fit, and the rest 55 percent, or 329 boys, were sick in their quarters, and, whilst not explicitly stated, it suggests another 120 boys had either died or been invalided back to Britain.[36] Whilst these figures are dire, George Brenton Laurie, the official historian of the 86th Foot,

33 Laurie, *History of the Royal Irish Rifles*, p.64.
34 Laurie, *History of the Royal Irish Rifles*, pp.64-65.
35 TNA: WO 17/185: Monthly Returns for the 65th Foot, 1 October 1803.
36 TNA: WO 17/185: Monthly Returns for the 65th Foot, 1 December 1803.

lists only 105 boys of the 65th still with Murray's column, which potentially suggests the actual fighting fit element of the regiment was much lower, and most of the boys may already have returned to Bombay to recuperate. By 17 December 1803, Murray's total force equalled 4,695 Europeans, *sepoys* and artillerymen and of these men and boys, 22 percent were on the sick list.[37] Thankfully for the 65th, within a week peace had been declared between the British, Scindia, and Bhonsle, bringing the war to a close and offering the promise of time to recuperate.

## Deluges and Sickness

Returning to August 1803, just before Murray led the 65th on a dithering march across Gujarat. On the other side of India, plans were being made to secure the land route between Calcutta and Madras. Bhonsle of Nagpur, like his ally Scindia, had an opening to the sea through the province of Orissa. The city of Cuttack, sitting upon the Carnatic Coast, blocked the land route between Calcutta and Madras. Additionally, the nearby fortress of Barabati commanded the Barmul Pass, which, if controlled by the Marathas, would enable them to raid the British territories with impunity. The expedition planned against Bhonsle's Orissa province was intended to both secure the land route between Calcutta and Madras whilst distracting Bhonsle and encouraging him to detach men from the vital Deccani theatre of operations, where Major General Wellesley's offensive was directed. For all these reasons, the province had to be taken.

As early as 13 July 1803, the Governor General had 'desired to ensure the necessary orders for … two complete Companies of His Majesty's 22 Regiment to be in

37 Laurie, *History of the Royal Irish Rifles*, pp.64-65.

readiness to embark on Ship Board to proceed on Service at the shortest notice…',[38] their orders were to sail to Ganjam and join a force from the Madras Presidency sent to reduce Cuttack. The two companies selected were not identified in the letter, but the muster rolls list two centre companies as 'on command' throughout the campaign. The boys selected came from the commandant's company commanded by Captain Henry Thomas Hurlstone and Captain Patrick McNeight's company. In total, 200 NCOs, drummers, and rank and file embarked for Ganjam, alongside the two captains, were Lieutenants Joseph Baines and William A. Bury serving in the commandant's and McNeight's companies respectively. While medical support was provided by Assistant Surgeon James Hacking.[39]

At the same time these preparations were in progress, 21 boys of the 22nd were detached to serve aboard the East Indiaman *Preston* as marines.[40] The boys selected came from the centre companies commanded by Captains John Otto Bayer, Matthew Hutton, G.B. Tucker and Christopher Wilson.[41] Their days seemed to have passed by watching the ebb and flow of tide and time at Kedgeree (Khejuri) harbour at the mouth of the Hooghly River.[42] With the exception of one mission escorting a deserter and five suspected French citizens to Calcutta, this small party of boys remained aboard ship for six months, until they returned to their regiment before March 1804.[43]

As the drift towards open conflict continued, plans were set in motion for the offensive against Cuttack, eventually coming to fruition in early September 1803, when the march into Orissa commenced. Command of the expedition had initially been given to Lieutenant Colonel Alexander Campbell of the 74th (Highland) Regiment of Foot, who started the advance from Ganjam. When the campaign commenced, Campbell was struck down with fever and had to relinquish the force to Lieutenant Colonel George W.R. Harcourt of the 12th (East Suffolk) Regiment of Foot.

Harcourt caught up with the column at Prayagi, some 10 miles from Ganjam, where he continued the march northwards to Cuttack. The path they trod consisted of 'a sandy beach, near the sea-side';[44] unfortunately, this was far from a seaside promenade. The supply chain started to break down, with water being particularly difficult to find, a problem further exacerbated by the intense tropical sun. Soon the progress of the column became marked by the bodies of men from both British and *sepoy* regiments who dropped out of the line with heatstroke. In a desperate attempt to slake their thirst, some soldiers attempted to dig in the sand for water, but their attempts proved fruit-

38 BL: IOR/F/4/173/3033, Detachments of H.M. 10th and H.M. 22nd Regiment of Foot, the Bengal Marine Regiment and a Company of Artillery are ordered to embark for service in Cuttack, p.3.

39 TNA: WO 12/3878: General Muster Books and Pay Lists, 22nd Foot 1st Battalion, 1803, July–August 1803.

40 TNA: WO 17/1749: East Indies, October 1803.

41 TNA: WO 12/3878: General Muster Books and Pay Lists, 22nd Foot 1st Battalion, 1803, October 1803.

42 BL: IOR/L/MAR/B/307C, Journals, Ledgers and Pay Books of the *Preston*, August 1803 – March 1804.

43 TNA: WO 17/1750: East Indies, March 1804.

44 Plummer, *The Journal of Samuel Plummer*, p.14.

less; due to their proximity to the sea the excavations only turned up brackish liquid. At one point Plummer – whilst serving as a private in McNeight's company – almost succumbed to a 'fainting fit', only managing to recover because he mixed some 'bad brackish water with ... some pepper'.[45] Regarding the boys around him, Plummer felt their close confinement in barracks had hindered rather than helped their acclimatisation, as they appeared to suffer more than regiments who had previously manoeuvred out in the open. Fortunately for the boys, all they had to focus on was marching. As was customary in India, the boys of the 22nd had bullocks to carry their equipment or used boats because of the number of rivers in this part of the Northern Circars. All armies in India at this time had a long logistical tail, one contemporary, William Thorn, described 'all necessaries must be provided before-hand or obtained from a train of followers ... Hence the line of march increases these appendages to an army'.[46] From this source Plummer claims the boys of the 22nd were supplied with rations of broiled goat and rice, served with 2 drachms of rum, roughly equivalent to ½ tablespoon (8ml) a day, 'as no provision could be purchase[d] for any price.'[47]

Having passed through Prayagi, Harcourt's column marched onwards, skirting the eastern shore of Lake Chilika to reach Mithakua on 13 September. Whilst the column pressed forward, the Marathas had prepared a force of 5,000 infantry to oppose the British advance at Manikapatna. Plummer appears to offer a description of this action, which occurred when the British attempted to ford a river, and the Marathas fired several volleys until a 6-pounder dispersed them with grape shot.[48] It took another five days for Harcourt to reach Puri after a march of 70 miles.

At the beginning of the campaign, the sun had dominated the heavens, but as the column neared Manikapatna the monsoon rains opened up and deluged Harcourt's army. The rainstorms flooded the roads, turning them into a quagmire, hindering any pursuit of the Marathas, and making cooking impossible, forcing the 22nd to sustain themselves on cold rice. The desperate lengths the boys resorted to were illustrated by Plummer, who had to wade 'up to the shoulders in water, to a house of one of the natives, where I met with a little sweet rice.'[49] When he returned to the regiment, the lack of supplies had become so desperate that one of his officers, either Captain McNeight or Lieutenant Bury, begged Plummer to share some of his haul.

The fatiguing marches taxed the boys to their limits, whilst their Nagpuri foes offered little respite during the frequent skirmishes with the British column. Plummer recalled that some Marathas had hidden in bushes, 'from whence they fired upon us, but only wounded one man. We pursued them with a running fire, and drove them off the field.'[50] All the while the rain remained relentless. To add to the boys' dearth of food, they also lacked tents, which did not arrive until late September. Amid the driving rain,

45 Plummer, *The Journal of Samuel Plummer*, p.15.
46 William Thorn, *Memoir of the War in India conducted by General Lord Lake* (London: Military Library, 1818), p.84.
47 Plummer, *The Journal of Samuel Plummer*, p.18.
48 Plummer, *The Journal of Samuel Plummer*, p.18.
49 Plummer, *The Journal of Samuel Plummer*, p.19.
50 Plummer, *The Journal of Samuel Plummer*, p.19.

some of the boys were forced to lie down through sheer exhaustion and fall asleep in running water, often with a stone under their head to avoid drowning in their sleep. Whilst Harcourt was anxious for the welfare of his soldiers, he was equally concerned about aggravating the Orissan people. He accordingly allowed his men to seek shelter in huts abandoned by the locals, on the condition that the British troops did not molest either the natives or their property.[51] While the rain continued to harangue the column, it was not the only force of nature stalking the British lines.

During the night, the Raja of the Indian jungle made its appearance: the Bengal tiger. Both Mansfield and Plummer mention sentries and children from the column being snatched from the British encampment by tigers. Mansfield recalled how a captain from the Madras Army attempted to lure some of the tigers into a shoot, which he did by slaughtering a bullock and hanging the carcass in a tree. Watching the shoot, Mansfield observed the tigers pass beneath the carcass and, true to the fickleness of felines, they failed to show any interest.[52]

Under these trying conditions the column continued to press on for Cuttack. By early October there were several serious actions involving the column's vanguard. Plummer describes one of these engagements in great detail, whilst Mansfield – who served as a serjeant in the commandant's company – only mentions a running pursuit, and his account of the incident mentioned by Plummer consists of a single line. When this is compared to Mansfield's later detailed description of the attack on Barabati, the lack of specifics recounting the skirmish might suggest that his company did not fight alongside Plummer's, or that Mansfield, who can be a laconic memoirist, felt the 22nd's role was not as important.

The subsequent action detailed by Plummer started after the vanguard had passed through a large rice paddy, 'covered with water, like a sea'.[53] The vanguard consisted of 300 *sepoys*, 100 Europeans, including elements from the 22nd, and eight artillerymen. The British force found a piece of dry ground next to some woodland where they formed up in battle array. As the men closed up, the horrific scream of rockets played across the sky. True to the traditional style of fighting in India, where cavalry had been queen of the battlefield for centuries, the Marathas launched their horsemen at the British detachment. A 6-pounder initially unseated the Maratha commander with round shot, before switching to grape as the cavalry closed. Finding the fire too hot, the Marathas withdrew and attempted another charge at the trot, but they could not close with the vanguard and were forced to retreat. The British column offered three cheers, which in turn were answered by Nagpuri infantry in the wood. They commenced a persistent fire which turned the wood into 'one blaze of light.'[54] Two-hundred men were detached to flank the trees and subsequently drove the Marathas out.

The vanguard had nearly expended its ammunition when a detachment of 300 *sepoys* arrived with fresh supplies. Plummer and the rest of the vanguard had to maintain their square and watch the Marathas throughout the night, the front rank ready with their

51 Plummer, *The Journal of Samuel Plummer*, p.19.
52 CMM: 0003.01/16: Personal reminisces of QM William Mansfield, 1798–1834, pp.6–7.
53 Plummer, *The Journal of Samuel Plummer*, p.20.
54 Plummer, *The Journal of Samuel Plummer*, p.21.

Maratha Cavalry. (Paul F. Brunyee)

muskets. Relief was spaced out to occur every hour as the front ranks were replaced with men from the rear, until dawn came, and the soldiers of the vanguard were ordered to return to camp.[55] Undaunted by this action, the Marathas continued to skirmish with the British until they had retreated to the tenth-century fortress of Barabati.

Situated to the north of Cuttack, the fortress sat on an apex of a delta formed by the rivers Mahanadi in the north and the distributary channel, the Kathajodi, in the south, presenting a formidable obstacle. There was only one point of access, a bridge spanning a wet ditch, which at some points was 35–135 feet (11–41m) across, and 20 feet (6m) deep.[56] Behind the bridge, access to the fort was guarded by three gates, which any would-be storming party must unlock. An additional hazard was the crocodiles, which Mansfield observed swimming in the ditch.[57]

The British reached Cuttack on 10 October and set about constructing a battery to tackle Barabati's guns. This was completed on the 13th and by 11:00 a.m. the next morning, the fort's guns had fallen silent under the fire from the Company's artillery. Despite this success, the British still had to storm the gate. During the bombardment, a ball went through the top of the first gate, and as a consequence the Marathas

55 Plummer, *The Journal of Samuel Plummer*, p.21.
56 Anderson, *The History of the Twenty-Second Cheshire Regiment*, p.113.
57 CMM: 0003.01/16: Personal reminisces of QM William Mansfield, 1798–1834, p.7.

threw up a wicket fence to protect the approach.[58] To storm this formidable defence, Harcourt turned to his Europeans, in particular the boys of the 22nd Foot, to act as his fortress busters. The boys were selected because it was believed by most British officers, even commanders like Lake, who spoke highly of the bravery of the company's *sepoys*, that Europeans from the King's or Company regiments were much better at facing the onslaught when charging a breach. In conformity to this notion, the assault upon Barabati was led by the two centre companies of the 22nd, followed by the 9th and 19th Madras Native Infantry (MNI) and the 20th Bengal Native Infantry (BNI).[59] The now 22-year-old Mansfield, a former boy recruit from Essex, volunteered to lead the forlorn hope, the rather pessimistic title given to the initial set of volunteers sent to storm any breach or gate.[60] Whilst Mansfield led from the front, Plummer also accompanied the storming party, escorting a 6-pounder gun to unlock the gates.[61]

As the 'forlorn hope' advanced to the doors, they had to destroy the wicket fence, a task which left them exposed to potshots from the Marathas for 40 minutes.[62] Passing through the first gate, the boys discovered that within the second gate, the defenders had erected a battery with three guns in front of the doors. Plummer recalls the boys gave three shouts before charging up to the second gate with the 6-pounder. The boys maintained an active fire on the Maratha trenches, whilst the British gun fired what Plummer calls double-headed shot (or bar shot), usually reserved for tearing the rigging off of ships, at the doors. This failed to make an entrance, so the gun was loaded with a blank cartridge and then hauled up until its muzzle almost touched the doors, then the gun was fired. With a roar, the gates burst open violently, and the boys squeezed inside one at a time.

Faced with the third entrance, the 22nd found another Maratha gun loaded with canister shot ready to sweep the storming party into oblivion. A shot rang out from the stormers which knocked down the artilleryman with a lighted match just as he was in the act of laying the fire to the touchhole. Plummer's account mentions a serjeant, possibly Mansfield, rushing forward with his pike and skewering the Nagpuri. The stormers rushed on and pushed aside the Nagpuri soldiers attempting to close the third gate. When the 22nd entered Barabati, Mansfield pulled down the Maratha standard and hoisted a soldier's red coat in its place, which informed the rest of Harcourt's force that the 22nd had succeeded. By the time relief arrived, Mansfield was 'wounded and worn out with Fatigue'.[63] According to Plummer, 400 defenders were killed during the storm, before they surrendered. In contrast, the boys of the 22nd had come off lightly, with only two boys killed, Captain Hurlstone and eight boys wounded, and one left permanently disabled.[64] Barabati marked the end of

58 Plummer, *The Journal of Samuel Plummer*, p.21.

59 Anderson, *The History of the Twenty-Second Cheshire Regiment*, p.113.

60 CMM: 0003.01/16: Personal reminisces of QM William Mansfield, 1798–1834, p.7.

61 Plummer, *The Journal of Samuel Plummer*, p.23.

62 Bhabani Charan Ray, *The British Conquest and Administration of Orissa, 1803–1819* (PhD thesis, University of London, 1956), pp.23–24.

63 CMM: 0003.01/16: Personal reminisces of QM William Mansfield, 1798–1834, p.7.

64 Plummer, *The Journal of Samuel Plummer*, p.24.

Hurlstone and McNeight's boys' active involvement in the Orissa campaign, although they remained on command until March 1804 when they rejoined the remainder of the 22nd garrisoning Fort William.[65]

The operations in Gujarat and Orissa were supplementary and remain an obscure part of the Maratha Wars, side-shows to Lake's campaigns in the north and the beginning of Wellesley's rise to become one of Britain's foremost generals. However, these two peripheral campaigns formed a vital part of the overall strategy of overwhelming the Marathas and forcing their armies to spread themselves thinly across the Confederacy, as John Company's forces closed in. By late 1803, following the victories at Assaye and Laswari and the capture of several important fortresses, the Marathas sought peace. In the subsequent treaties, Bhonsle gave up Cuttack and Orissa to the HEIC as part of the treaty signed on 17 November 1803. Whilst Scindia surrendered Baroach and made several concessions in Gujarat. This was in addition to major concessions in Hindustan, including protection of the Mughal Emperor and his court in Delhi, which were transferred to the Company.[66]

To secure this conquest in either late October or November 1803, the light and grenadier companies of the 22nd Foot commanded by Captain Effingham Lindsay and Captain James Menzies were sent to the Upper Provinces of the HEIC.[67] Before the flank companies departed, trouble broke out amongst the boys, as Shipp, who had just been promoted to corporal in Lindsay's company on 10 October, recalled. When the flank companies received their orders to march, 8 rupees were stopped from their pay without explanation. The boys took the matter up with their officers, who could offer no explanation. With tempers rising the boys sought redress from the local military authorities in Fort William and the flank companies marched on their quarters forthwith. To their horror they discovered the stoppage was to cover the costs of their burial if they died on campaign. Incensed by this sombre precaution, the flank companies returned to their barracks, topped up their cups with liquor, and called for a mutiny.

Anxious to control the situation, Lindsay, Menzies, and their lieutenants attempted to calm the rebels and explain that a mutiny would hinder rather than help their claim, as it would stop the officers from being able to intercede on the boys' behalf. Always a charismatic figure and described by Shipp as 'one of the bravest soldiers in his majesty's army'.[68] Lindsay seems to have managed to convince the light company to back down, with the boys exclaiming '"March us before the enemy, that we may wipe away this our first disobedience"'.[69] In contrast, Menzies' grenadiers would not budge. Finally, the tall figure of Lieutenant Colonel Mercer was called upon to quieten the ranks. Both Shipp and Plummer talk about Mercer with considerable respect. Shipp even went so

65 TNA: WO 12/3879: General Muster Books and Pay Lists, 22nd Foot 1st Battalion, 1804, March 1804.

66 Martin R. Howard, *Wellington and the British Army's Indian Campaigns 1798–1805* (Barnsley: Pen and Sword Military, 2020), p.144.

67 TNA: WO 12/3878: General Muster Books and Pay Lists, 22nd Foot 1st Battalion, 1803, October 1803.

68 Shipp, *The Extraordinary Military Career*, p.46.

69 Shipp, *The Extraordinary Military Career*, p.61.

far as to claim 'he was a father to his men'.[70] Mercer's appearance before the angry and drunken boys did calm them, until the adjutant, Lieutenant Hugh Stewart, arrived. Stewart was hated by the boys, although Shipp does not give a reason why; he does describe his appearance eliciting shouts of '"Kick him out!"'.[71] Stewart beat a hasty retreat, and the boys eventually were returned to their quarters an hour later. Despite the ruckus, their demonstration had persuaded the authorities and the next day they returned the 8 rupees stoppage. The morning after, the regimental band struck up their instruments and announced the flank companies' departure from Fort William, playing them through the streets of Calcutta, where they were 'hailed by all assembled'.[72] It took the two companies three months to reach Lake's army on 12 February 1804, where they found the Grand Army encamped near Hindaun, about 67 miles (100km) south-west of Agra.[73] They arrived just as tensions in India were beginning to simmer once again.

At the close of 1803 it had seemed that the HEIC had finally mastered Hindustan. With the Maratha rajas under the sway of the British, peace appeared to be in the air for India. Despite the growing calm, there remained one Maratha strongman who had not faced John Company in the field and was now waiting to spring onto the political stage.

70 Shipp, *The Extraordinary Military Career*, p.61.
71 Shipp, *The Extraordinary Military Career*, p.61.
72 Shipp, *The Extraordinary Military Career*, p.61.
73 William Thorn, *Memoir of the War in India*, p.330.

# 8

# Holkar Enters the Fray

Despite helping to initiate the Maratha civil war, which in turn sparked British involvement in Maratha politics, Yashwantrao Holkar, Raja of Indore, had remained aloof from the conflict with the HEIC. As 1803 faded into 1804, Holkar took an increasingly intransigent tone with the Company. He threatened to plunder vast swaths of HEIC territory and the lands of allied rajas, unsettling the British at a time when India appeared to have been secured for the Company. Furthermore, Holkar's posturing was not an idle threat, as the Raja maintained his army in the field and used their muscle to provocatively attempt to exact tribute from several Company allies. Many of these allied kingdoms, including Jaipur, had recently signed treaties with the HEIC following Lake's victories on the Gangetic Plain. Incensed by Holkar's raids and threats, in April 1804, Lord Wellesley ordered John Company's armies back into the field to end Holkar's depredations.[1]

Holkar's forces were known to be nimble, particularly his cavalry, which operated in the true Maratha style, conducting raids deep into enemy territory. Anxious to take the fight to Holkar, Lake launched an offensive towards Jaipur. During the march, Shipp notes there were frequent skirmishes with roving bands of *pindaris* – irregular horsemen who accompanied Maratha armies – notorious for despoiling the countryside and harrying enemy columns. Brushing aside the swarms of *pindaris*, the British eventually secured Rampura between 15–16 May. By this point in the campaign, Lake was increasingly concerned about the effect the blazing summer sun had on his European soldiers, as heatstroke thinned the army's ranks. According to William Thorn, who served with the Grand Army, 'Young men who set out in the morning full of spirits, and in all the vigour of health, dropped dead immediately on reaching the encampment', the men, 'suddenly turned giddy, foamed at the mouth, and as instantaneously became lifeless.'[2] Rising deaths from the heat coupled with the looming threat of Maratha raids in the Company province of Bundelkhand distracted Lake from his pursuit of Holkar's main army. With the Raja nowhere to be found, the General decided to withdraw his King's Regiments, including the 22nd, north-eastwards to Cawnpore (Kanpur). Meanwhile, to arrest the progress of the Marathas, Lake left a detachment comprised of *sepoys*,

1 Howard, *Wellington and the British Army's Indian Campaigns*, p.147.
2 Thorn, *Memoir of the War in India*, p.346.

commanded by Lieutenant Colonel William Monson of the HM 76th (Hindoostan) Regiment of Foot, to observe Holkar's movements. In addition to defending against Maratha incursions, Lake's orders provided Monson with the latitude to continue advancing into Holkar's domains to maintain pressure on the Raja's forces.

Whilst Monson's detachment prepared to shadow Holkar, Major General Wellesley ordered the British forces in Gujarat, including Murray's army, into the field with orders to cooperate with Lake. When Wellesley composed his orders on 7 May 1804, he remained uncertain of Lake's plans, so he offered a scenario to Murray; if Lake planned on a decisive battle to destroy Holkar's army, then Wellesley ordered Murray to, 'post yourself in such a manner as to stop Holkar, embarrass and impede his flight as much as possible, and if you can, to engage him.'[3] To achieve this, Wellesley surmised that with the coming monsoon season, Holkar would, in all likelihood, try to retire before Lake towards Ujjain and the Malwa plateau, where there were fewer rivers to impede his army's movements. Accordingly, if Lake adopted an aggressive stance, then Murray should direct his march to Malwa and combine his strength with Scindia's army, as following his defeat, the Raja of Gwalior had become an ally of the HEIC.[4] If, however, Lake did not intend to fight Holkar's army, Murray was to avoid any unnecessary sieges, as this would tie down his force, leaving the operational initiative with the Marathas.[5] Wellesley's vague, almost distracted orders were further muddled by a paragraph in his letter where he mulls, 'It is difficult to point out the place to which you ought in the first instance to direct your March'.[6] Wellesley then suggested that Murray's 'local knowledge' might serve best to direct his movements. This letter demonstrates a lack of communication between Wellesley and Lake coupled with a continued underestimation of Murray's abilities as an independent commander. A dilatory officer at best, Wellesley's vague instructions left Murray without a clear plan of action and at the same time shackled him to Gujarat, which he was ordered to defend if Holkar appeared in force.[7]

The army Murray took into the field consisted of approximately 5,300 men including the boys of the 65th. The brief respite between December 1803 and April 1804 gave the 65th time to recover from the pervading sickness in their ranks. The result of this intermission is demonstrated in a regimental return taken on 1 May 1804, which shows the regiment numbered 543 rank and file, 462 of whom were fit for service, with only 15 percent of the regiment listed sick.[8] With his army ready, Murray commenced his march from Gujarat, and by 12 June he had re-occupied Dahod, before continuing his plodding progress north-eastwards, across the Mahi River, reaching Badnawar by 30 June.[9] Just like his previous campaign with the 65th, Murray's army fared poorly. Major

3 BL: IOR/H/626: Papers concerning the war with Holkar, pp.268–269.
4 Laurie, *History of the Royal Irish Rifles*, p.66.
5 BL: IOR/H/626: Papers concerning the war with Holkar, p.271.
6 BL: IOR/H/626: Papers concerning the war with Holkar, p.272.
7 K.G. Pitre, *The Second Anglo-Maratha War 1802-1803* (PhD thesis, *University of Poona*, 1984), pp.235–236.
8 TNA: WO 17/185: 65th Foot Monthly Returns, 1 May 1804.
9 Pitre, *The Second Anglo-Maratha War*, p.238.

General Wellesley wrote to the Colonel on 28 June, 'I am concerned to hear of the sickness of your Europeans'.[10] For the boys of the 65th, the rate of sickness remained steady, causing the death rate to mount. On 1 July, 491 boys were recorded on the monthly returns, with 17 percent of the rank and file listed as sick, a slight increase from May.[11] Over the same period in June 1804, the 65th Foot suffered their worst month for casualties for the year, losing 40 boys during Murray's command.[12] Whilst the cause of death was not provided, most of these boys probably succumbed to sickness, as the Colonel's column did not fight a major action during the campaign.

Meanwhile, Monson had continued his pursuit of Holkar's main army, storming the ancient fort of Hinglajgarh, on either 1 or 2 July. Despite this success, Monson's detachment, like Murray's column, was too small to consider fighting Holkar alone and with the better part of Lake's army now ensconced in Cawnpore, they needed to cooperate. Even though both commanders were aware of their individual weakness, there was no direct correspondence between Monson and Murray. Instead, both commanders were groping through the dark towards each other, hoping to catch Holkar in the middle.

Some form of communication was briefly opened when Murray reached Badnawar and found two letters waiting for him from Monson. In a subsequent letter to Lake, written the same day, Murray does not elaborate on their contents, but the intelligence within caused the startled Colonel to retreat back across the Mahi away from Monson.[13] Murray's reasoning was that he felt any attempt to occupy and defend Ujjain would leave his force open to being singled out by Holkar. The Colonel was quite happy to use Wellesley's commonsense stricture, 'to avoid exposing my [Murray's] Corps to the sole operation of Holkar's Army'[14] and Lake's withdrawal to Cawnpore as the rationale he needed to turn tail from the Marathas and focus on defending Gujarat. Having dispatched a letter to Monson informing him that without sufficient provisions he had to withdraw, Murray and the sickly 65th began to retire. Almost as soon as the retreat commenced, the Colonel changed his mind again, possibly when news reached him that Holkar was not in pursuit. Murray retraced his steps and reached Ujjain on 8 July, where he constructed a magazine before sending off a detachment to occupy Holkar's capital Indore.[15] Murray had returned too late; the damage had already been done.

Murray's letter arrived at Monson's camp on 7 July and accordingly Monson, who had only pushed so far south to cooperate with the Gujarat column, commenced his own retrograde movement. Monson's army faced a horrific ordeal during their retreat northwards, as Holkar fixed his attention on the retiring column and harassed them mercilessly. Even the elements turned against the retreating *sepoys* when the monsoon struck with a vengeance, turning the roads into quagmires. By the time Monson's force struggled into Agra on 31 August, discipline had almost completely broken down

10 Howard, *Wellington and the British Army's Indian Campaigns*, p.152.
11 TNA: WO 17/185: 65th Foot Monthly Returns, 1 May 1804.
12 TNA: WO 17/185: 65th Foot Monthly Returns, 1 June 1804.
13 BL: IOR/H/626: Papers concerning the war with Holkar, Raja of Bharatpur, Sindhia and Raja of Berar, p.53.
14 Pitre, *The Second Anglo-Maratha War*, p.238.
15 Laurie, *History of the Royal Irish Rifles*, p.66.

amongst both officers and men. The final collapse started on the 28th, when Holkar's guns fired on Monson's encampment, causing panic and confusion amongst the harried camp followers who disrupted the *sepoys* and the army subsequently collapsed as, 'order could no more be restored, the troops fairly broke and fled'.[16]

## Lake's Vengeance

The disastrous retreat had cost Lake dearly; he lamented the loss of, 'the flower of the army, and how they are to be replaced at this day, God only knows'.[17] There was no time to refit and refresh his already tired soldiers, as Holkar was on the march again. The Raja had followed the British retreat, but he had later tarried awhile after taking the city of Mathura. His position in the town had successfully interposed Holkar between Lake and the British garrison in Delhi. Anxious to restore British prestige in the subcontinent and take the fight to Holkar, Lake set out from Cawnpore on 3 September, with the monsoon rains pelting his column.[18]

By 27 September, Lake had re-assembled the Grand Army at Secundera, 5 miles west of Agra.[19] What followed was a series of marches and counter-marches as the General continued to seek a decisive battle to end the campaign, whilst Holkar played for time to complete his siege of Delhi. Around 3 October Lieutenant Colonel Patrick Don, commander of the Reserve Brigade, including HM 22nd's flank companies, 1/12th and 2/12th BNI, and 2/21st BNI, reoccupied Mathura. Despite being an allied town, this did not prevent Shipp and several of his compatriots from a 'glorious plunder', particularly of shawls and silks. Shipp himself broke into a locked storeroom and was about to make off with a bale of shawls when he froze, transfixed by a pair of eyes. Shipp initially fled the scene but later decided to return only to discover he had been spooked by a Hindu idol, and in retribution he decided to commit an act of iconoclasm and strike the statue across the face with a sword.[20]

After retaking Mathura and anxious to crush Holkar's army, Lake was soon on the march again. Before daybreak on 7 October 1804, the Grand Army was a mere 4 miles from Holkar's camp at the village of Aurung. Lake ordered his men into three columns; Don's reserve with the 22nd formed the centre, flanked by the cavalry on the right and another brigade of infantry on the left commanded by Major General John Henry Fraser. True to the often-dispiriting nature of Maratha warfare and setting the tone for the campaigns against Holkar, by the time the British had reached the Maratha's encampment, the Raja had withdrawn. This frustrating war of manoeuvre was repeated on 10 October and again on the 12th, when Lake caught wind of the

16 J. Bailey Fraser in James Skinner, *The Recollections of Skinner of Skinner's Horse* (Driffield: Leonaur, 2006), p.165.
17 Provan, *Bullocks, Grain and Good Madeira*, p.137.
18 Howard, *Wellington and the British Army's Indian Campaigns*, p.153.
19 Provan, *Bullocks, Grain and Good Madeira*, p.140.
20 Shipp, *The Extraordinary Military Career*, p.63.

Viscount Lake. (Anne S.K. Brown Collection)

siege of Delhi and advanced to its relief.[21] Still harassed on their line of march, the Grand Army reached the metropolis on the 17th and discovered the city had been ably defended by Colonel David Ochterlony, despite its crumbling walls. Foiled in his attempt to take Delhi, Holkar withdrew and returned to raiding the HEIC's possessions and allies in Hindustan.

Lake needed to destroy Holkar's army to bring the war to a swift conclusion, as the longer Holkar kept the British at bay, the more it sapped their prestige with their Indian allies. The first signs of unrest appeared as early as 29 October, when reports arrived at the British camp in Delhi that Ranjit Singh, Raja of the Jat kingdom of Bharatpur, had decided to side with the Marathas.[22] Whilst these reports were unsubstantiated, further delay could encourage more rulers to throw their lot in with Holkar. To bring matters to a head, Lake divided his forces, taking the bulk of the cavalry squadrons and Don's brigade across the Yamuna River in pursuit of Holkar's cavalry.[23] As the British pursued the Marathas, Shipp vividly recalls the trail of destruction they left in their wake, 'we passed several villages that had been burned to the ground, and plundered creatures, men, women, and children; burning corn-fields; dead elephants, camels, horses, and bullocks'.[24]

Meanwhile, Fraser, now in command of the remaining infantry and cavalry, began to retire towards Mathura on 5 November. Four days later, Fraser learnt that Holkar's infantry were sheltering under the walls of Deeg, within the Kingdom of Bharatpur. Advancing to attack on 13 November, Fraser secured the decisive victory Lake had sought. He crushed Holkar's infantry, scattering them, but he could not destroy them completely due to the fire from the Jat defenders of Deeg. Fraser's victory was swiftly followed by Lake's success at Farrukhabad on the 17th. Here the Grand Army's cavalry caught Holkar – allegedly hungover after a night of drinking – and his horsemen unawares in their camp, dispersing them across the countryside.[25] Luck seemed to be on the 22nd flank companies' side as, apart from their strenuous marching, they played no active role in either engagement. With Holkar's army scattered, the end of the war was in sight; only Ranjit Singh and the Jats had to be brought back into line.

Lake was incensed that Ranjit Singh had allowed Holkar to shelter in his kingdom, particularly as Bharatpur had sought an alliance with the HEIC, following the General's triumphant 1803 campaign. Lake had promised Lord Wellesley that he would endeavour not to bring the Jats into the war, but with the remnants of Holkar's infantry still hiding under the walls of Deeg, the General felt he had no option and could not let that 'treacherous fool' Ranjit Singh off.[26] By 5 December, Lake's army was back before Deeg and preparations were in hand to lay siege to the fortress.

21 Thorn, *Memoir of the War in India*, pp.371–372.
22 Pester, *War and Sport*, p.339.
23 Thorn, *Memoir of the War in India*, pp.382.
24 Shipp, *The Extraordinary Military Career*, p.65.
25 Howard, *Wellington and the British Army's Indian Campaigns*, pp.155–156.
26 Provan, *Bullocks, Grain and Good Madeira*, p.147.

## 'Gallantry and Zeal': The Storming of Deeg

Deeg had been constructed amid a flood plain, surrounded by marshes, making it virtually impenetrable during the rains. The first line of defence was formed by the *pettah* wall, which encircled the town and was peppered with round towers and guarded by a ditch. Betwixt the wall and the main citadel in the north-east of the town lay Deeg's palace, bazaar, and gardens. To besiege Deeg, Lake initially encamped to the west and commenced his siege lines opposite the *Shahburj*, a miniature fort with four bastions, which also acted as the main barracks for the garrison. Despite the presence of this formidable structure, Lake was forced to lay his siege lines in front of the *Shahburj*, as the approach to the walls had no ditches or impedimenta to forestall the advance of his assault parties.[27]

During Lake's investment of Deeg, his army had to clear the defenders from the ground chosen to establish the British batteries. On 13 December 1804, the army had taken up its final position for a siege. Before them sat the *Shahburj*, whilst at an angle to their right rested the old Gopalghur fort, which the British kept on their right flank. To limit the impact of shots from matchlock men inside the Gopalghur, Don and his Reserve Brigade, including the 22nd Foot, were sent to occupy a *tope* or grove in front of the *Shahburj*.[28]

Shipp later recalled the night of the 13th, 'as dark as pitch, and bitterly cold.' The working party consisted of Europeans including some boys of the 22nd and *sepoys* from the 12th BNI, all carrying entrenching tools to begin construction of the siege lines. In the darkness, Don's column marched towards a small village – burnt down by the defenders – situated amidst the *tope*. By 11:00 p.m., Don's men were amongst the trees, where they split up and searched for the best positions to lay the siege lines. Meanwhile, Shipp was sent to find out what lay beyond the village. As he passed the burnt-out husks of the buildings, the apprehensive Shipp was startled by three malnourished bullocks. Beyond the ruins he espied a blue light hanging on the walls of Deeg and he advanced so close to the walls that he could hear voices from the battlements. Then a challenge rang out in the stillness of the night, as a Jat soldier called out, '"*Khon Hie?*" … Who is there?'[29] Shipp attempted to hide but trod on a fire near one of the smouldering buildings and had to dive into a hut for cover. Whilst the Jats debated if they heard something, Shipp was cornered. In a desperate bid for freedom, he darted back out into the night, swiftly followed by shots from the matchlock men. Shipp did not stop running until he reached a British picquet.

Whilst Shipp recovered from his misadventure, Don had successfully occupied the *tope*, ordering the boys to dig a shallow depression in the earth to protect them from the enemy's fire. By sunrise, these depressions had become 300 yards of trenches, including batteries for mortars and 6-pounder cannons.[30] Over the course of December further

27 Provan, *Bullocks, Grain and Good Madeira*, p.148.
28 Thorn, *Memoir of the War in India*, p.408.
29 Shipp, *The Extraordinary Military Career*, p.65.
30 Thorn, *Memoir of the War in India*, p.408.

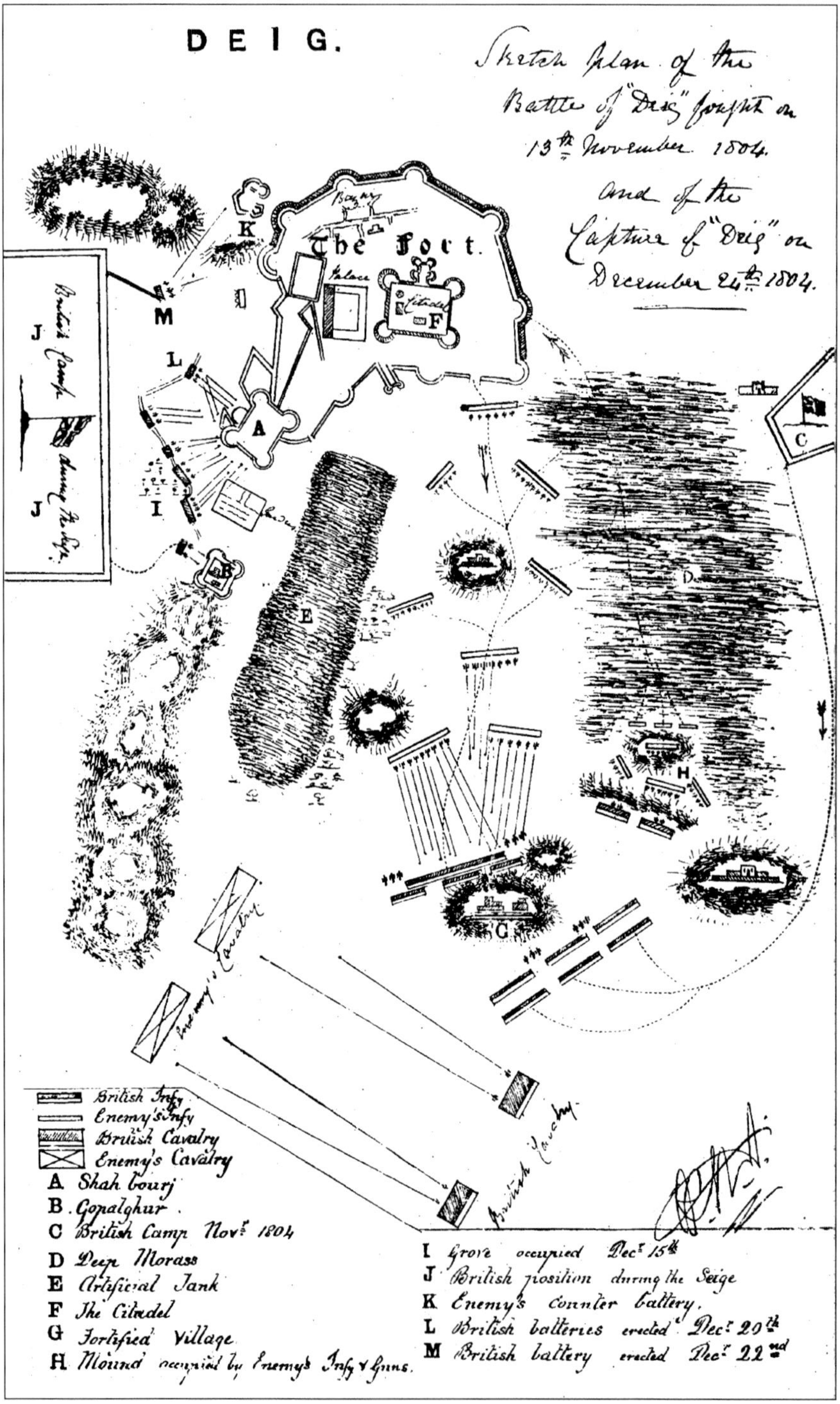


A map of the Battle of Deeg and subsequent Siege of the town, 1804.
(William Thorn, *Memoir of the War in India*)

batteries were constructed and the lines enlarged, while the Jats maintained a constant fire on the working parties.

By 23 December, under fire from the British artillery, many of the enemy's guns had fallen silent and a practicable breach had been made. At 11:30 p.m., during 'as dark and cold a night as ever blew from the heavens',[31] Lake's storming parties marched into the trenches. The General had divided his force into three columns for the assault, the right column was ordered to attack the Jat trenches and batteries, established on a piece of high ground near the *Shahburj*. Whilst the left column's objectives were to seize another set of earthworks. The main assault was given to the centre column led by Lieutenant Colonel Kenneth Macrae, whose men were tasked with storming the breach. Macrae's command consisted of the flank companies of the HM 22nd and 76th Foot, alongside those of the HEIC's European Regiment, and the entirety of 1/8th BNI.[32] The signal to advance was the rising of the moon, and in that pale light the stormers could see the formidable host arrayed before them, 'spears on the ramparts as thick as plants in a new-set forest.'[33] Blue lights lit the ramparts and time was marked by the occasional roar of a gun, or the scream of a rocket, which 'played beautifully in the air'.[34] As the boys waited, an old veteran in the 76th, who had spent 20 years in the east, offered Shipp two pieces of advice. Firstly, always bayonet a body before passing it, as many defenders pretended to be dead before springing up and striking their opponents from behind. Secondly, whenever a shell or rocket landed close-by, Shipp should throw himself to the ground close to it. Shipp came to rely on this advice in the years to come.

The boys of the 22nd led the assault on Deeg, initially with Serjeant Garnett Bury, of the grenadier company at their head. Whilst the boys waited to advance, Bury was injured, so Shipp volunteered to take his place. With the young corporal leading the way, the column pressed forward. During the advance, the British found the ground broken, which disordered the cohesion of the infantry's ranks. John Pester, advancing with the right column described, 'the troops were as silent as death on our approach, but we were no sooner discovered from the works than the whole face was completely illuminated by the enemy's cannon and musketry.'[35] Fortunately for the stormers, the guns in the enemy entrenchments were elevated too high, which meant that most of their shot passed over the assaulters' heads. The column rushed forward, between the boys of the 22nd and the breach was a battery erected by the Jats. Captain Effingham Lindsay of the light company led his lads into the entrenchments, 'cheering and boldly leading us on'.[36]

The fighting in the trenches was intense, as they were defended by the stalwart remnants of Holkar's infantry and the determined soldiers of the Raja of Bharatpur. In the ensuing *melée* Lindsay was struck in the arm by a spear and received a severe sabre blow, but despite his injuries he refused to retire and continued to lead his boys from

31 Shipp, *The Extraordinary Military Career*, p.69.
32 Howard, *Wellington and the British Army's Indian Campaigns*, p.159.
33 Shipp, *The Extraordinary Military Career*, p.69.
34 Shipp, *The Extraordinary Military Career*, p.69.
35 Pester, *War and Sport*, p.365.
36 Shipp, *The Extraordinary Military Career*, p.69.

the front. Shipp meanwhile had spotted a cannon turned towards the advancing flank companies and with three comrades rushed towards it. He was in the act of looking for the touchhole to spike the gun when a *golundaz* (artilleryman) lit the fuse. The resulting recoil threw Shipp into the trench with the *golundaz* hard on his heels. Fortunately, a grenadier, possibly Private Joshua Share although Shipp spells his name as Shears, shot the artilleryman, saving Shipp's life. Having cleared the trenches, the boys pressed forward for the breach.

Nearing the foot of the wall, with shot flying in all directions, Shipp was struck on the head by a matchlock ball. Stunned and bleeding profusely, he rose to his feet and was carried into the breach by the stormers. Before them, the tenacious defenders were 'throwing immense stones, pieces of trees, stink-pots, bundles of straw set on fire, spears, [and] large shots'.[37] Despite the veritable fusillade, the 22nd carried the breach, and the assault turned into brutal street fighting. Shipp recalled that the defenders had taken up positions in the second storeys of the buildings, and many of the streets had a cannon parked at the end to sweep the approaches.

Lindsay was hemmed in at a street corner, bleeding profusely and forced to one knee surrounded by five assailants, when Shipp and some of the boys came to their Captain's rescue. Later in the midst of the pell-mell of the assault, Shipp ran into Lindsay again, and always concerned about the boys, the Captain asked Shipp how he was faring with his injuries. By 2:00 a.m., on Christmas Eve, the British had cleared much of the town, although skirmishing continued and the citadel remained in the hands of the defenders. Shipp had managed to escape, with a 2-inch scar across his head where a musket ball had grazed his skull, and severe bruising on his side from the pressure of the cannon blast, the effects of which he would suffer for months afterwards.[38]

Whilst Shipp sought medical attention, the battle in the streets of Deeg carried on in fits and starts. As dawn broke on the bloody breach, Pester tried to find a way into the town from the *Shahburj* with 160 men. Despite the night's bloody work, he still had to fight to secure a gateway into the heart of Deeg. When Macrae heard of Pester's prize, he brought the 8/15th BNI to Pester's assistance; at their head were 200 men of HM 76th and 80 boys of HM 22nd. After uniting with Pester, Macrae's passage was relatively quiet until they reached the Palace of Deeg. The palace was only a 'half-musket shot' distance from the citadel, and as the British approached, the defenders opened a smart fire on their ranks. Several men in the front ranks were injured, and accordingly Macrae withdrew into the palace. Some Jats attempted to fire their cannon into the buildings the British occupied, but as they were too close to the citadel, the Jats could not lower the elevation on their guns sufficiently, so most of the shots whistled overhead. Inside of this 'elegant … and most stylish' building, the boys of the 22nd found numerous fountains, nestled amidst extensive groves of orange and myrtle trees. There was even a pond where Ranjit Singh liked to feed fish in his garden. As the shots occasionally whistled overhead, the boys helped themselves to the unripe oranges in the groves and liberally doused themselves and each other in the rose water that furnished every room. Amid

37 Shipp, *The Extraordinary Military Career*, p.69.
38 Shipp, *The Extraordinary Military Career*, pp.70–71.

his exploration of the palace, Pester encountered a boy of the 22nd, returning from the Raja's ponds, carrying 'a very fine fish'. When he asked how the soldier had acquired it, the boy replied, '"With a sharp-pointed bayonet, sir; that's how I catch my fish"', before gesturing to the pond where his comrades were likewise spearing the seemingly innumerable fish crammed into the 30-foot (9m) pools.[39]

Preparations were in hand to assault the citadel, but fortunately for the boys, during the night of the 24th, the last of the defenders evacuated Deeg, retiring to Bharatpur. The storming of Deeg had proven to be a light *repas* for Lake's army. In total, 27 men were killed, 121 wounded, and five men reported missing after the storming. Of these, one serjeant and five privates of the 22nd were killed. The wounded included Captains Lindsay and McNeight, who had led the 22nd at Cuttack, along with Lieutenants William Creswell and Stephen Sweetenham. Two serjeants, one drummer, and 16 privates were also injured during the assault.[40] Unsurprisingly, Lake praised Lindsay in particular, noting his 'highly meritorious' conduct. The Grand Army had won another victory, and the tide of the war appeared to be in Lake's favour. Holkar's army was broken and with one of Ranjit Singh's citadels in British hands, Lake now prepared to give his final chastisement to Ranjit Singh, and assault his capital, Bharatpur.

39 Pester, *War and Sport*, pp.367–370.
40 BL: IOR/H/626, Papers concerning the war with Holkar, Raja of Bharatpur, Sindhia and Raja of Berar, p.877.

# 9

# Britannia at Bay

On 28 December, Lake left Deeg, and by 2 January 1805 his army was encamped in the shadow of the fortress at Bharatpur. Like Deeg, the fort lay in a plain surrounded by water and jungles. Lake described the town as:

> … every where strongly fortified. A mud wall of great height and thickness, and a very wide and deep ditch, everywhere surround it. The Fort … is of a square figure. One side of that square overlooks the country; the remaining three sides are within the Town. It occupies a situation that appears more elevated than the town; and its walls are said to be higher, and its ditch of greater width and deepness. The circumference of both Town and Fort is upwards of eight miles, and their walls in all that extent are flanked with bastions at short distances, on which are mounted a very numerous Artillery.[1]

Despite the fort's formidable appearance, Lake was champing at the bit to punish Ranjit Singh. The British encamped to the south-west of the town, and like at Deeg, the working parties used the cover of a *tope* to protect themselves whilst they constructed the siege lines. Shipp, who had been promoted to serjeant on 3 January 1805, recalled how the working parties from the 22nd were responsible for digging trenches and batteries during the cold winter nights. Regularly, a cry rippled through the siege works of, 'Shot' and the boys had to throw themselves to the ground. In the face of this danger, as is the habit of British soldiers, the besiegers passed the time thinking up nicknames for the enemy, including a massive gun mounted upon the walls of Bharatpur. This behemoth was estimated to be a 72-pounder, and its 'report was like that of an earthquake',[2] but its roar was much worse than its bite, and the boys took to calling the gun 'Civil Tom', as most of the shots flew overhead.

Toiling tirelessly through the chilly winter nights, the working parties continued to enlarge the siege lines, whilst the British guns battered the mud brick walls. Eventually, by 9 January 1805, a practicable breach had been made and the storming party was

1 J.N. Creighton, *Narrative of the Capture of Bhurtpore, in the province of Agra, upper Hindustan, by the forces under the command of Lord Combermere* (London: Privately Printed, 1830), p.ix.

2 Shipp, *The Extraordinary Military Career*, p.78.

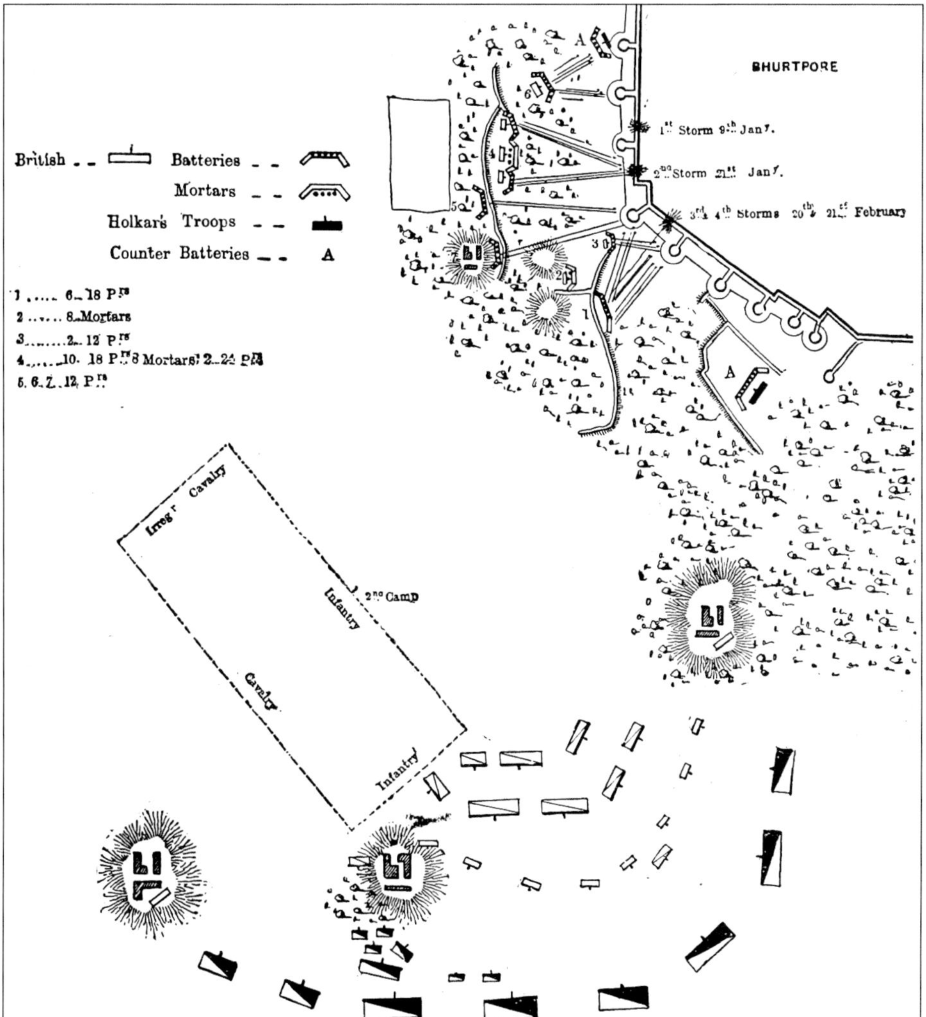


The Siege of Bharatpur 1805. (William Thorn, *Memoir of the War in India*)

ordered to attack that same evening.[3] True to form, Lake divided his attacking force into three columns. The left column was ordered to assault a gateway, whilst the right was directed to support the centre column by attacking a battery of guns erected by the Jats in front of the walls. The centre column's commander, Lieutenant Colonel James Maitland of HM 75th Foot, was ordered to storm the breach. Maitland led a force composed of the flank companies from HM 22nd, 75th and 76th Foot and the HEIC

3 Thorn, *Memoir of the War in India*, p.416.

European regiment, supported by an unnamed battalion of *sepoys*.[4] At their head was the 20-year-old John Shipp, who had volunteered for the forlorn hope. Before the storm, Shipp had spent the day replacing the flint of his musket and pointing his bayonet, as rumours abounded that the Jats used padded jackets to stave off thrusts. When he left for the trenches, Shipp bid farewell to his pony Apple and his favourite dog Wolf, as the camp guns sounded at 8:00 p.m., the appointed hour for the attack.[5] Upon entering the siege lines, Shipp's comrades asked if he had left a will, he stated his last will and testament would be to lead them into the breach.

As the storming party advanced, they found the ground broken up with swamps and pools, which forced the centre column to open out, delaying the march and confusing the men. Some of the disorientated soldiers drifted too close to the other columns and became mixed up with them.[6] The centre column remained undetected until they had reached within 50 paces of a ditch in front of the breach and then all hell broke loose, 'rockets were flying in all directions; blue lights were hoisted; and the fort seemed convulsed to its very foundation. Its ramparts seemed like some great volcano vomiting tremendous volumes of fiery matter'.[7] Racing forwards, Maitland's soldiers came up against a ditch, some 20 yards wide and four or five feet deep, which was overlooked by two guns set up on an island by the Jats, who poured a steady fire on the stormers. Pioneers rushed forward and threw gabions and fascines – bundles of sticks – into the ditch to help the forlorn hope across, but 'they were as a drop of water in the mighty deep'.[8] The flank companies of the 22nd had to jump into the ditch and wade through the chest-high water to clear the island and push onwards to the breach. Thorn states only 23 boys of the 22nd Foot crossed and mounted the destroyed walls. A herculean effort had been required to mount the breach, as when the boys reached the base, they discovered that in many places the walls had not been completely reduced to rubble and were still perpendicular. Scrabbling about, the only footfalls available to the boys came from stones and pieces of wood cast down by the defenders. To make matters worse, to their right a sizable bastion covered in timber was fired by the defenders, lighting up the Rajasthani night as if it were 'noonday'.[9] Amidst this chaos, the walls echoed with the martial tunes of *The Grenadier's March* and *God Save the King*, and failing that, three rousing cheers to encourage the boys to press their advance.[10]

In the first salvo from the bastion, Maitland was killed by grapeshot while the boys climbed into the breach three abreast. Any hopes that still lay within them must have been dashed as soon as they crested the ruined walls. The area had been refortified with wooden emplacements, through which a forest of spears bristled. During the fighting Lieutenant Creswell was almost cut to pieces. The breach was heavily fortified, and the 22nd were too few to turn and mount the walls to attempt to dislodge the guns.

4 Thorn, *Memoir of the War in India*, p.416.
5 Shipp, *The Extraordinary Military Career*, p.81.
6 Thorn, *Memoir of the War in India*, p.417.
7 Shipp, *The Extraordinary Military Career*, p.82.
8 Shipp, *The Extraordinary Military Career*, p.82.
9 Shipp, *The Extraordinary Military Career*, p.82.
10 Provan, *Bullocks, Grain and Good Madeira*, p.155.

Consequently, the boys were initially ordered to sit down to avoid the incessant fire, whilst Lieutenant George Mansergh of the grenadier company sought help. The 22nd waited in vain; eventually they were forced to beat a retreat back across the ditch and leave behind many of their wounded comrades. The assault had cost the 22nd dearly, five privates killed, while both Lieutenants Sweetenham and Creswell were wounded, along with four serjeants, a drummer, and 49 privates. The hardest pill to swallow was a missing serjeant and three boys, who it was assumed, would have been offered no quarter by the defenders.[11] Shipp had come off comparatively lightly; the wound on his forehead reopened, a spear cut his finger, and he received several smaller cuts possibly from an exploding pot. Other casualties suffered by the boys included copper coins embedded in their flesh from exploding bombs. Amongst the fallen was Serjeant Bury.[12] In his memoirs, Shipp places Bury's death at Deeg, where he writes that Bury had been wounded, but decided to return to the assault and fought through the night, before he was killed by a cannon round the next day as he looked over a parapet. It is more than likely that Shipp blurred the memory of the two events, and the unfortunate Bury probably met his fate looking over a parapet at Bharatpur, not Deeg.

Realising the initial breach was impracticable, Lake's engineers started to work on creating a fresh breach in Bharatpur's walls further east.

## The Second Assault

It took nearly two weeks to prepare the second breach, but finally on 20 January the new opening in the walls was ready. To make sure the previous mistakes estimating the depth of the ditch were not repeated, Lake's command needed intelligence regarding the size of the ditch in front of the new breach to ensure the ladders were long enough. Through a cunning ruse, a *havildar* and two *sowars* of the 3rd Bengal Native Cavalry approached the walls of Bharatpur disguised as turncoats and reconnoitred the ditch. With this intelligence, the British knew the extent of the ditch before the walls. Following the cavalrymen's report, Lake settled on 21 January for the assault. The attack's forlorn hope advanced with Serjeant Shipp once again volunteering to lead them into the breach. Behind him came 50 boys of the HM 22nd led by Lindsay, who reportedly 'threw away his crutch and marched with his left arm in a sling'.[13] The remainder of the column consisted of 120 men of HM 75th, 150 of HM 76th, and 100 men of Bengal Europeans. If the advance party succeeded in mounting the breach, the rest of these regiments would follow, and behind them further reinforcements from the native infantry were on hand. Part of the thorough planning for the second assault detailed that the 75th and 76th should cover the ladder parties – whilst they were lowered across the ditch – by firing on the walls and keep the defenders' heads down.

11 BL: IOR/H/626, Papers concerning the war with Holkar, Raja of Bharatpur, Sindhia and Raja of Berar, p.883.
12 TNA: WO 12/3880: General Muster Books and Pay Lists, 22nd Foot 1st Battalion, 1805-1806, February 1805.
13 Thorn, *Memoir of the War in India*, p.423.

With the plans for the assault carefully crafted, the attack was scheduled to commence at 3:00 p.m. on the 21st. Shipp remembered almost instantly coming under fire. The column pressed on, with soldiers falling left and right until the stormers approached the ditch. Here the storming party discovered that since the initial reconnaissance, the Jats had dammed the ditch lower down, causing the water level to rise in front of the breach. One tall grenadier jumped in to test the depth and discovered it was 12 feet (3.65m) deep.[14] The ladders were now too short, and despite the best efforts of the British, Shipp could only watch hopelessly as the ladders drifted loose in the current. Some soldiers managed to swim across but were quickly recalled by Macrae, who beat a hasty retreat.

Casualties had been high amongst the 22nd; one serjeant and seven privates were killed. Whilst three serjeants, four corporals, two drummers, and 32 privates were listed as wounded.[15] Amongst the casualties was the redoubtable Lindsay, whose right knee was smashed by a *jingal* gun – a large wall-mounted musket. The damage caused by the *jingal* ball meant Lindsay later had to have his leg amputated below the knee. Shipp did not escape unscathed either and received another ball across his forehead, which grazed his skull and caused a large flap of skin to drop over his eye. He subsequently spent several days blind and in high fever. [16]

## 'The latest job': The Third Assault

Whilst Lake's army had been marching back and forth across northern India, Colonel Murray, who we last saw occupying Indore, was also on the move. As early as October 1804, Lake had urged Murray to link up with his army and bring desperately needed reinforcements to aid the tired veterans of the Grand Army. After a fresh supply of equipment, Murray started out from Ujjain on 19 October. Back in Bombay, Major General Wellesley frustrated with Murray's tardiness, demanded the Colonel's replacement. Despite a reluctance to change horses in midstream, the Bombay Presidency eventually relented, and Murray was replaced by Major General Richard Jones of the Bombay Artillery.[17]

Jones caught up with Murray on Christmas Day 1804 and quickly discovered the grim situation in the ranks. Most of the Europeans, including the boys of the 65th, were riddled with sickness, with 164 of the total 651 Europeans listed as sick. He also found most of the *sepoys* were new recruits, calling into question their reliability in action. It took Jones' column another month before they neared Bharatpur on 10 February 1805. Approaching the fortress, they were assailed by Maratha cavalry, who forced the column to march in square and frequently unlimber their guns to keep the horsemen in check. By the time Jones' column marched into Lake's encampment on the 11th, the soldiers were described as presenting 'a motley appearance; their worn-out uniforms

14 Pester, *War and Sport*, p.379.
15 BL: IOR/H/626, Papers concerning the war with Holkar, Raja of Bharatpur, Sindhia and Raja of Berar, p.886.
16 Shipp, *The Extraordinary Military Career*, pp.88–89.
17 Laurie, *History of the Royal Irish Rifles*, p.67.

were patched with various colours, or replaced by red cotton jackets; many of the men wore sandals in the place of shoes and turbans instead of hats'.[18] Despite their disparate appearance, Lake was naturally pleased by this fresh injection of manpower.

The boys of the 65th did not have long before they too joined their brothers in the 22nd Foot in assaulting the walls of Bharatpur. On 6 February, a couple of days before Jones' column marched into camp, Lake had shifted his attention towards a bastion near the Anar Gate, south-east of the two initial storming attempts.[19] By the 18th, another breach had been made and the British trenches were brought as close to the ditch as possible, almost to the brink. In front of the breach the British had also constructed a mine to blow up the counterscarp and create a sloping path for the stormers.[20] Whilst they laboured in the trenches, above the heads of the British working parties, the Jats waved the clothes and weapons of the men and boys who had been left behind in the two previous assaults, reminding the besiegers of their previous failures.[21]

Orders were issued for the storming parties to enter the trenches on the morning of 20 February, and wait for the artillery to destroy any stockades the Jats had constructed in the breach during the night. The British appear to have habitually abandoned the mine during the night and retired into the trenches. Observing this routine, during the night of the 19/20th the Jats entered the siege lines to steal entrenching equipment and dismantle the mine. Their work appears to have gone unnoticed until the Jats sallied into the trenches, drums beating and the cold steel of tulwars and spears flashing in the morning light. Both Thorn and Shipp suggest the attack landed just as a relief was taking place and the flank companies of the 22nd were advancing to their usual spot at the head of the storming party. Although it must be noted that the injury to Shipp's head had left him *hors de combat* for this attack and Thorn appears to have gained his information later, as he was serving away from Bharatpur during this part of the siege. Pester, who remained with Lake's army, confirms that the attack caused confusion and forced the men in the trenches to fall back.[22] Whilst some officers swiftly organised a mixed body of men from the 76th and *sepoys* to drive the Jats out, the 22nd, led by Lieutenant William Wilson, entered the trenches. Wilson's boys advanced with the bayonet and drove the Jats out of the siege works. Pester mentions the mixed European and *sepoy* force chased the Jats almost to the Anar Gate before they retired to the British lines. Although an unnamed officer in command of the 76th refused to reoccupy the trenches and was later forced to leave the regiment. A sad portent of what was to come.[23]

The sally had unnerved the besiegers, particularly the British, but despite their misgivings the third assault had been scheduled to go forward that afternoon. Accordingly, the force was split into three columns. The main storming party, commanded by Don, was positioned on the left, and consisted of the flank companies of the 22nd, with the battalions of HM 75th, 76th, the Bengal Europeans and the 1/12th, 2/12th and 1/15th

18 Laurie, *History of the Royal Irish Rifles*, p.68.
19 Provan, *Bullocks, Grain and Good Madeira*, p.160.
20 Thorn, *Memoir of the War in India*, pp.450-451.
21 Provan, *Bullocks, Grain and Good Madeira*, p.160.
22 Pester, *War and Sport*, p.383.
23 Thorn, *Memoir of the War in India*, p.451.

BNI. To their right, the centre column was ordered to carry a series of gun placements and trenches constructed by the Jats before the walls. Whilst the right column, consisting of 300 boys of HM 65th Foot and the 1st Grenadier ByNI and 1/3rd ByNI, would attack the Bhim Narayan Gate and try to force the gates with cannon.[24]

Around 3:30 p.m., the start of the centre column's attack on the outworks was the signal for the remaining storming parties to advance. Of the three columns, the centre fared the best, managing to capture 11 guns and haul them back to the British camp. In contrast, as Don ordered HM 75th, 76th and Bengal Europeans to advance, they refused, declaring 'they would not go to be slaughtered'.[25] The morning attack by the Jats had left the Europeans jittery. To add to their nervousness, it was known that the Jats had occupied the mine, and they feared this had been rigged to blow on their approach. On top of this, many of their comrades who had been injured during the sally had not been evacuated and were still plaintively calling out for aid. This was a grave crisis for Don's assault. As already noted, the British felt the only troops steady enough to lead an attack against a breach were King's Regiments or the HEIC's Europeans, and their refusal to march left the contest for the walls as good as over.

As the low roar of the guns mixed with the whistle of passing shots and the lamentations of the wounded, Don tried to harangue the mutinous Europeans to advance. He informed them that such conduct was 'unprecedented and such as British soldiers were supposed incapable of'.[26] All to no avail, the Europeans would not budge. Don turned to the men behind, who had belonged to what had been nicknamed the 'ragged battalions', men who had served under Don when he commanded the Reserve Brigade and had chased Holkar across Hindustan and charged through the walls of Deeg – the boys of HM 22nd and the *sepoys* of the 12th BNI. Don called on 'the glorious 12th Regiment of Native Infantry to follow him. This distinguished corps, to the eternal disgrace of the Europeans' names, in an instant obeyed their gallant and well-known commander',[27] followed by the boys of HM 22nd Foot.

Don led the way as HM 22nd and the 12th BNI, supported by two 6-pounders, 'left the trenches in the best order'.[28] The guns vomited forth canister upon the breach, whilst the infantry advanced. A tall *sepoy* tried to test the ditch, which was 'like a sea' and became fully submerged.[29] Turning aside from the breach and the threat of fresh mines, the stormers edged towards a nearby bastion and, to the surprise of onlookers, including the artillery officer James Young, 'they clambered up within a few feet of the top, where they stuck like bees'.[30] As they pulled themselves up, a boy from the 22nd tried to enter an embrasure, but was blown from the gun at the moment he dropped

24 Hugh Pearse, *Memoir of the Life and Military Services of Viscount Lake, Baron Lake of Delhi and Laswaree 1744-1808* (Edinburgh: William Blackwood and Sons, 1908), p.378.
25 Pester, *War and Sport*, p.384.
26 Pester, *War and Sport*, p.384.
27 James Young quoted in Provan, *Bullocks, Grain and Good Madeira*, p.162.
28 Pester, *War and Sport*, p.384.
29 Pester, *War and Sport*, p.384.
30 Young quoted in Provan, *Bullocks, Grain and Good Madeira*, p.162.

in. In the face of tremendous odds, the tenacious boys and *sepoys* managed to place the colours of the 12th BNI atop the bastion.[31]

At this moment in the assault, the Jats blew their mines in the breach, assuming the main part of the centre column was close by. The explosion widened the breach and, according to Thorn, made the approach easier, but the Europeans would not budge. With no reserves to support the 22nd and the 12th BNI, Don called off the attack and ordered the soldiers to retire. The third assault had failed.

On the other side of the battlefield, the right column had also fared poorly. As Don's soldiers fought around the bastion, the 65th tried to advance on the Bhim Narayan Gate, but they could not bring their guns to the entrance. The assault column had been halted by a body of Maratha horse, who threatened their flank.[32] The subsequent delay meant that as the British neared the walls, the defenders could turn their full attention towards them, with some precise shots knocking out the wheels of the stormers' gun, and destroying several scaling ladders.[33] The right column still attempted to approach the walls, but with their scaling equipment destroyed the attack had to be called off.

Casualties were once again heavy, the 22nd suffered one serjeant and 11 privates killed, whilst one serjeant and 19 privates were wounded. In the 65th, Captain Ralph Bates, Lieutenants Richard Bates and Thomas Hutchins were all wounded. The list of dead included two serjeants and 11 privates, whilst two privates had been wounded. Most harrowing of all were the two missing privates, their unknown fate adding to the uncertainty of the day's events.[34] In his dispatch to Lord Wellesley, Lake glossed over the mutiny in the trenches, merely stating 'The Troops, most confident of success, commenced the attack and persevered in it for a considerable length of time with the most determined bravery', but he could not hide the casualties, totalling 147 Europeans and *sepoys* killed, 732 wounded, and 15 missing.[35] Despite the overwhelming losses, the siege had to go on.

## 'Once more unto the breach, dear friends': The Fourth Assault

The next morning, Lake appeared on the parade ground before his battered army. In his life, Lake had been something of an old dandy, keen to appear in full general's attire. Indeed, his tendency to examine the trenches at Bharatpur in full dress and feathers earned a request from his men that he might refrain from doing so in the future, as it tended to attract the enemy's fire. It can easily be imagined, as he stood before his assembled European infantry, the kind of figure the old swashbuckler cut on the parade ground. The soldiers gathered before him had just finished burying the bodies from

31 Thorn, *Memoir of the War in India*, p.453.
32 Thorn, *Memoir of the War in India*, pp.453–454.
33 Pearse, *Memoir of the Life and Military Services of Viscount Lake*, p.378.
34 BL: IOR/H/626, Papers concerning the war with Holkar, Raja of Bharatpur, Sindhia and Raja of Berar, p.897.
35 BL: IOR/H/626, Papers concerning the war with Holkar, Raja of Bharatpur, Sindhia and Raja of Berar, p.897.

the attack on the 20th. When Lake addressed the assembled European infantry, he 'most strongly expressed his disapprobation and disgust at their conduct yesterday'.[36] Lake's admonishment and shaming of the European infantry had the desired effect; they immediately volunteered to retrieve their lost reputation.

The assault was planned to go in at 3:00 p.m. on the 21st and was directed against the bastion HM 22nd and the 12th BNI had attempted to mount in the third assault. To reduce the bastion, Lake's artillery had expended the last of their ammunition to produce a practicable breach. The regiments selected for the fourth assault comprised the entirety of the Europeans, including the boys of HM 22nd and HM 65th, under the command of Monson. Despite his injuries, which left him with a throbbing headache, Shipp would not be denied the opportunity to lead the forlorn hope once more. Shipp was joined by Lieutenant Templeton of the 76th, described by Shipp as a little man with the heart of a lion. Templeton gave the young serjeant his hand and apologised, 'Shipp, I am come to rob you of part of your glory; you are a regular monopolist of that commodity',[37] Templeton carried with him a small Union flag and had promised to place 'Old England's' banner on the bastion or die in the attempt.

The column set off for the final attack. As they left the British camp, the stormers passed under Lake's watchful eye, who, according to Shipp, addressed the 20-year-old saying, 'Sergeant, it is with sincere regret I again see you wounded, and again at the head of your little band of heroes. I will not check your praiseworthy spirit; go into glory, my lads, and may Heaven prosper your zeal, and crown you with triumph!'[38] Lake offered similar encouragement to every regiment that passed by, although it was claimed when the 22nd marched past, he had to turn away with a tear in his eye at the sorry state to which they had been reduced.

Despite the personal touches and speeches, Shipp and his comrades seemed more resigned to their fate rather than certain of victory, a feeling made much worse by the sight that lay before them. The fourth assault took place across the same ground as the assault on the 20th. Many of the men and boys' comrades who could not be buried remained strewn out in the open. Some of these poor souls, covered in blood, raised their hands imploring for aid. Whilst Shipp states this excited the soldiers to vengeance, it must have also added to the disquiet in the ranks.

The stormers found the breach at the bastion to be extremely steep; some shelter could be found near the base, but to ascend the bastion the soldiers had to expose themselves to the enemies' fire.[39] Shipp observed that the fire from the stormers was largely ineffective against the heavily armoured Jat defenders, as the balls were turned aside by their armour.[40] For an hour the attackers tried to find a way to mount the breach under heavy fire from the fortress' guns and matchlocks. Some soldiers tried to climb the bastion by driving their bayonets into the walls, using them like an ice axe. These enterprising individuals were knocked down by logs or other missiles thrown by the defenders. Others

36 Pester, *War and Sport*, p.385.
37 Shipp, *The Extraordinary Military Career*, pp.91–92.
38 Shipp, *The Extraordinary Military Career*, p.92.
39 Thorn, *Memoir of the War in India*, p.456.
40 Shipp, *The Extraordinary Military Career*, p.93.

A boy soldier mounting the breach at Bharatpur. (K.D.)

tried to squeeze through holes in the walls made by the British artillery, but in most places only a couple could attempt to enter, and they were easily overwhelmed.[41]

Minutes into mounting the breach, Shipp was shot in the back and tumbled down to the base, knocking several men over. During his fall, a grenadier's bayonet penetrated the fleshy part of Shipp's foot, stabbing under his big toe. At the base of the breach, Shipp was helped up by a boy from the light company who was killed in the attempt. Meanwhile, true to his word, Templeton planted the Union flag near the top of the bastion before he was cut in two. Menzies, who formerly commanded the grenadiers of the 22nd and was now aide-de-camp to Lake, attempted to lead a party into the breach 'where, by his animating language and heroic example, he greatly invigorated the troops' but he was also killed after gaining the top of the bastion.[42]

As the dazed Serjeant Shipp took in the scene, a flaming projectile struck his cartridge pouch, causing them to explode. Shipp blacked out, and when he came to, he discovered he was at the base of the breach with his legs dangling in the water. 'I was much hurt from the fall, my face was severely scorched, my clothes much burnt, and all the hair on the back of my head burnt off.'[43] Shipp crawled over to another soldier and sat there for a while until a cannon ball struck close by, showering them in mud, 'This added greatly to the elegance of my appearance'.[44] At this moment, after two gruelling hours,

41 Thorn, *Memoir of the War in India*, p.456.
42 Thorn, *Memoir of the War in India*, p.456.
43 Shipp, *The Extraordinary Military Career*, pp.93–94.
44 Shipp, *The Extraordinary Military Career*, p.94.

Monson sounded the retreat. Bharatpur had bested the Grand Army of the HEIC, causing horrendous casualties to the Bengal and Bombay establishments.

In the final assault, two privates of the 22nd were killed. Lieutenant Wilson was injured again alongside Serjeant Shipp and one private. Whilst in the 65th, one serjeant, one drummer, and eight privates were killed. Captains Symes, Warren, and Watkins were wounded, as were Lieutenants Hutchins, O'Brien, Hinde, Clutterbuck, and Harvey, in addition to nine serjeants, 11 corporals, a drummer, and 78 privates. Two corporals and nine privates were marked as missing.[45]

Of the 9,400 men who had served under Lake at Bharatpur, 3,000 were listed as casualties. The 65th had suffered severely; of the 463 rank and file serving with Lake's army, as many as 121 were recorded as killed, wounded or missing. Whilst out of 19 NCOs and drummers, 14 were listed as killed or wounded, which meant that of the eight companies deployed, 29 percent had become casualties. The figures for the 22nd were even more stark: 193 rank and file from the flank companies had been deployed to Bharatpur; out of this total, 28 were either killed or missing and 117 wounded. This meant that as many as 75 percent of the flank companies had been casualties during the siege.[46]

Bharatpur brought the seemingly irresistible wave of Lake's conquests in northern India to a shuddering halt. The day after the last assault, Lake withdrew his guns from the batteries. Outwardly he still seemed confident of victory, but he made no attempts to continue the siege. Ranjit Singh had been anxious to negotiate with the British since Holkar's armies had been crushed in December 1804, and his representatives were permitted to enter Lake's camp to negotiate. The eventual treaty agreed that an indemnity of 20 *lakhs*, or two million rupees, was to be paid to the HEIC, and in return Ranjit Singh was able to keep his territory. By 10 April, the battered remnants of the Grand Army had retired from Bharatpur towards Agra.[47]

The boys had performed prodigious service during the siege, especially the battered flank companies of the 22nd Foot, who were always willing to lead in every assault. A testament to their bravery against overwhelming odds. Not only did the boys in red coats have to face the tenacious Jat defenders, but they also had to reckon with a dearth of siege artillery. Due to cost-cutting on the part of the HEIC government and a lack of foresight on Lake's part, the Grand Army's siege train did not have any guns of a sufficient calibre to breach Bharatpur's walls. The lack of adequate artillery helped to make the assaults exceedingly brutal as the boys were faced with almost insurmountable obstacles just to reach the breach.[48]

Amid a melancholy camp, there was one bright point. Serjeant Shipp's courageous role, leading multiple forlorn hopes against the breaches, had been noted by Lake. Accordingly, in March 1805, Shipp – who had just celebrated his twenty-first birthday

45 BL: IOR/H/626, Papers concerning the war with Holkar, the Raja of Bharatpur, Sindhia and the Raja of Berar, pp.898–899.

46 BL: IOR/H/626, Papers concerning the war with Holkar, the Raja of Bharatpur, Sindhia and the Raja of Berar, pp.883–899.

47 Provan, *Bullocks, Grain and Good Madeira*, p.168.

48 E. Buckle, J.W. Kaye (ed.), *Memoir of the Services of the Bengal Artillery* (London: Wm. H. Allen & Co., 1852), pp.274–276

– was given a commission in the 65th Foot, becoming an ensign. Moving from one boy regiment to another, Shipp found, 'From the whole of this regiment, I received the most marked attentions; and whenever I served with, or met them afterwards, I experienced from them the most disinterested friendship.'[49]

Upon his promotion, Shipp, now kitted out as an officer, dined in Lake's tent, where he was asked to sit beside the General and regale him and his son, the Honourable George Augustus Frederick Lake, with his account of fighting in the breach. Whilst Shipp does not state where he received his new uniform it may have come from Lindsay who funded some parts of his officer's kit. The day after dinner, Shipp was called to see Lake, who declared, 'Shipp, I have been thinking a good deal about your case. You of course, have not much money. I know your generous Lindsay will do anything to serve you, but must really leave a little for me to do. You may therefore draw on me, through the field paymaster, for what you want.'[50] As good as his word, Lake provided Shipp with a tent, two camels, and a horse, whilst Lindsay provided Shipp with the remainder of his equipage. Shipp's time with the 65th was brief, as within three weeks Lake had used his patronage to promote the young man to lieutenant in the 76th. In the popular imagination, rising from the ranks was rarely achievable in the British Army during the Napoleonic Era, however, the reality was quite different. Many serjeant majors often became adjutants through long service or by demonstrating their ability as capable administrators. Occasionally, individuals like Shipp demonstrated not only capability but extraordinary bravery, such as Serjeant Charles Ewart, who combined long service and the feat of capturing the eagle of the *45e Régiment de Ligne* at Waterloo that won him an ensigncy. Likewise, Shipp demonstrated his capability and determination by learning to read and write and, in the space of eight years, went from being a destitute ward of the parish and an illiterate ranker to an educated subaltern aged just 21.

Not all of Shipp's comrades were so lucky. Following the siege, several boys were invalided home in September 1805. Upon their return, their details were noted down by the Royal Hospital Chelsea, which provides a brief glimpse into the lives of the boys. Serjeant George Howe, a former weaver from Fife, 19 years old in 1805, had been left lame in his left leg following a 'Gun Shot' wound. Another former weaver, Private John Erroll from Lanarkshire, who had enlisted at 15, also suffered the effects of gunfire. Whilst William Dale, who had left Congleton and followed the drum at 16, was discharged having lost his left hand. Finally, the 22-year-old Corporal Roger Burns from Armagh left the 22nd having lost his index finger on his right hand and most of his middle finger from a gunshot wound; he had enlisted in 1796 at the age of 13.

Over 20 years later, following the second and successful siege of Bharatpur, James Skinner, famed soldier and founder of Skinner's Horse, reflected on the boys and men he had served with in 1805. For Skinner, despite Lake's failure, he still spoke highly of, 'His acts, and those of heroes whom he led, require no mention here: they stand immortal and unrivalled, and ever must do so.'[51]

49 Shipp, *The Extraordinary Military Career*, p.95.
50 Shipp, *The Extraordinary Military Career*, p.96.
51 Skinner, *The Recollections of Skinner*, p.258.

# 10

# The Hunt for Holkar

Lake's failure at Bharatpur left his army mauled whilst his main opponent, Holkar, still roamed unchallenged throughout the countryside. During the siege, the remnants of Holkar's army had hovered around the siege lines, maintaining a respectful distance from the British. With the failure at Bharatpur, Lake turned his attention back to Holkar. During the dawn of 2 April 1805, the British cavalry, reserve, and horse artillery arrived at the Raja's encampment, scattered his army and pursued them over 7 miles.[1] Following this disaster, Holkar fled across the River Chambal, as the river marked the limit of British influence. Lake initially pursued his quarry, but as the monsoon rains battered his column, he withdrew his forces to Mathura and Agra before spending the summer of 1805 encamped away from the frontier.

When the flank companies of the 22nd arrived at their summer quarters, they found the rest of the battalion had travelled up country to join the Grand Army. The main body of the 22nd had left Calcutta in December 1804, and as they passed through the city, they saluted the Governor General before commencing their 800-mile (1300km) journey to Cawnpore.[2] During the march, Plummer's prayer group conducted their meetings in a tent derisively nicknamed 'the Methodists tent'. Their devotions must have been sombre affairs, as they restricted themselves to reading the hymns rather than singing them, still nervous of drawing attention to themselves and potentially causing another scuffle.[3] Whilst Plummer fixated on these furtive prayer meetings, Mansfield notes with considerable irritation the number of thefts which had taken place in the camp. This appears to have been an especially irksome bugbear for the British during this time, as both Shipp and another officer and memoirist, Robert Grenville Wallace, describe in great detail how thieves operated in India. They both claimed that some robbers shaved all the hair from their bodies and oiled themselves up so they could creep into the British camps. If these burglars were detected, the oil allowed them to literally slip through their pursuers' fingers.[4] During the march to Cawnpore, Mansfield describes the thefts of several items, including the regimental bandmaster's new coat

1 Thorn, *Memoir of the War in India*, p.461.
2 Plummer, *The Journal of Samuel Plummer*, p.42.
3 Plummer, *The Journal of Samuel Plummer*, pp.43–44.
4 Robert Grenville Wallace, *Fifteen Years in India* (London: Longman, Hurst, Rees, Orme, and Brown, 1823), p.295.

and his wife's petticoat.[5] Despite these trials and tribulations, the centre companies reached Cawnpore on 28 February 1805 after nearly two months marching up country.[6] As the regiment established itself in the town, Plummer observed 'a number of carts coming down the country, full of wounded men'.[7] Some of these casualties came from the mauled flank companies of the 22nd, who had travelled almost 300 miles (483km) to reach Cawnpore. Plummer described their appearance as being 'in a very miserable and wretched condition. Some of the men had lost their limbs; and their wounds, owing to the heat and the want of proper care, were full of maggots'.[8]

In the meantime, Holkar fled northwards, towards the northwest of Delhi, outmanoeuvring Jones' Bombay division, including HM 65th Foot, which tried to intercept the Marathas along the way. This was the 65th's last operation in the war as subsequently they retired to Dahod, garrisoning the town for the remainder of 1805.[9]

Having given the Bombay Division the slip by September 1805, Holkar had found refuge in the Punjab – the land of the five rivers – ruled at the time by Maharaja Ranjit Singh of the Sikh Empire.[10] Whilst hiding in the Sikh court, Holkar hoped to persuade Ranjit Singh to join an anti-British coalition and throw the formidable Sikh army known as the *Khalsa* against the HEIC. When Lake received intelligence of his mission, the old general set out in pursuit, determined to bring Holkar to the negotiating table and quash any potential coalition between the Raja of Indore and the Sikhs. Accordingly, in October 1805, Lake gathered his forces and, placing the boys of HM 22nd Foot in the Reserve Brigade, he set out towards the Punjab.[11]

As the British approached the Sikh rajas, Holkar attempted to incite them to fight Lake's army, but his efforts proved futile, and the Raja was forced to flee across the Sutlej, one of the major rivers that marked the frontiers of the Punjab.[12] By 2 December, the British had reached Ludhiana, a town situated on the Sutlej, which had been abandoned by the inhabitants at the approach of the Grand Army. With Holkar ensconced beyond the river at Jullundur, Lake was anxious to enter the Punjab and bring the campaign to an end. Accordingly the General encouraged Skinner and his horsemen to cross the River Sutlej and lead the way for the Grand Army, including the 22nd Foot.[13]

Pressing onwards into the Punjab, Lake directed his soldiers towards the holy city of Amritsar where Holkar had encamped with his army.[14] As they passed through the Sikh Empire, Lake maintained a tight leash on his men, plundering was prohibited and damage had to be paid for.[15] Lake subsequently crossed the Beas River and set up camp on the south bank of the Ravi River across from Amritsar. On 19 December, Ranjit

5 CMM: 0003.01/16: Personal reminisces of QM William Mansfield, 1798–1834, p.8.
6 TNA: WO 17/1751: East Indies Monthly Returns, 1805, 1st January–March 1805.
7 Plummer, *The Journal of Samuel Plummer*, p.51.
8 Plummer, *The Journal of Samuel Plummer*, p.52
9 TNA: WO 17/1751: East Indies Monthly Returns, 1805, March–December 1805.
10 James Grant Duff, *A History of the Mahrattas* (Calcutta: R. Cambray & Co., 1912), vol.3, p.306.
11 Thorn, *Memoir of the War in India*, p.479.
12 Thorn, *Memoir of the War in India*, p.480.
13 Skinner, *The Recollections of Skinner*, p.207.
14 Thorn, *Memoir of the War in India*, p.488.
15 Pearse, *Memoir of the Life and Military Services of Viscount Lake*, p.406.

Singh's *vakil*, or representative, Fateh Singh Ahluwalia came to the British camp to act as a mediator between the Company and Holkar.[16] Whilst negotiations dragged on, Mansfield noted the richness of the countryside, describing it as 'a very fine country, it has plenty of Game, Fruit and Vegetables very cheap.'[17] He also noted that local Punjabis frequently entered the camp, curious to see the strangers in their land. At the same time, Plummer and his prayer group seem to have kept themselves apart from the hubbub of the British camp, as he busied himself constructing 'a booth' where his prayer group could meet.[18]

Over the course of December, the war was brought to its conclusion. Wellesley's tenure as Governor General came to an end with his recall to London, and with his departure the aggressive 'forward policy' of the last seven years ended as well. Instead, Wellesley's replacement, the Marquess Cornwallis, had been given a brief to conclude the Maratha War and reduce HEIC expenditure. However, Cornwallis' tenure proved to be short-lived as he died on 5 October 1805 and was temporarily replaced by Sir George Barlow, who intended to follow his predecessor's orders and end the war.[19] Accordingly, under instructions from Calcutta, Lake agreed to restore Holkar to his throne in Indore and by 24 December the conflict was over.

Before Lake had packed up his camp and returned to Hindustan a singular event took place, which appears to have left a lasting impression on the Sikhs. For some time, the Sikh commanders had repeatedly asked Lake for a review of the British troops, which the General arranged to take place on 31 December. The subsequent demonstration of European tactics included a brigade of cavalry and infantry, the latter composed of HM 22nd Foot and two battalions of *sepoys*. The parade commenced at three o'clock that afternoon, with Lake riding out accompanied by the Sikh generals, including Fateh Singh Ahluwalia. Having passed the line, Lake positioned himself opposite the centre of his brigades mounted upon an elephant. The infantry began the manoeuvres, with the 22nd and the *sepoys* advancing in close columns before deploying into line in front of the reviewing party. Once deployed, the battalions went through the motions of loading and firing, although it must have been an uncanny display, as there were no blank cartridges in the British camp, so the parade ground resounded with the clicks of a thousand empty Brown Bess flintlocks.[20]

Changing front, the British deployed into square, which was followed by a charge from the cavalry brigade and a few rounds fired by the horse artillery.[21] According to Skinner, this caused the Sikhs to exclaim, 'Oh saints, oh saints, it is all witchcraft!'[22] Whilst Thorn asserts that the generals whispered amongst themselves, 'thank God that we did not go to war with the English.'[23] Whilst this may not have been the exact

16 Thorn, *Memoir of the War in India*, p.491.
17 CMM: 0003.01/16: Personal reminisces of QM William Mansfield, 1798–1834, p.10.
18 Plummer, *The Journal of Samuel Plummer*, p.60.
19 James Mill, *History of British India*, (London: Madden, 1858), pp.566–567.
20 Thorn, *Memoir of the War in India*, p.493.
21 Skinner, *The Recollections of Skinner*, p.207.
22 Skinner, *The Recollections of Skinner*, p.207.
23 Thorn, *Memoir of the War in India*, p.494.

words exclaimed by the suite of Sikh generals, the appearance of British troops in the Punjab appears to have left a lasting impression on the Sikhs. Ranjit Singh's biographers, Patwant Singh and Jyoti M. Rai, both assert the Maharaja's exposure to Lake's army encouraged him to continue to reform the *Khalsa*.[24] These reforms would in time produce the formidable Sikh army which gave the British and Company regiments a bloody nose, 40 years later, during the First Anglo-Sikh War.

Finally, as the last treaties were signed, the British Army began the laborious journey back to the Upper Provinces of the HEIC, on 9 January 1806. During their march home, both Plummer and Mansfield remark that the army was continually tormented by regular thefts and robberies. Lieutenant Colonel Mercer had his coat and epaulettes pinched from his table whilst he was shaving, and a captain lost his silver teapot.[25] Passing near Delhi, the army halted for 20 days in February, and during the pause the Grand Army was broken up and sent to encampments across India.[26] The 22nd Foot were ordered to Mathura, which they reached on 17 March 1806. Upon their arrival, the regiment had to wait a further two months in the hot and arid countryside around the town whilst proper quarters were built for them.

As they waited, Plummer dutifully set about finding another location for his prayer meetings, as he hoped to avoid the scorching winds, named the *Loo*. These hot and dry winds are renowned for roaring across the Gangetic Plain; their scorching temperature turned foliage brown and raised the risk of heatstroke. The worst storms kicked up enough dust to cover the plains in darkness for hours. Plummer describes one example where, 'The heavens looked like fire during the whole storm, till the rain came on; and so dark, that we could not see each other at a yard distance.'[27] Fortunately for Plummer, he discovered a hill which offered shelter from the worst of the winds and his prayer group set about constructing an underground meeting place. Digging into the hill, Plummer's prayer group used a camel leg bone and a large turtle shell to construct a room for eight persons at a comfortable height of six feet.[28] With the war at an end, the three boy regiments were able to take stock and account for those that remained from the first boys who had enlisted almost a decade ago.

24 Patwant Singh and Jyoti M. Rai, *Empire of the Sikhs: The Life and Times of Maharaja Ranjit Singh*, (London: Peter Owen Publishers, 2013), pp.99–100.
25 CMM: 0003.01/16: Personal reminisces of QM William Mansfield, 1798–1834, p.12.
26 Plummer, *The Journal of Samuel Plummer*, p.62.
27 Plummer, *The Journal of Samuel Plummer*, p.64.
28 Plummer, *The Journal of Samuel Plummer*, p.63.

# 11

# 'Who am I sent upon Fort-duty'

## Nine Years with the Colours

The boys had spent almost nine years soldiering and six of those were half-way across the globe. They had faced conquest, war, starvation, and disease throughout their time with the colours, and whilst many had endured, and some won fame on the fields of India, many never returned to Britain. The 1806 Statement of the Periods of Service for all NCOs and Men provides some indication of how many of the boys remained with their regiments. The Statement was created at a time when the Secretary of State for War and the Colonies, William Windham, proposed introducing limited or short-service of seven years for recruits joining the line infantry regiments.[1] Since the outbreak of the war with France in 1793, various amendments to enlistment into the army meant there could be some variance in the service terms agreed by enlisting recruits. The 1806 Statement was an attempt by Parliament to gain a clearer idea of the manpower at its disposal by understanding how long the men had served in the army, how many were available for service abroad, and therefore might form part of any future expeditionary forces against Napoleonic France.

To complete the statement, the regimental staff had to provide details including enlistment dates, age at enlistment if they were under 18, and their date of birth. The British Army monitored the birth dates of all underage recruits, as it was standard practice in the early nineteenth century to make deductions from a soldier's pension for every year they were under the age of 18. For instance, Private Thomas Attwood of the 22nd Foot enlisted at 15 years old on 19 December 1799. By the time the statement was recorded on 24 June 1806, Attwood was 20 years old. If he survived to retirement, his pension would be deducted for every day he was under 18; this would amount to a loss of four years and 19 days.[2]

This practice provides invaluable insight into the numbers of underage soldiers who were serving in the boy regiments, with the only exception being the 65th Foot, who do not appear to have recorded the birth dates of the soldiers in their ranks. The

1 Linch, *The British Army,* p.141.
2 TNA: WO 25/944: 22 Foot, Statements of the Periods of service, 24 June 1806, p.1.

regimental staff do not provide any justification as to why this was the case, and the rest of the regimental paperwork leaves no clues as to the reasoning behind the omission in the register.

The administrative records are more comprehensive for the 22nd and 1st battalion 34th Foot (1/34th). When the statements were taken on 24 June 1806, they recorded 809 serjeants, drummers and rank and file in the 22nd and 1,014 in the 1/34th.[3] By this time the 34th Foot had also acquired a second battalion. Whilst the 1/34th sweated in a South Indian garrison during 1805, changes in the recruiting law in Britain – such as legislation allowing men to transfer from the militia into the army – produced a surplus of manpower. With these extra men the army was able to raise second battalions for several regiments. These battalions were intended to serve in Britain and Ireland and then send periodical drafts to the first battalion serving overseas. This system quickly had to give way to exigencies of war and many second battalions ended up serving overseas on campaign.[4] The 34th Foot are a prime example of one of these regiments; their second battalion was raised at Ashford in 1805. The men of the 2/34th had limited interactions with the 1st Battalion in India, as the 2nd battalion served in Europe principally in the Peninsular War (1808–1814) with no record of any former boy soldiers transferring to the second battalion.[5] Nevertheless, for the purposes of clarity, the 1st Battalion shall henceforth be referred to as the 1/34th.

To give an assessment of how many boy soldiers – raised under the Duke of York's orders – survived until 1806, all underage recruits who enlisted before 2 December 1797, when York and Fawcett issued their order, were eliminated from this book's examination of the number of boys, because the boys who enlisted before 2 December 1797 were signed up as drummers. Likewise, any recruits who enlisted after 1800, when the three regiments embarked for the Cape, have also been eliminated. This is because after the regiments departed for service in India, the age of enlistment appears to have been relaxed, enabling adults to take the King's shilling in the 22nd, 1/34th and the 65th Foot. Additionally, these later enlistees did not serve under the regulations outlined in the Duke of York's letter, which included a minimum of two to three years' service at home. With these provisions, when added up, 60 boys, or about 6 percent of the 1/34th, were still with the regiment in 1806. Most of these boys had directly enlisted into the 1/34th, but seven were draftees from the 4th Foot who had been sent to the 1/34th on 19 December 1798. Four of the boys had been promoted to serjeant and a further five were serving as corporals.[6]

In the 22nd Foot the proportion was much greater; 18 percent were former boys recruited during 1797–1800, including 10 serjeants, nine corporals, four drummers, and 122 privates. Like the 1/34th, most of these boys had been recruited by the 22nd, but there were also a significant number of draftees. Unsurprisingly, the

3 TNA: WO 25/944: 22 Foot, Statements of the Periods of service, 24 June 1806; TNA: WO 25/964: 34 Foot, Statements of the Periods of service, 24 June 1806.

4 Linch, *The British Army,* p.74.

5 Steve Brown, *King George's Army: British Regiments and the Men who led them 1793-1815: Volume 3: 31st to 60th Regiments of Foot* (Warwick: Helion, 2024), p.61.

6 WO 25/964: 34 Foot, Statements of the Periods of service, 24 June 1806.

largest group were from the 4th Foot, who sent 100 boys and men on 19 December 1798, although almost eight years later only 16 boys from the 4th Foot remained with the regiment. The next largest group of draftees came from the 32nd Foot, who had also recruited boys, amounting to 10 soldiers, followed by two former boys of the 9th Foot and one boy of the 52nd. These numbers suggest a substantial loss of boys from the 1797–1800 cadre.

The last six years of conflict had taken its toll, with disease running rampant through the boys, particularly those of the 1/34th and 65th who had served in Ceylon. In contrast to the substantial loss of boys, the statement lists several adults who enlisted at the turn of the century and survived the rigours of disease. In the 22nd Foot, 26 percent of the regiment were over 20 years old in 1799 compared with seven years later in 1806, when 19 percent of the battalion were from this original over 20 years old cadre who had enlisted before 1800.[7] The smaller losses experienced by the men in the 22nd Foot might suggest that older recruits were more resilient and survived the spectre of disease better than the boys. This would account for the significant drop in boy recruits in the regiments, as in 1799, both of these battalions' boys amounted to 73 percent of the rank and file in the 22nd and 63 percent of the privates in the 34th. Experiencing such significant losses, with a 57 percent loss in the 34th and a 55 percent fall in the 22nd Foot, could have been due to a range of factors, including wounded boys being pensioned off, some deserting, and many falling in battle or succumbing to sickness.

A poignant reminder of the age of these boys is evidenced in the statements for 1806, as one of the youngest recruits was Private William Edwards. Born on 1 January 1791, Edwards was only eight when he enlisted in the 22nd Foot, on 25 August 1799. Due to his age, he appears to have been detained in England until 19 January 1803, when, at barely 12 years old, his service in the East Indies commenced. Edwards was initially posted to Lieutenant Colonel Mercer's Company when he arrived in India in late 1803. Whilst he appears to have missed the major battles fought by the 22nd, Edwards still had to endure the relentless pursuit of Holkar into the Punjab and face inspection upon the parade ground by a host of Sikh generals, all before his fifteenth birthday.

## 'Brooding on Ancient Fame', the 34th in Madras

Whilst the 22nd and 65th Foot endured siege, slaughter, and sickness, the 1/34th posted to the Madras Presidency faced the prospect of idling away their days in the stifling barrack rooms of the Carnatic. Between 1804–1809, much of the battalion's time was spent in garrisons, first in Madras and then later moving to Walajabad, a town just outside Madras in September 1804. By January 1805, the 1/34th had recalled most of the boys who had been stationed on Ceylon and were reunited at Walajabad.[8] In April 1805, 355 rank and file were sent north to the fortress of Vellore, which had been

7 TNA: WO 25/944: 22 Foot, Statements of the Periods of service, 24 June 1806
8 TNA: WO 17/1751: East Indies, January 1805.

ceded by Tipu Sultan of Mysore during the 1790s. At the time, the fortress was a prison for Tipu's sons and their families and for the 1/34th, the fort promised yet more time sweltering within the confines of one of India's sixteenth-century forts.[9]

During the summer of 1805, the 1/34th's headquarters moved across the Carnatic, first to Damul, present-day Dambal in Karnataka state, and then to Peroor. Eventually in August 1805, the battalion marched north to Bellary (Bellari), a town situated between the northern frontier of Mysore and the southern border of the dominion of the Nizam of Hyderabad.[10] By January 1806, the 1/34th were posted to the medieval fort of Gooty, constructed on a rocky outcrop several miles east of Bellary.[11] The battalion spent three years garrisoning Gooty alongside regiments from the Madras Army. This prolonged period of inaction was occasioned by the relatively peaceful atmosphere across southern India following the fall of Seringapatam in 1799 and the death of Tipu Sultan, events that secured the Carnatic for the Company. Despite some resistance to British rule, by 1806, in the words of historian James W. Hoover, 'South India was almost completely demilitarised'.[12] Local outbreaks of violence or policing duties were handled by the Madras Army, whilst the King's Regiments were reserved for active operations against external threats that rarely materialised.

Whilst records from the 1/34th's time in Madras are sparse, there are a few that provide a tentative glimpse into regimental life. On 10 July 1806, a mutiny broke out in Vellore amongst some of the *sepoys* of the Madras Native Infantry. Several British officers were killed, including Lieutenant Colonel St John Fancourt of the 1/34th, and although the mutiny was swiftly repressed, it led to a wave of panic amongst many officers of the Madras Army.[13] Their fear led to accusations of plots flying through the balmy Carnatic air during 1806 and 1807.

Over a year after the mutiny at three o'clock in the afternoon of 20 November 1807, Rama Samy, a *naik* – equivalent to a corporal – in the 1/25th MNI, came to the office of the fort adjutant of Gooty, Lieutenant George Carnegie of 1/34th. The *naik* had attempted to speak to his own colonel but had been refused entry. Rama Samy eventually found a soldier of the 1/34th who brought him to Carnegie, where he relayed the dire news that a conspiracy was afoot intent on massacring the 1/34th during their unarmed exercises – in this case a cricket match.[14]

Rama Samy named several conspirators, including some *subadars*, a rank equivalent to captain. The conspiracy had been planned during a festival in July and was intent on capturing the fort of Gooty and slaughtering the unarmed soldiers of the 1/34th. Rama Samy also claimed the mutiny had been delayed at least once because the 1/34th had been ordered to watch a punishment, possibly a flogging and could not be taken

9 James W. Hoover, *Men without Hats: Dialogue, Discipline and Discontent in the Madras Army, 1806-1807* (New Delhi: Manohar Publishers & Distributors, 2007), p.49.
10 TNA: WO 17/1751: East Indies, June–September 1805.
11 TNA: WO 17/1752: East Indies, January 1806.
12 Hoover, *Men without Hats*, p.51.
13 Hoover, *Men without Hats*, p.60.
14 BL: IOR/F/4/293/6692: Report of a Native Infantry Battalion to attack the His Majesty's 34th Regiment, p.12.

unawares.[15] Whilst this report may have raised the alarm, it proved to be a false accusation by Rama Samy, who was already under inspection for offences in his regiment and was seeking revenge. Whilst this was the only threat of mutiny experienced by the 1/34th, the incident provides a glimpse into some of the routine of garrison life in 1807. Day-to-day in barracks revolved around routine exercises 'every second day',[16] and watching punishments on the parade ground. Although the effectiveness of these public displays of corporal punishment is debatable.

Between 1805–1808 several criminal cases were brought before the civil court at Fort St George in Madras. Whilst none of the cases involved former boy soldiers, their unsavoury character gave the battalion an unwholesome reputation. Most of the court cases related to the murders of native camp followers and servants. The first case was brought against Private George Bevan, who had joined the 1/34th on 16 February 1801 and was not listed as underage.[17] Bevan was accused of murdering a regimental cook, Nagapen (otherwise known as Mustopha) on 27 September 1805. Without a previous quarrel, Bevan shot the cook, claiming at his trial on 25 January 1806 that he had been suffering from mental derangement, caused by fits, usually brought on by a night of drinking and the heat. The jury debated for two hours and finally found Bevan not guilty, intimating they considered his mental instability compelling evidence to recommend diminished responsibility. Their verdict flew in the face of the presiding judge, who had stated, during his summing up of the case that there were no compelling grounds to find the defendant not guilty and stressed the dangerous effects of drink.[18]

A year later, on 24 July 1807, Private William Parkinson, who enlisted 15 December 1800 and was not underage, was executed for the murder of another camp follower, Yankoo. The propensity for violence against camp followers suggests a deterioration in the management of the battalion. This steady decline culminated on 21 January 1808 with a speech given to the Grand Jury of Madras by the Honourable Sir Thomas Strange, Chief Justice of Madras.

Strange did not preserve his ammunition and swiftly let fly a volley at the 1/34th, despairing, 'that in a Battalion of one of His Majesty's Regiments … there appears to have diffused itself such a spirit of rancour, and such a hardened wantonness exists'.[19] Strange also feared that if left unchecked, the canker of indiscipline would fester and might produce 'scenes of horror'.[20] The session included several cases of larceny not detailed in the report printed by the *Government Gazette* published in India, in addition to another two cases of murder. In the first case the accused was William Cogan, tried alongside a separate case involving William Smith. Cogan enlisted on 31 December 1800, but Smith is harder to identify, as there are three different Smiths in the battalion

15 BL: IOR/F/4/293/6692: Report of a Native Infantry Battalion to attack the His Majesty's 34th Regiment, p.28.
16 BL: IOR/F/4/293/6692: Report of a Native Infantry Battalion to attack the His Majesty's 34th Regiment, p.26.
17 TNA: WO 25/964: 34 Foot, Statements of the Periods of service, 24 June 1806.
18 *Government Gazette (India)*, 6 February 1806.
19 *Government Gazette (India)*, 4 February 1808.
20 *Government Gazette (India)*, 4 February 1808.

who all enlisted around 1797–1799, but like Cogan, none of them was listed as underage when they joined the regiment.

The report on Cogan's case reveals he was accused of murdering *Sepoy* Roshumbeg of the 2/7th MNI on 27 September 1807, whilst they both stood guard over several prisoners. The corporal of the watch discovered the murder when a shot rang out, and he found Cogan returning to his post with Roshumbeg stretched out on the ground. Cogan initially claimed the *sepoy* had shot himself, but upon closer examination it was discovered the ball had entered Roshumbeg's back. During the investigation, a corporal and two other private soldiers claimed Cogan had stated he would either kill himself or someone else before he went off guard and 'in fourteen days he [Cogan] would be on his way to Madras.'[21] The jury found Cogan guilty of murder, and it was the testimony of Corporal William Woodcock that led the judge to conclude that Cogan's attack had been premeditated. After sentencing, Cogan was sent from Madras back to Bellary so that his execution could be witnessed by the entirety of the 1/34th to serve as a warning to the soldiers and an exhibition of justice to the Madras Army and the locals.

Whilst the precise wording of Woodcock's testimony was not recorded in the *Government Gazette* or the *Madras Courier*, the *Courier* does mention that Woodcock provided a positive character witness for Cogan, possibly highlighting to the judge the defendant's ability to coldheartedly plan a murder. The major difference between Woodcock and the defendant was that Woodcock had been a boy soldier. Enlisting on 7 December 1800, Woodcock was 15 years old when he joined the 32nd Foot and was later transferred to the 34th on 13 April 1801, suggesting the 32nd continued to occasionally recruit boys before transferring them to the main boy regiments after some training.

The other case involved William Smith, and whilst the report is sketchy, it appears that Smith killed 'the companion of your bosom',[22] which suggests it was a comrade in the regiment. Unlike Cogan, Smith avoided the gallows and was convicted of manslaughter, receiving a 12-month sentence in gaol and a fine of 100 pagodas (gold coinage issued by both the HEIC and local rulers). A condition of Smith's sentence was that he remain in prison until the fine was paid.

Part of the reason there appears to have been so much violence in the barracks at Gooty, particularly against local camp followers was highlighted by Strange, who commented, 'Whence the delusion has sprung, I know not; but it would seem to be the opinion of the privates of this corps [1/34th], that, in order to be discharged from it, they have only to commit murder, and, for this purpose it would appear to be sufficient with them at all times, that a Native is at hand.'[23] These scenes of wanton violence seem to have – especially in Strange's case – aroused considerable alarm, particularly in the shadow of the recent mutiny at Vellore and the fear these murders would eventually provoke the *sepoys* of the Madras Army. To crush these sentiments, the convicted men of the 1/34th needed to be made examples of to dissuade other European regiments

21 *Madras Courier*, 27 January 1808.
22 *Government Gazette (India)*, 4 February 1808.
23 *Government Gazette (India)*, 4 February 1808.

from following their precedent. For the 1/34th stuck out on the fringes of the Madras Presidency, life must have been a tedious round of routine, with the ever-creeping spectre of senseless violence omnipresent in the corners of every barrack room. The problem was further compounded by many of the 1/34th's officers being absent from the regiment, a problem also experienced by 22nd Foot, leading to similar scenes of disorder amongst the regiment.

## 65th in Gujarat

Following their failed attempt to block Holkar's escape into the Punjab, the 65th remained encamped at Dahod on the border of Gujarat. Much like the 1/34th, only sparse details have filtered through regarding how the regiment was occupied. In January 1806 the 65th left Dahod and marched out of the interior to the coast, where they entered cantonments in Brachie, near Surat, remaining in the town until 1809.[24] Whilst stationed in Brachie, on 11 January 1807, Lieutenant Colonel Maddison, who had led a detachment of the 65th during the brutal Ceylon campaign, retired and was presented with a plate by his officers.[25] Aside from this passing reference, the 65th simply fade into temporary obscurity, with the voices of the remaining boys in the battalion disappearing from the historical record.

## Mismanagement and Misbehaviour in Mathura

During this period of quiet garrison life, the 22nd remained at Mathura, in the Upper Provinces of the HEIC. This was an important post as it lay close to the frontier with the Maratha Confederacy. While the peace held, the Company were anxious to stave off any potential raids from Maratha freebooters crossing the border into HEIC territory. During the doldrums of 1806–1809, life in the barracks of Mathura appears to have been much the same as any other. Plummer's memoir focuses on his prayer group's continued antagonism with many of their comrades, while Mansfield neatly skipped past this period in his diary and recommences his narrative in 1810. Both memoirists do not mention a prescient event in the history of the 22nd, which is also absent from the pages of the regiment's official history.

Early in the morning of 26 May 1807, Major General Richard Mark Dickens, commander of the garrison at Mathura, was disturbed by the sudden and unexpected appearance of the entirety of the 22nd's private soldiers arrayed before his quarters. Each company advanced in turn to deliver a statement of grievances to Dickens. Today the Indian Office Records at the British Library hold a copy of the five complaints laid before Dickens by the grenadiers of Captain Thomas Buttle's company. The first complaint stated that the regiment's pay was seven months in arrears from November

24 TNA: WO 17/185: 65th Foot Monthly Returns, 1806–1808.
25 *Calcutta Gazette*, 19 February 1807.

1806 to May 1807, referring to the Articles of War, the petitioners quoted the 79th section, which stated no soldiers' pay could be stopped for more than a month. Secondly, they complained the soldiers were two years in arrears for complete clothing and allowances, which had forced the men to pay for replacement white shirts without compensation. Thirdly, the men complained about the meagre quality of their provisions. Fourthly, they objected to an arrack godown (warehouse), established within the regiment that was unfairly charging 4 rupees per gallon, of which an extra rupee had been added by the 22nd's commanding officer Lieutenant Colonel William Frome. Finally, the men complained Frome had banned any natives in the regimental bazar from supplying credit to the privates, as a consequence of their refusal to accept arrears of pay for February, whilst the soldiers still awaited payment for November 1806 to January 1807.[26]

On receipt of these notes, Dickens ordered the companies to disperse and return to their regimental lines. Initially, the 22nd complied, but once they reached their encampment, the men reassembled and broke into the regimental guard house, releasing all the prisoners. Dickens laid bare the circumstances in a letter, stating the regiment, 'in short were in a state of absolute Mutiny.'[27] As the situation deteriorated, Dickens seized the initiative, ordering out a regiment of Bengal native cavalry and two battalions of infantry from the garrison, and set out for the 22nd's camp. His swift response enabled him to disarm the battalion without any loss of life and then confine them to their regimental lines.

Following the incident Dickens was naturally anxious to quickly remove the 22nd Foot from the frontier. Equally shocked, the HEIC officials accepted his proposal, but were keen to understand why the misconduct had occurred. A flurry of letters followed as Dickens first sought and then obtained permission to pay the arrears of the 22nd until March 1807, hoping to mollify the irate men. Whilst Dickens attempted to pacify them, he did not want the 22nd to come off lightly. He confiscated their colours and their arms, stating in a letter written on 2 June that these should be withheld for some time, 'at least as a mark of Disgrace' or until he received positive orders from the provincial Commander in Chief to reinstate them.[28] Whilst Dickens fumed at what he perceived to be a long-fermented plan to mutiny, the HEIC focused on tracing the missing money. The subsequent investigation revealed a host of problems, which appeared to have festered in the 22nd Foot for over a year prior to 26 May 1807.

The cause of the unrest at Mathura was investigated by a Special Court of Enquiry organised by Dickens. The enquiry was presided over by Lieutenant Colonel Samuel Need of HM 24th Light Dragoons; alongside him were Paymaster John Wardell and Captain William Wallis, also from the 24th, whilst the HEIC's officers were represented by Captain William Agnew of 11th BNI and Lieutenant Arnold, Deputy Paymaster to the Honourable Company's Forces.[29] The enquiry first met on 22 June

26 BL: IOR/F/4/322/7378: Discontent of the rank and file of HM 22nd Regiment of Foot at Muttra, September 1806 – November 1807, pp.10–13.
27 BL: IOR/F/4/322/7378: Discontent of HM 22nd Regiment, p.7
28 BL: IOR/F/4/322/7378: Discontent of HM 22nd Regiment, p.37.
29 BL: IOR/F/4/322/7378: Discontent of HM 22nd Regiment, pp.150–151.

1807, commencing with an investigation of the men's first allegation, the arrears in pay since November 1806.

By this time, Frome was in a frail condition, with most of his evidence provided from his quarters where he lay on his sickbed. During his testimony, he provided background to the challenges he had encountered after taking command of the 22nd Foot due to the lack of discipline in the regiment. Frome had only recently joined the 22nd, initially as a major on 14 February 1805.[30] On 25 September 1806, Frome took command of the battalion as a lieutenant colonel, and what he found at Mathura gave him cause for concern, as many of the officers had been absent for some time. The tall, stalwart figure of Mercer, who had quietened the boys before they had marched to join Lake's army, had been absent with leave in Europe since June 1806, and the redoubtable Lindsay had spent a year recovering from his injuries inflicted at Bharatpur. McNeight who had stormed Barabati, and received wounds at Bharatpur, had also been on a leave of absence since May 1806. In addition, Major Robert Kelso, who had done much to ensure the boys behaved at the Cape, had been sick at Cawnpore since October 1805, and had still not returned by 1806.[31]

When Frome took command in September 1806 from Captain William Shaw – another old regimental hand who had served with the boys since 1798 – the regimental staff were represented by the adjutant, the surgeon and assistant surgeon, both the quartermaster and the paymaster were absent with leave along with almost 40 percent of the officers absent as well. Some of the original officer corps were present, including Captains Hutton and Hurlstone, who had fought at Barabati, as both had remained on duty.[32] Despite the support of these experienced officers, Shaw's tenure as acting commanding officer left much to be desired. The day after Frome took command, he ordered Shaw to take the battalion through 'any Manoeuvres he might think proper'. Frome found a want of drilling had left the boys of the 22nd clumsy and 'not capable of going through one movement with precision.' Frome ordered the non-commissioned officers to parade before him, and 'found they were as ignorant as the Men.'[33]

To remedy the situation, Frome instituted daily drill for an hour for Serjeant Major Dugald McInnes and the drill serjeant, until both men were refamiliarised with the King's Regulations. By 7 October, Frome was satisfied with their progress and decided to include all the serjeants, including Mansfield, in the daily drilling. Despite this progress, Frome did not feel sanguine about the rank and file and thought the battalion would take some time to become fighting fit due to 'the extreme ignorance of the Serjeants.'[34] As Frome put the NCOs through their paces, he ordered the rank and file to parade at sunset; their sole manoeuvre was wheeling into line and standing at attention.

30 Steve Brown, *King George's Army: British Regiments and the Men who led them 1793-1815: Volume 2: Foot Guards to 30th Regiments of Foot* (Warwick: Helion, 2024), p.288.
31 TNA: WO 12/3880: General Muster Books and Pay Lists, 22nd Foot 1st Battalion, 1805–1806, February 1805.
32 TNA: WO 12/3880: General Muster Books and Pay Lists, 22nd Foot 1st Battalion, 1805–1806, September 1806.
33 BL: IOR/F/4/322/7378: Discontent of HM 22nd Regiment, p.275.
34 BL: IOR/F/4/322/7378: Discontent of HM 22nd Regiment, p.276.

In addition to reestablishing drill discipline, Frome also kept the battalion in close confinement to the regimental lines until 'there was an appearance of more respect paid to the orders of their officers.' In addition to slack parade discipline, the privates of the 22nd had formed the habit of leaving the camp at any time, sometimes venturing as far as 4 or 5 miles. Frome was particularly concerned about these excursions because they were marred with the 'grossest Brutality', including an incident on 30 September, when nine soldiers of the light company stole from some civilians. The fugitives were captured by a group of *sepoys*, but before they could face military discipline, the light bobs escaped from their gaolers as the soldiers neared the barracks. The culprits from the 22nd quickly disappeared amongst their comrades and could not be identified. It may have been some of these fugitives who, in a later show of defiance, removed a flag marking the boundaries of the light company's section of the camp as a protest against Frome's orders.[35] Despite their demonstration, Frome was implacable and continued to dispense punishment for absence without leave, including a court-martial decision to issue 200 lashes to a soldier for running into camp at full speed after absconding for the night.

Discontent continued to simmer, with the first warning signs appearing at eight o'clock on the night of 6 October 1806, when three privates came to the tent of Lieutenant Thomas Poole. They presented a letter to Poole's servant, who conveyed the letter to the officer's mess. This letter listed just two complaints; uppermost were Frome's orders to confine the regiment to barracks, which the privates felt was unjust as they thought they had not committed any crime 'deserving of this ill treatment'. The second complaint concerned the arrears in pay. The privates, 'one and all in General', felt compelled 'to give the present warning in hopes of redress' and wanted their situation returned to 'the same as when Colonel Mercer Commanded'.[36] Undaunted, the morning after the letter was received, Frome ordered the regiment out on parade and had the Articles of War read to them along with the letter, stating if the culprits behind it were not found, he would report the matter to the commander of Mathura.[37] Irrespective of Frome's actions, the men were not identified as Poole's native servant had not been able to distinguish their faces in the dark.

Whilst the absenteeism of the men and the letter of complaint suggest there was a mutinous spirit loose in the regiment, even Frome blamed the ill-discipline on a minority of the rank and file. His most stringent criticism was levelled at the officers and NCOs, who he had observed in his orders confining the 22nd to barracks, 'pass soldiers of their Corps in the act of disobeying orders without taking any notice'.[38] The military hierarchy had broken down with the departure of so many officers, and a growing laxity in those that remained. Whilst it is not possible to identify all of the individual miscreants in these cases, there is a high chance that some of them where former boy soldiers, particularly in the larger demonstrations. For the boys, who by 1807 had spent nearly 10 years in the 22nd Foot, the sudden departure of the officers they were familiar with

35 BL: IOR/F/4/322/7378: Discontent of HM 22nd Regiment, pp.277–279.
36 BL: IOR/F/4/322/7378: Discontent of HM 22nd Regiment, p.283.
37 BL: IOR/F/4/322/7378: Discontent of HM 22nd Regiment, p.279.
38 BL: IOR/F/4/322/7378: Discontent of HM 22nd Regiment, p.159.

must have been jarring. Without their usual oversight, the structures of discipline withered and a growing attitude of laxity spread like a canker from the remaining officers through the NCOs to the 22nd's rank and file. With discipline and morale at a low ebb, trust had become a rare commodity, making the regiment a perfect tinderbox waiting for a spark.

The coming trigger related to pay and first appears in a letter from Frome written on 7 October. The letter was sent to Colonel de Castro, commander at Mathura. Frome outlined that most of the King's Regiments' pay was issued monthly, as soon as enough money was available from the Paymaster General's Office, but the 22nd had been paying a weekly subsistence in advance and not their full wages.[39]

The problems with pay stretched back to October 1805, when the regimental paymaster, John McKinnon, was taken ill at Cawnpore and did not follow the regiment into the Punjab.[40] Usually when a paymaster could no longer fulfil their duty, matters of pay were settled by a committee appointed by the regiment; however, in this instance McKinnon asked his friend Captain James Cullen, as a favour, to take over the role of paymaster. Prior to his departure, McKinnon had been paying the men a subsistence rate, which was maintained by Cullen until he too took a leave of absence. The role of paymaster subsequently passed to the commanding officer, Shaw, on 25 August 1806. At that time, the regiment had been paid in full up to May 1806 and in subsistence until September. When the court asked Shaw why the regiment had not been paid in full, he laid the blame on the Paymasters Department at Calcutta.[41] The court pressed Shaw, asking if this was standard practice for the paymaster to advance subsistence money rather than paying the regiment in full, but he was not able to give an immediate answer. As the session was near the end of the day, the court adjourned until the morning, when Shaw was finally able to answer the question with an emphatic, 'No!'[42]

The confusion besetting the regiment appears almost palpable in the enquiry documents and letters investigating the incident. Over the course of the enquiry, it became clear the fault rested with McKinnon. The 22nd had been drawing advances for subsistence before October 1805, when Lake authorised the regiment to continue doing so whilst they were serving with the Grand Army.[43] Despite leaving Lake's army in February 1806, the 22nd continued to pay subsistence until the mutiny a year later. Further complications with the regiment's finances were outlined by Frome in a letter sent in April 1807 to Dickens. Frome noted that McKinnon had accrued a considerable debt of over 34,000 rupees to the Paymaster Department in Calcutta. Naturally keen to bring the regiment's accounts in order, Frome had commanded McKinnon to rejoin the regiment, but as the paymaster neared Mathura, in January 1807 he died, leaving Frome with the task of finding a replacement. In the meantime, Paymaster J. Hall, from the King's Troops Pay Office at Fort William, had attempted to mitigate

39 BL: IOR/F/4/322/7378: Discontent of HM 22nd Regiment, pp.280–281.
40 TNA: WO 12/3880: General Muster Books and Pay Lists, 22nd Foot 1st Battalion, 1805–1806, October 1805.
41 BL: IOR/F/4/322/7378: Discontent of HM 22nd Regiment, pp.164–165
42 BL: IOR/F/4/322/7378: Discontent of HM 22nd Regiment, p.165.
43 BL: IOR/F/4/322/7378: Discontent of HM 22nd Regiment, pp.172–173.

the debt by lowering the monthly remittance to the regiment from 16,000 to 12,000 rupees. Receiving no complaints from Shaw, who seems to have been paying the officers in full whilst leaving the NCOs and other ranks on subsistence, Hall continued to make these reduced payments until a letter arrived from Frome requesting 6,925 rupees to clear the debt for February. Hall complied but remained uneasy about the state of the 22nd's debts, which now stood at about 15,618 rupees. Hall even considered withholding payment but refrained from doing so until a new paymaster was appointed in the 22nd.[44]

The enquiry found McKinnon's management of the accounts to be irregular. According to the paymaster serjeant, John Ward, he had previously remarked to McKinnon that the paymaster should keep a cash book, to which McKinnon replied it was his responsibility and Ward, 'had no business with it.'[45] Further examination of the regimental accounts from March 1805 revealed that, of the two payments due to King's Regiments in India, McKinnon only drew King's pay from HM Treasury for the same period as HEIC pay. Because of this unusual arrangement, the men of the 22nd were a month's pay behind their peers in the other King's Regiments. These problems were ultimately compounded by several large payments McKinnon drew from August 1805, including the subsistence for the flank companies from August to October 1805, and several other advances made to the regiment, amounting to four payments totalling 50,630 rupees. These large payments were made to the 22nd Foot due to the pay of the flank companies having been delayed because they were on command with Lake. Additionally, one of the payments covered the costs of a detachment of artillery that had been temporarily attached to the 22nd Foot whilst serving with Lake.[46]

Although the enquiry dealt with complaint five at the end of the court proceedings, it is just as well to cover this complaint at this point as it relates to subsistence pay. The privates complained that on Frome's orders they had been refused credit for goods in the regimental bazaar. Elaborating on his orders, Frome stated that whilst trying to right the regiment's finances he had cancelled subsistence pay and commanded the bazaar to give credit, with the regiment's officers answerable for the payment. Frome's one proviso for the merchants in the bazaar was that they could not give credit beyond a month's pay.[47] Both Poole and the contractor's *sirkar*, Ram Churn, agreed this had been the spirit of Frome's orders and had complied with them prior to the unrest on 26 May. It seems, however, these orders were not clearly expressed to the men of the battalion.

With these payments outlined, the board moved on to examine the second complaint made by the rank and file of the 22nd. Similar to the matters of pay, this complaint concerned arrears of two years for clothing and the resulting expense the rank and file incurred maintaining their uniforms. Frome offered the enquiry an outline of the situation as of 26 May 1807, when at the time, the regiment's men were still wearing uniforms issued for the year commencing on 25 December 1804. He explained the uniforms for 1805–1806 were expected from the regimental agent in Britain, but Frome deferred the order

44 BL: IOR/F/4/322/7378: Discontent of HM 22nd Regiment, pp.20–26.
45 BL: IOR/F/4/322/7378: Discontent of HM 22nd Regiment, p.177.
46 BL: IOR/F/4/322/7378: Discontent of HM 22nd Regiment, pp.307–308.
47 BL: IOR/F/4/322/7378: Discontent of HM 22nd Regiment, p.229.

as he considered the current state of the regiment's uniforms was sufficient. In contrast, the money for what Frome calls white clothing, which appears to be referring to undress uniforms and underclothing including, white jackets, – possibly an adaptation to local conditions – shirts and vests, had not been paid to the rank and file for 1805. Whilst the men had paid for their white jackets, the money for vests and shirts had not been distributed. Frome had attempted to mitigate the problem by deferring any payments from the men until they were in credit and reporting the issue to his superiors, but he had no notion as to why the 'vest and shirt money' had not been paid before he took command.[48]

When questioned, Pay Serjeant John Ward highlighted McKinnon's prolonged absence, as he claimed the vest and shirt money was usually drawn on 25 December each year. On Christmas Day 1806, the regiment was stationed in the Punjab, and due to McKinnon's absence, Cullen had drawn the money on his behalf and had it sent directly to McKinnon in Calcutta. The paymaster planned to bring the money with him when he returned to the regiment, but this meant the regiment's men were left without any money to cover their vests and shirts.[49] Before Mercer's own leave of absence, the quartermaster issued nankeen jackets and pantaloons to the men. On 24 May 1806, Mercer ordered Cullen to enter the charges into the accounts and credit the shirt money. Once Mercer had left and Ward prepared the books, Cullen sent a note to Ward, ordering him to enter the charges but not to credit the shirt money. Ward later speculated that Cullen did not want to draw the money from a bill issued to cover the regimental pay, as there was still no sign of McKinnon with the shirt money. To understand how the men viewed the situation, the enquiry interviewed an undisclosed number of serjeants and privates, who confirmed they had received the clothing for 1804–1805 but were still waiting for the uniform issues for 1805–1807.[50]

The court proceeded to examine points 3 and 4, which related to the quality of provisions. Complaint 3 stated that the privates had not received adequate provisions whilst complaint 4 focused on the price and quality of rum issued by the regimental godown. Two grenadiers were initially questioned, and they claimed that, before they had delivered the letter to Dickens, the privates of the 22nd frequently complained of bad food and the 'not so strong as it ought to be' liquor,[51] commenting that 'the meat appeared black and in our opinion unwholesome', and the soldiers often simply threw it away.[52] The privates had reported their concerns about the poor quality to the duty officer, but the two grenadiers did not recall any action being taken. Quartermaster William Edmonds was called to describe the process of selecting meat for the regiment. Edmonds explained he would inspect the cattle before slaughter and when the meat was brought to the centre of the camp each company's orderly NCO also had the opportunity to inspect the meat. It was confirmed throughout this entire process the privates could reject the rations and ask for them to be exchanged.[53]

48 BL: IOR/F/4/322/7378: Discontent of HM 22nd Regiment, p.185.
49 BL: IOR/F/4/322/7378: Discontent of HM 22nd Regiment, pp.192–193.
50 BL: IOR/F/4/322/7378: Discontent of HM 22nd Regiment, pp.194–196.
51 BL: IOR/F/4/322/7378: Discontent of HM 22nd Regiment, p.213.
52 BL: IOR/F/4/322/7378: Discontent of HM 22nd Regiment, pp.199–200.
53 BL: IOR/F/4/322/7378: Discontent of HM 22nd Regiment, pp.201–202.

When questioned if the privates had regularly rejected the meat and spirits, Edmonds stated they had not, only recalling two instances when the liquor was rejected. This in turn had been disputed by the officer of the day, who refused to offer the men an exchange because he believed it was the same as the regular issue. After the preceding testimony, Corporal Osbell Barton was called before the enquiry. Barton was a former boy soldier who had enlisted in 1799 at the age of 17 and had risen to become orderly corporal for Captain Hector Hall's company. Barton refuted Edmonds' claim that the boys and men had rarely complained about the rations. He recalled an incident a week before 26 May, when his company complained to him of the quality of the meat. The matter was reported to Captain Thomas Buttle, officer of the day, and duly exchanged. Barton did back up Edmonds' statement that complaints about the liquor were brushed aside with claims no better spirits were available.[54] More orderly NCOs were called to provide testimony, including Corporal Mark Fields, another boy soldier who had enlisted in 1799 at the age of 16. All the NCOs agreed that complaints had been made, but they did not agree on the frequency of the reports, or how often the information made its way up the chain of command.

Eventually the contractor's *sirkar* and regimental rum supplier, Ram Churn, was called to account for the quality of the rum. It became clear that, contrary to Company regulations, which stipulated the rum must be Bengali, Churn's supply came from Agra and was delivered in casks from the producer in Georgemow. When Frome was questioned, he attested he thought the rum was not as strong as it should be, but his undisclosed illness hindered any meaningful investigation before the mutiny.

The final complaint was levelled directly at Frome, who was accused of adding an extra rupee to the price of rum in the regimental godown, in direct contravention of the Articles of War. Frome explained how he had established the godown in November 1806 on the advice of the regimental surgeon, James Hacking. The surgeon suggested that opening a regimental godown would control the soldiers' access to spirits, as he proposed only opening the building in the morning and the evening. Hacking hoped that an official godown for alcohol would prevent the men from hanging around the cookhouses, where the native cooks were in the habit of bringing a liquor called *paniah*, which the soldiers would drink until they were inebriated. Impressed with the surgeon's plan, Frome ordered the regimental *sirkar* and an orderly serjeant to establish the godown. Prices for rum were initially fixed at 3 rupees, but in January 1807, the *sirkar* complained to Frome that the privates had been cheating him out of rum and, in one incident, they managed to pilfer a full cask.[55] Poole offered further details about the case, which took place on Christmas Day 1806, when a party of soldiers forced their way into the godown and filled their mugs from a cask. Although they did pay for the spirits they took, Poole had destroyed the remnants of the liquor the privates had taken at Christmas and shut the godown for the day.[56] Frome initially gave the *sirkar* the liberty to choose whom

54 BL: IOR/F/4/322/7378: Discontent of HM 22nd Regiment, pp.204–205
55 BL: IOR/F/4/322/7378: Discontent of HM 22nd Regiment, pp.215–219.
56 BL: IOR/F/4/322/7378: Discontent of HM 22nd Regiment, p.222–223.

he would serve, but when he complained of a loss of income, Frome permitted the *sirkar* to charge 4 rupees, at the godown.[57]

Upon further examination, *Sirkar* Ram Churn revealed he had been charging the regiment 4 rupees from as early as 16 November, subsequently obtaining permission from Frome and the contractor's agent, Mr Mercer.[58] Churn also claimed he had been directed by Frome to make a five percent adulteration on the rum sold and to pass the profits back to Frome. This scheme included Churn and the butcher. With this fresh twist in the tale, the enquiry examined the butcher, who had been pressured into paying the *sirkar* 50 rupees in March 1807; the money was allegedly part of Churn's agreement with Frome.[59] The butcher was the last witness questioned, bringing the enquiry to a close on 4 July 1807 after nearly two weeks.

The enquiry's findings laid the blame for the regiment's finances principally at McKinnon's door due to his prolonged absence and unorthodox decision to draw the King's pay at the same time as the Company's, which had delayed the men's pay. In addition, he failed to keep proper records or provide any details of how he intended to lower the regiment's deficit or note down any agreements between himself and Paymaster Hall. The enquiry also blamed Hall for delays of several weeks before funds were distributed to the regiment, due to the distance between Calcutta and the Upper Provinces. The enquiry condemned the subsistence system, stating it would have been prudent to have paid the privates 'at the expense of the Officers'.[60]

Whilst the court noted that Cullen's and Shaw's accounts were correct and had been paid, they could not help admonishing the irregularity of both these officers assuming the role of paymaster without committee oversight. There was also a large payment drawn by Cullen, which could not be explained as he had departed India. The only party to escape with mild censure was Frome, who the enquiry noted had consistently tried to bring the 22nd's financial affairs in order.[61]

Moving on to the complaints regarding clothing, the court found that the privates had no cause for complaint about the issue of regimental coats; indeed, Frome had acted for the good of the service by withholding the regiment's red coats for a year. Although the enquiry acknowledged the poor management of the shirt money, and McKinnon was once again found at fault. Complaints three and four were dealt with at the same time by the enquiry, who would have concurred with Frome, the quartermaster and the orderly corporals, that the provision for meat and spirits was not a problem, but Churn's and the butcher's testimony changed their opinion. They found that money was being siphoned off by the *sirkar,* and poor-quality victuals presented instead. During an investigation on 28 and 29 June 1807, the enquiry questioned if the rum issued was the same quality as usual; the men said it was better than usual. Using this consignment of rum as a control, the court concluded that if the adulteration of 5 percent had been applied by the *sirkar* to previous issues of the liquor, it would have been a third weaker

57 BL: IOR/F/4/322/7378: Discontent of HM 22nd Regiment, p.219.
58 BL: IOR/F/4/322/7378: Discontent of HM 22nd Regiment, p.233–234.
59 BL: IOR/F/4/322/7378: Discontent of HM 22nd Regiment, p.241.
60 BL: IOR/F/4/322/7378: Discontent of HM 22nd Regiment, p.246.
61 BL: IOR/F/4/322/7378: Discontent of HM 22nd Regiment, pp.244–255

than the regulations. The rules for rum quality stated that soldiers should be issued with a Bengal rum aged for three years, whereas the rum provided by the *sirkar* came from Cawnpore and was regarded as new and freshly distilled. Following the investigation, in August 1807, the contractor's *sirkar* was ordered to Calcutta to account for 'exorbitant and fraudulous charges', whilst providing rum to the 22nd Foot.[62] The results of the case were not recorded with the letters relating to the misconduct at Mathura. The final allegation levelled by the privates of the 22nd was quickly dismissed by the court, as they felt every effort had been made to give credit to the privates and explain to them why the system had changed.

The whole saga revealed the dangers of officers taking long absences from their regiments, particularly in India, where officers could be absent for over a year. The case also demonstrated how the lack of a firm hand, like Mercer's, enabled discipline to slip amongst the regiment. When Frome assumed command and attempted to bring the regiment in order, he was met with a mutinous rank and file. This rebellious spirit appears to link directly to the breakdown in regimental structures; as familiar officers left, the remainder seem to have taken a lackadaisical approach to the battalion's management. This laxity created the perfect conditions for the collapse of the regimental accounts and hence the boys' and men's trust in their officers. Anger spread amongst the rank and file caused by what they perceived was a breakdown in the agreement between them and their officers as represented by the Articles of War, which the men of the 22nd used as the basis for framing their grievances. It took several months for these wounds to fester, until they eventually burst out into mutiny and revealed a concerning collapse in regimental discipline and administration that was difficult to restore.

Whilst the court acknowledged some of the men's grievances, there was still concern about the defiant presentation of their complaints to Dickens armed with bayonets and the subsequent rioting. These acts of intimidation and violent protest could not be ignored, and after the enquiry Dickens maintained his refusal to return the regiment's colours and arms, as he felt there was no sense of contrition from the men. On 1 July 1807, Dickens ordered the 22nd Foot to depart for Berhampore, whilst he sent their colours and arms ahead of them down the River Jumna.[63] Dickens testily remarked in his letter, 'I never was Witness to so obstinate a perseverance in Error ... as has on this occasion been shewn by His Majesty's 22nd Regt.'[64] Subsequently, seven privates were tried by courts martial for their role in the mutiny. It is difficult to determine who they were or what their sentences were, as they are not listed on the register of courts martial held at the National Archives.

The 22nd Foot left Mathura in early July 1807, and as they progressed, they were not without sympathisers. The provincial Commander in Chief, Major General Ewen Baillie, felt something must have been amiss for the regiment to behave as they had done. Baillie wrote on 8 July to express his hope that Dickens would return the arms to the centre companies, because they had 'expressed sentiments of regret' but not

62 BL: IOR/F/4/322/7378: Discontent of HM 22nd Regiment, p.325.
63 BL: IOR/F/4/322/7378: Discontent of HM 22nd Regiment, p.92.
64 BL: IOR/F/4/322/7378: Discontent of HM 22nd Regiment, p.92

the flank companies who remained truculent.[65] Despite Baillie's hopes for the 22nd Foot, the regiment had to endure a gruelling march to Berhampore in Bengal. During their journey, Plummer recalled seeing rain before them and behind them, whilst they remained, 'excessively hot' with many privates dropping down dead by the roadside.[66] Frome was amongst those who did not survive the journey, passing away on 19 July 1807, living just long enough to give his evidence at the trial and start the march with the 22nd.

The regiment reached Cawnpore in late July, where they were forbidden from communicating with the 8th Light Dragoons and the 17th (Leicestershire) Regiment of Foot, as elements within the 22nd Foot remained defiant about the mutiny.[67] The 22nd eventually reached Berhampore before 1 September 1807.[68] It had been a sordid situation, but in time Baillie restored the regiment's colours and arms. The 22nd's new station was sited in a poor location, with the regiment's official historian Bernard Rigby noting it was a particularly sickly one.[69] Following the drama of the near mutiny, the 22nd spent three relatively quiet years garrisoning Berhampore.

65 BL: IOR/F/4/322/7378: Discontent of HM 22nd Regiment, p.100.
66 Plummer, *The Journal of Samuel Plummer*, p.65.
67 BL: IOR/F/4/322/7378: Discontent of HM 22nd Regiment, p.141.
68 TNA: WO 17/1753: East Indies, September 1807.
69 Rigby, *Ever Glorious*, p.136.

# 12

# Pirates, Privateers, and Pindaris

As the first decade of the nineteenth century drew to a close, fresh opportunities for service overseas appeared for the few remaining boys of the 'experimental battalions'. By 1809, France dominated Europe, with the exception of the ongoing 'Spanish Ulcer' and the British expeditionary force sent to help. In contrast, in the Indian Ocean, French influence had drastically dwindled away, as Britain rose to pre-eminence in India and controlled the approaches to the Indian Ocean through the Cape Colony and St Helena. Despite Britain's ascendency two trouble spots remained: the last major French outpost on the Île de France, present-day Mauritius, and the Persian Gulf. Both were connected, but it was the Gulf that initially concerned the HEIC's government.

Whilst HEIC convoys sailed around the foot of Africa, laden with their cargoes, the old overland route between India and Europe was also frequently used by the HEIC. Rather than carrying goods, this route started in the Persian Gulf, passed overland from Basra to Constantinople, and conveyed correspondence. To protect these packet ships, the Bombay Marine patrolled the Gulf with a range of light ships, including frigates, brigs and sloops, these vessels were sent on cruising missions and became known as cruisers when on patrol. In addition to this correspondence, Indian merchants from the HEIC's territories also plied their trade in the waters of the Gulf.

Aside from this tentative British presence, there were two major powers in the Gulf, the Ottoman Empire and Qajar Iran. Beneath these two, several Arab rulers managed most of the region's trading fleets. Foremost amongst them was the Imām of Muscat, who ruled from present-day Oman and the Qawāsim, a confederation of tribes ruled by the Al-Qāsimī dynasty. At the time, the Qawāsim's principal harbour was Ras al Khaimah, now located in the United Arab Emirates.[1] Both kingdoms had access to extensive fleets of dhows and baghlas, great 300-ton vessels with which Muscat traders carried goods from Mesopotamia to the Dutch East Indies. During the early nineteenth century there was considerable competition between the Qawāsim and Muscat over the carrying trade, which frequently led to bursts of violence in the Gulf and with it the potential for piracy.

1 Fahad Ahmad Bishara and Patricia Risso, J.E. Peterson (ed.), 'The Gulf, the Indian Ocean and the Arab World', in *The Emergence of the Gulf States* (London: Bloomsbury Academic, 2016), pp.168–169.

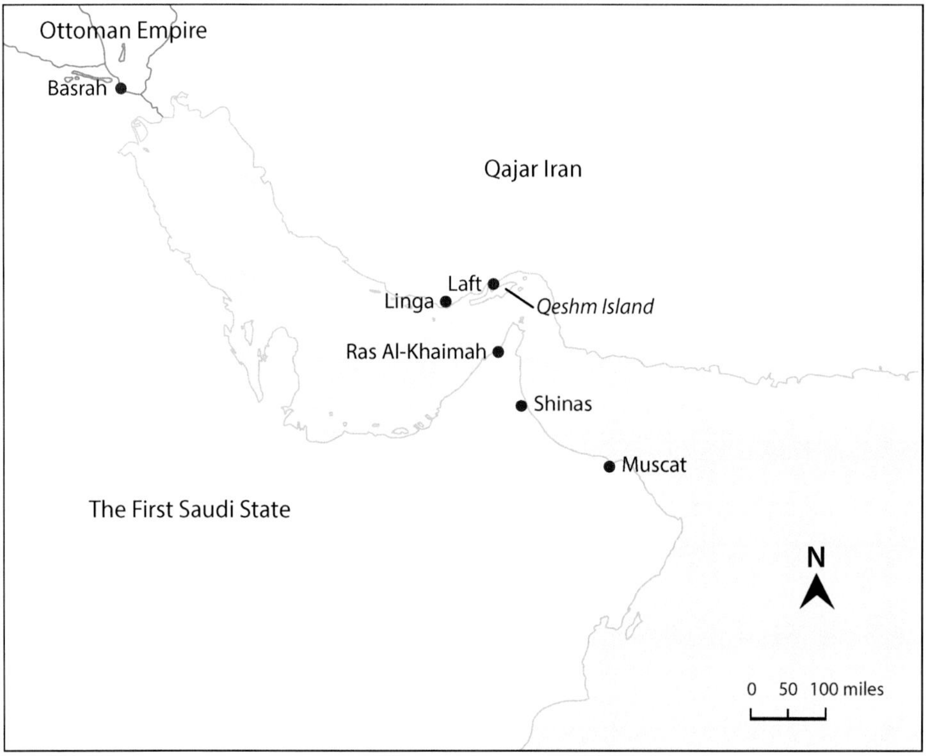


The Persian Gulf campaign 1809.

As early as 1778, accusations of piracy had been levelled at the Qawāsim by the British and had remained a lingering concern thereafter.[2] With the renewed war with France in 1803, there was growing disquiet in the HEIC regarding French interest in the Gulf. French privateers operating from Mauritius visited the Gulf and Muscat, threatening to cut off Britain's communications through the Middle East.[3] In 1798, the HEIC had concluded a deal with the Imām, which stopped any communication or trade with France, and considerably improved Anglo-Muscat relations.[4] Despite this agreement, the region remained unstable; for instance, in 1805, the Bombay cruiser *Mornington* was forced to see off piratical dhows.[5]

Part of the region's instability came from the rise of a powerful new branch of Islam, Wahhabism, founded by Muhammad ibn Abd al-Wahhab. The subsequent Wahhabi movement was adopted by the Emirate of Dir'iyah, the first Saudi state, in the middle of the eighteenth century and helped to drive Saudi expansion as they fought 'against

2 Sultān Muhammad al-Qāsimī, *The Myth of Arab Piracy in the Gulf* (Abingdon: Routledge, 2016), p.32.
3 BL: IOR/H/MISC/479: Wellesley Papers, p.545.
4 al-Qāsimī, *The Myth of Arab Piracy*, p.31.
5 al-Qāsimī, *The Myth of Arab Piracy*, p.181.

all of their own faith who deviated from the injunctions from the Qur'an.'[6] By 1805, the Saudis had become the overlords of the Qawāsim, which brought them into the Wahhabism sect. The Qāsimī sheikhs were encouraged by the Saudis to raid shipping in the Gulf, attacking both the fleets of Muscat and the Indian merchants sailing under the colours of the Company.

By April 1809, the Bombay Presidency obtained permission from the Governor General, Gilbert Elliot-Murray-Kynynmound, the Earl of Minto, to dispatch an expedition to the Persian Gulf and attempt to suppress the piratical raids of the Qawāsim. Minto's orders limited operations to naval actions and descents on the coast, in conjunction with the forces of the Imām of Muscat.[7] The expedition was composed of two ships from the Royal Navy and 10 vessels of the Bombay Marine, commanded by Captain John Wainwright, whilst the land forces were led by Lieutenant Colonel Lionel Smith, with his main strike force being his own regiment, the 65th Foot.[8] Smith was described as a systematic officer, who, when he took command of the 65th in 1807, had banned whiskers 'deeming it easier to shave the face to the tip of each ear, than to raise a crop of hair where nature never intended one to grow.'[9] Smith had at his disposal 829 men from the 65th and the flank companies of the 47th (Lancashire) Regiment of Foot, alongside 529 *sepoys* and eight 6-pounder guns.[10] This force was ordered to raid Qawāsim ports, destroy any vessels found within and liberate all British or Indian captives and their property.

The expedition planned to sail once the monsoon had abated, and Wainwright was ready to leave Bombay on 14 September 1809. After leaving India, the fleet was delayed by contrary winds and finally reached Muscat on 23 October. Here Wainwright and Smith had to wait for 10 days whilst they brought on board fresh supplies of water. Finally, on 11 November the fleet sighted its main objective, Ras al-Khaimah, the seat of the al-Qāsimī sheikhs. As they approached the harbour, the British had a stroke of luck when several dhows and the captured Company cruiser *Minerva* sailed out of Ras al-Khaimah. Upon sighting the British fleet, the Qawāsim crews turned about and raced for home, all escaped except the *Minerva*, which ran aground under a small fort. The fort was bombarded, and the *Minerva was* set ablaze as she could not be towed away. The British fleet then turned their attention to Ras al-Khaimah itself.[11]

The town sat on a peninsula, and the beaches were defended by an array of batteries. South of the town was a high wall drawn across the peninsula and strengthened by four towers, whilst inside the British estimated there were 5,000 defenders.[12] For three hours on 12 November, the fleet bombarded Ras al-Khaimah, whilst Smith planned his

6 H. Moyse-Bartlett, *The Pirates of Trucial* Oman (London: Macdonald, 1966), pp.28–29
7 BL: IOR/F/4/343/7962, Operations of the Naval and Military forces employed against the Joasmee Pirates, p.5.
8 J.G. Lorimer, *Gazetteer of the Persian Gulf* (Calcutta: Superintendent Government Printing, 1915), vol.1, pp.183–184.
9 Wallace, *Fifteen Years in India*, pp.414–415.
10 al-Qāsimī, *The Myth of Arab Piracy*, p.135.
11 al-Qāsimī, *The Myth of Arab Piracy*, p.135.
12 Moyse-Bartlett, *The Pirates of Trucial Oman*, p.50.

Private Richard Temple of the 65th Foot's depiction of the landings at Ras al-Khaimah. (Yale Center for British Art, Paul Mellon Collection)

descent on the coast. Smith organised a feint to the north of the town to distract the Qawāsim from the main landing, which was led by the 65th and made landfall on the shore south of the wall. At 2:00 a.m. on the 13th, the sky was pitch black as the 65th were ferried towards their landing ground. As dawn broke, HMS *La Chiffonne* and two gunboats dashed for the harbour. The Qawāsim raced to intercept the northern feint, whilst the 65th were rowed to their landings in the south. Smith lauded the soldiers, particularly their 'coolness and good order in which they debarked shoulder high in water and charged the Enemy in heavy sand was beautiful and truly soldierlike.'[13] As the first troops began to disembark in the surf, the Qawāsim tried to charge them in the flank, but were checked by grape shot from the nearby ships. The 65th and the 47th then drove off the defenders and Wainwright later described the landings as carried out 'in great style'.[14]

As the sun continued its inexorable progress, the field artillery was brought ashore. Covered by the shot of the 6-pounders, the 65th pressed forward into the teeth of the Qawāsim's fire. As the 65th entered Ras al-Khaimah, the battle quickly devolved into street fighting as the British drove the defenders from the houses. By 10:00 a.m. the town was in British hands. During the assault, the fire from the field artillery had managed to set some houses alight, and by 4:00 p.m., a great swath of Ras al-Khaimah, 50 dhows, and all the naval stores had been destroyed.[15] When the cost of the day's action was accounted for, the 65th had come off lightly; Captain William Mallet Dansey was killed by a spear, whilst Captain Dunlop Digby, one serjeant, and two rank and file were wounded.[16]

13 BL: IOR/F/4/343/7962, Operations of the Naval and Military forces employed against the Joasmee Pirates, p.285.
14 Wainwright quoted in al-Qāsimī, *The Myth of Arab Piracy,* p.137.
15 Wainwright quoted in al-Qāsimī, *The Myth of Arab Piracy,* p.137.
16 BL: IOR/F/4/343/7962, Operations of the Naval and Military forces employed against the Joasmee Pirates, pp.281–283.

The 65th Foot storm a storehouse in Ras al-Khaimah, whilst Captain Dansey is led away for treatment. (Yale Center for British Art, Paul Mellon Collection)

The expedition did not enjoy its success for long, as on 14 November reports reached Smith that a large force of possibly Saudi troops was headed towards Ras al-Khaimah. Anxious not to create a general conflagration in the Gulf, Minto's instructions for Wainwright and Smith precluded them from fighting the Saudis. In compliance with their orders, the two commanders quickly reembarked their men before the arrival of the Saudi army. The historian J.G. Lorimer noted that the Qawāsim's 'spirit was still unbroken, [and they] defiantly re-occupied the town.'[17]

By 15 November the expedition had set sail across the Gulf, towards Iran; this was at the request of the local Iranian Governor, who had asked the British to clear any Qawāsim pirates from the coast.[18] For centuries Arab communities had grown up along the southern shores of Iran, including the Qawāsim, who had a sizable community in the trading town of Linga or Bandar Lengeh. As the fleet approached the port on 17 November, the inhabitants fled, and all the ships found in the harbour were set alight.[19]

The next raid was planned against the fort of Lāft, situated on Qeshm island. Wainwright attempted to negotiate with the commander of Lāft, Mulla Hussain, but when this failed, Smith landed 300 troops on the afternoon of 27 November. The raiding force included half a company from the 65th, who were ordered to assault the 14-foot(4m) thick walls of Lāft. The Qawāsim held their fire until the British approached the gate, then their guns poured a deluge of shot upon the advancing assault party. Smith later reported 31 men were killed and wounded during the failed attack on the gate.

17 Lorimer, *Gazetteer of the Persian Gulf*, p.184.
18 Moyse-Bartlett, *The Pirates of Trucial Oman*, p.52.
19 al-Qāsimī, *The Myth of Arab Piracy*, p.140.

Fortunately for the British, cannon fire from the Bombay Marine ship *Fury* caused sufficient damage to persuade Hussain to yield the fort to Wainwright and Smith on behalf of the Imām of Muscat.[20] As the year drew to a close, the British fleet retired to Muscat, arriving on 7 December, where at the suggestion of Sa'īd bin Sulṭān, Imām of Muscat, a joint expedition was prepared to take the fort of Shinās, and restore it to the Imām.[21]

Whilst the Imām's army marched overland, the expedition set sail on Christmas Eve and arrived before Shinās on the evening of the 31st. On New Year's Day 1810, Smith summoned the fort to surrender, but the defenders refused. Smith had hoped a couple of shells would have compelled the enemy to capitulate, but this was not the case. The siege continued until 3 January, when a breach was made in the walls and a tower was knocked in. The assault was planned to commence at 2:00 p.m. with the King's Regiments leading the storm supported by the Muscat Omanis, however, due to some confusion, the Imām's men charged the breach first. Smith hastened to catch up with them, and the Omanis yielded the honour of capturing Shinās to the British. The fighting had been fierce, Smith later reported, 'It is impossible to contemplate a more obstinate resistance ... [the enemy's] defences were nearly battered to ruins and the greatest part of his garrison lay around in mangled heaps.'[22]

Near the end of the day, two towers stubbornly held out, bristling with spears and showering any would-be stormers with stones. Smith called on the defenders to relent, but they refused. To try and persuade them, Smith brought up several guns and set to battering the towers. After pounding the walls, he once again called on the defenders to relent, which they eventually agreed to and by 5:00 p.m. the fort once more belonged to the Imām of Muscat, although he did not keep it for long.[23] A large Saudi force was coming to the relief of Shinās, and by 5 January, Smith had embarked his men, again escaping a confrontation with the Saudis. During the assault, one rank and file was killed, and nine were wounded.

After the fall of Shinās the expedition sailed back into the Gulf, where Wainwright set about destroying more pirate vessels. Having completed its objectives of damaging the Qawāsim fleet, the expedition began its return to Bombay in February 1810, with the last troops leaving by April. The expedition had been an operational success and, for the moment, the Qawāsim had been beaten, however, they remained unbowed with many of their ships escaping the fires of the British expedition. Meanwhile as long as the Saudis remained unchallenged by the powers in the Gulf, Britain's ally, the Imām of Muscat, remained vulnerable to retribution from the Wahhabis and their allies, the Qawāsim. Whilst Muscat remained at risk, the 1809 expedition had managed to temporarily hush piracy in the region for British trade, allowing the HEIC to focus on the wider war against France in the Indian Ocean. Once the threat of French piracy had been removed, Britain slowly turned its attention back to the Gulf and launched another expedition in 1819, which included the 65th Foot once again. For their role in these anti-piracy operations, the 65th did receive some recognition when the regiment was given the unique battle honour for Arabia in 1823.

20 Wainwright quoted in al-Qāsimī, *The Myth of Arab Piracy*, p.141.
21 Lorimer, *Gazetteer of the Persian Gulf*, p.184.
22 Smith quoted in al-Qāsimī, *The Myth of Arab Piracy*, p.141.
23 Smith quoted in al-Qāsimī, *The Myth of Arab Piracy*, p.141.

Temple's depiction of the Storming of Shinās in 1809. (Yale Center for British Art, Paul Mellon Collection)

## Pindaris

Whilst the 65th set the coasts of Arabia ablaze, the 1/34th were also called upon to take to the field. As noted earlier, aside from the Vellore Mutiny, the Madras Presidency had remained relatively peaceful. Meanwhile, to the north, Maratha politics were a slowly simmering cauldron of intrigue. A key player in this manoeuvring, who had gained prominence serving under Holkar during the Second Anglo-Maratha War, was Amir Khan, a *pindari* warlord of Pathan descent. Khan had been a thorn in the side of Lake's army and continued to be a cause for concern for the British, when, in October 1808, his overlord Holkar succumbed to a fit of madness from which he never recovered.[24]

Sensing the moment was ripe, Khan, who had already been given a grant of land around Tonk by Holkar, set about expanding his influence. Accordingly, in January 1809, Khan led his horsemen into the lands of Bhonsle of Nagpur, a foe the boys of the 22nd Foot had fought in 1803.[25] Khan's offensive and subsequent occupation of Jabalpur alarmed the HEIC, as Bhonsle was now an ally of the Company. While Khan's advance placed him in a position where he could threaten both Bhonsle's and the Nizam of Hyderabad's territories. By 19 October 1809, the British resident in the Maratha capital Pune, Colonel Barry Close, had been appointed to command a field force to oppose Khan's raiding.[26] The force was assembled at Jalna and consisted of a cavalry and infantry division, including the 1/34th Foot, who marched overland to join the army.

24 R.S. Chaurasia, *History of the Marathas* (New Delhi: Atlantic Publishers and Distributors, 2004), p.71.
25 W.J. Wilson, *History of the Madras Army* (Madras: E. Keys, 1883), p.296.
26 BL: IOR/H/595a: Correspondence regarding Ameer Khan and the Raja of Berar, pp.1–2.

*Pindari* horsemen were notorious throughout India, known for their raids across the country. (Anne S.K. Brown Collection)

As Close assembled his force, Bhonsle, encouraged by the growing British force, launched an attack upon Khan and drove the freebooter into Bhopal. Despite this success, Close was still anxious to quash Khan's ambitions and in the middle of November 1809 departed Jalna and marched northwards towards Khan's capital Seronge in Tonk. It was not until 10 February 1810, after 'a long and difficult march' that Close reached Seronge, only to find the town had been deserted the day before. Crucially, Close's demonstration proved enough of a deterrent to convince Khan to end his deprivations. After making contact with a detachment from Bengal, sent to approach Seronge (Sironj) from the north, Close retired south, arriving at the Nerbudda river on 8 March. By 24 April he had reached Amravati, where Close broke up his command and retired with a part of his army, including the 1/34th, to Jalna. The battalion remained at Jalna for the rest of the year.[27] The campaign had proven to be anti-climatic, but it had allowed the British to contain Khan and avoid a general conflagration of violence between the Maratha states. In some way it must have also felt like a diversion from the humdrum of garrison life for the 1/34th.

27 Wilson, *History of the Madras Army*, pp.296–298.

## Privateers

As Amir Khan was chased back to Tonk, and the Qawāsim licked their wounds in Arabia, the British government set their sights on securing the Indian Ocean once and for all. As mentioned previously, the Île de France (Mauritius) was the last vestige of France's imperial pretensions in Asia. The island was governed by *général de division* Decaen, whose arrival at Pondicherry in 1803 with a regiment of infantry had caused a stir during the build-up to the Maratha War. Despite the anxiety he induced amongst the British, Decaen had fled the mainland before encountering John Company's armies. Decaen spent the intervening seven years on the Île de France, playing host to French privateers and keeping both British and Company diplomats up at night through his attempts to ferment discord amongst the HEIC's allies and territories. The presence of French privateers and diplomats at Muscat had raised the spectre of French frigates cutting off the communication route through the Persian Gulf.[28] Whilst the British government fretted about Decaen and the HEIC complained of the increasing number of ships lost to French convoy raiders, the sheer remoteness of the Île de France from the nearest British colonies and the cost of mounting an expedition dissuaded the government from embarking on any action.[29]

Matters changed in March 1809, when a French squadron of frigates, commanded by *capitaine de vaisseau* Jacques-Félix-Emmanuel Hamelin, arrived at the Île de France. Hamelin embarked on an extended raiding campaign across the Indian Ocean, destroying HEIC installations in Sumatra, and attacking East Indiamen from the shores of East Africa to the Bay of Bengal. Provoked into action by Hamelin's escapades, a blockade was placed on the Île de France and the Mascarene Islands. The first steps to occupy the islands began in August 1809, when the Île Rodrigues was seized as a staging post for the Royal Navy to establish a base for launching an attack on the Île de France itself.[30]

The capture of Rodrigues was followed almost a year later by the fall of the Île de Bourbon (Réunion) on 7 July 1810. The campaign seemed to be plain sailing until August 1810. Aware of the numerous coral reefs surrounding the Île de France, the commander of the British naval squadron, Commodore Josias Rowley, ordered the capture of several islets to ensure a smooth landing for the British and Company troops. The navy completed this task and managed to bottle up most of Hamelin's squadron in Grand Port at the south-eastern coast of the island. A subsequent attempt to cut the French ships out, however, led to one of the worst naval disasters suffered by the Royal Navy during the Napoleonic Wars. The Battle of Grand Port on 22–23 August 1810 temporarily knocked out Britain's frigate squadron in the Indian Ocean, when during the battle two frigates were scuttled and two captured, resulting in the total loss of all British warships engaged.[31]

28 Mikaberidze, *The Napoleonic Wars*, pp.491–492.
29 Wilson, *History of the Madras Army*, pp.299.
30 Mikaberidze, *The Napoleonic Wars*, pp.496.
31 J.W. Fortescue, *A History of the British Army* (London: Macmillan and Co., Limited, 1912), vol.7, p.600.

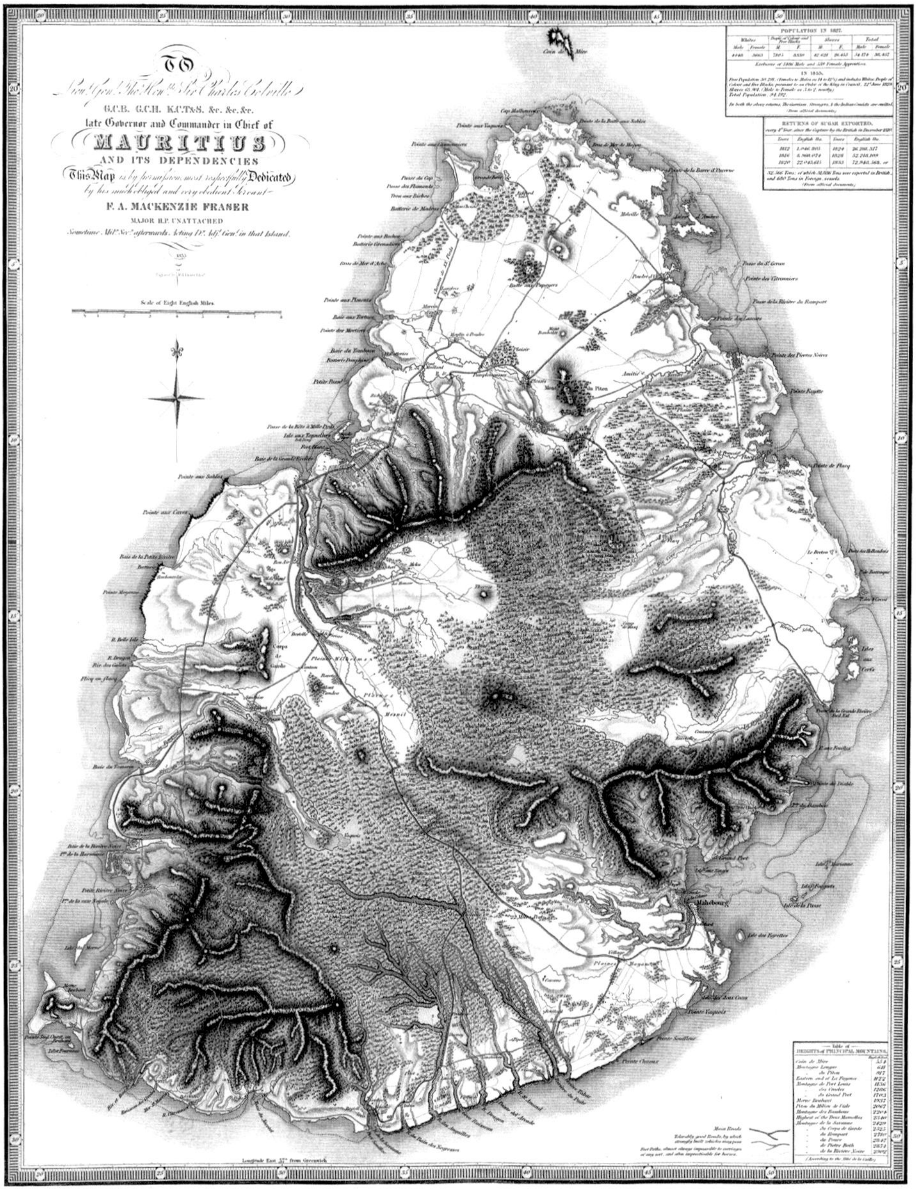

An 1835 map of Île de France (Mauritius). (Anne S.K. Brown Collection)

The shock of Grand Port spurred the British government in India into action, launching one of the largest military operations in the Indian Ocean. Each presidency provided a detachment, with two of the boy regiments selected to take part. In August 1810, the 22nd Foot were ordered to leave Berhampore and join the Bengal contingent, while the 65th Foot joined the Bombay detachment with orders to rendezvous at Rodrigues before the assault on the Île de France. The troops from Bombay arrived first, reaching the island on 22 October. Meanwhile, the 22nd Foot left Calcutta on 16 September aboard the *Hugh Inglis*. From the moment they set sail, Plummer recalled the vessel had a high proportion of men on the sick list. To comfort their bedridden comrades, Plummer wrote that his prayer group 'made a chapel of the large boat, where we sung the praises of the Lord'.[32] After a long passage, where Major General the Honourable John Abercromby fretted over whether the Bengal ships would arrive in time, the 22nd Foot eventually reached Rodrigues by 21 November.[33]

Upon their arrival, the 22nd Foot were placed in Lieutenant Colonel John Picton's First Brigade, alongside HM 12th Foot and the right wing of the Madras volunteer battalion. Their comrades in the 65th joined the Fifth Brigade, which included HM 25th Light Dragoons and the 1st Bengal Volunteers, led by Smith of the 65th Foot.[34]

With his forces assembled, Abercromby's expedition departed on 22 November and a week later they reached Grand Baie, located at the northern end of the Île de France. The navy had carefully plotted a route through the numerous reefs, which dotted the bay, and the redcoats had been ordered to 'sit still in the boats, even if the French should fire upon us.'[35] Fortunately, the landings were made without mishap, despite the occasional pot-shot from the shore, and the army made landfall by two o'clock in the afternoon. Abercromby's force advanced south towards Port Louis, whilst the 65th and the Fifth Brigade secured the landing, and brought up supplies.[36]

The British marched 'over bad roads'. Mansfield recalled that the 22nd 'got a guide to lead us for there was no roads'.[37] After five miles the army halted and set up camp for the night. Up ahead, Abercromby's vanguard, spearheaded by the Reserve Brigade, skirmished with the French. The next day the march resumed. Plummer 'suffered much from thirst, as we brought no water from the ships'. However, they received succour from local French planters who ordered their slaves to supply the British.[38] Eventually the redcoats reached the area of Moulin à Poudre, the powder-mills, and discovered a drove of bullocks, which Abercromby ordered the soldiers to shoot for dinner. Whilst they thus were engaged, a party of French infantry and cavalry burst on the British pickets. A detachment from the army's light companies reinforced the pickets whilst some 'sharpshooters' flanked the French. During the ensuing conflict Decaen's men set fire to some huts behind the British and the woods before them, creating 'one continued blaze for a mile distance.'[39] Eventually the French were driven off and after rest and resupply from the fleet, the British column pressed on.

On 1 December, after marching another 3 miles, the vanguard approached the River des Pamplemousses, where Decaen had established a battery of guns. The British brushed

32 Plummer, *The Journal of Samuel Plummer*, p.71.
33 Wilson, *History of the Madras Army*, p.309.
34 Fortescue, *A History of the British Army*, vol.7, pp.601–602.
35 Plummer, *The Journal of Samuel Plummer*, p.72.
36 Fortescue, *A History of the British Army*, vol.7, p.603.
37 CMM: 0003.01/16: Personal reminisces of QM William Mansfield, 1798–1834, p.13.
38 Plummer, *The Journal of Samuel Plummer*, p.72.
39 Plummer, *The Journal of Samuel Plummer*, pp.72–73.

A contemporary depiction of the landings on the Île de France. (Anne S.K. Brown Collection)

these defences aside, and as the column advanced, they found another force of cannon at the Rivière Sèche. Mansfield later left a description of an action that he claims took place at the Moulin à Poudre, but the details do not tally with any of the other first-hand accounts, and it is probable he confused the skirmish at the mills with the action at the Rivière Sêche. In the following skirmish the French had placed sharpshooters amongst the rocky outcrops to harass the British as they made for the river. When they reached the water, the vanguard discovered another emplacement of guns, which, 'commenced their fires direct in our faces, with grape shot and shells'.[40] In response, Abercromby ordered a light infantry detachment to circle around the French right flank. As the 'light bobs' bore down on the French flank, Mansfield recalled, 'we [22nd] and the 12th Regt. Charged them [the guns] with Bayonet to Bayonet'.[41] The triumphant British pressed onwards, chasing the French up to the outskirts of Port Louis. As they neared the town, the British advance was brought to a skidding halt when a 24-pounder opened fire. The gun's shot signalled the presence of the remainder of Decaen's army, including several batteries of cannon, and the *Garde nationale* standing, 'with long pikes'.[42] The British retraced their steps, withdrawing towards the Montagne Longue, where they made camp for the night. On 2 December, Decaen sent a flag of truce out to Abercromby's camp, and to Mansfield's and the other British soldiers' disappointment, the negotiations succeeded, forestalling any hopes the British may have had of storming and plundering Port Louis.[43]

View from the deck of the Upton Castle transport. (Public Domain)

40 Plummer, *The Journal of Samuel Plummer*, p.73.
41 CMM: 0003.01/16: Personal reminisces of QM William Mansfield, 1798–1834, p.13.
42 Plummer, *The Journal of Samuel Plummer*, p.73.
43 CMM: 0003.01/16: Personal reminisces of QM William Mansfield, 1798–1834, p.14.

Abercromby was keen to secure the island and remove the threat of French piracy. Even though Decaen could not completely man the defences of Port Louis and remained vulnerable to an assault, Abercromby offered the French generous terms, including repatriating the general and his men to France. At a stroke, the last major outpost of the French Empire in the Indian Ocean was in British hands. The expedition was broken up, and by January 1811, the 65th Foot were back at sea on their way to Bombay, but the 22nd were ordered to remain. Abercromby felt, 'They were not only very sickly but the men in general are nearly exhausted by a long residence in a debilitating climate'; the lingering effects of the 22nd's ignominious posting to Berhampore were still affecting the regiment. When Abercromby left the island, he noted, 'upwards of 100 men were still sick' in the 22nd Foot.[44] Whilst the campaign to stifle France's privateers had drawn to a close, there was still one more operation in the Indian Ocean for the last remaining boys of the 22nd Foot.

## Slavers

The new governor of the now renamed British colony of Mauritius was an old-India hand, Sir Robert Farquhar, whose role involved implementing Abercromby's terms of capitulation offered to the French colonists. The terms included the preservation of the islanders' 'Religion, laws and customs', including slavery.[45] The plantation economy of Mauritius and the other Mascarene Islands was dependant on imports from Madagascar, this not only included slaves, but also bullocks and rice.[46] One of the principal ports for exporting goods to the Mascarenes, was Tamatavé (Toamasina) on the eastern coast of Madagascar. Despite the fall of Mauritius, the French continued to hold a factory in the port, which was used to smuggle slaves onto the Mascarene Islands.

Since the passing of the Slave Trade Act in 1807, the slave trade had been abolished throughout the British Empire, although slavery itself remained legal until 1833. The act encouraged Farquhar to engage with Madagascan politics, where he hoped to end the slave trade and eliminate French influence on the island.[47] A force was sent to occupy Tamatavé under the command of Commodore Lynne, which included a detachment of 65 soldiers from the 22nd Foot commanded by Captain Christopher Wilson.[48] Wilson's detachment reached Tamatavé on 18 February 1811, where Lynne called on the French Agent, Sylvain Roux, to surrender. Fortunately for the British, even if Roux felt like offering resistance, the small French garrison had not been paid and were marching about dressed in rags and so refused the agent's orders. Roux promptly capitulated and

44 Rigby, *Ever Glorious*, p.136.
45 Sidney Selvon, *A Comprehensive History of Mauritius* (Port Louis: Mauritius Printing Specialists Ltd., 2005), p.194.
46 Gwyn Campbell, *An Economic History of Imperial Madagascar 1750-1898* (Cambridge: Cambridge University Press, 2005), p.52.
47 Phares M. Mutibwa, *The Malagasy and the Europeans* (London: Longman Group Limited, 1974), p.24
48 TNA: WO 17/2172: Mauritius Monthly Returns, 1811, February 1811.

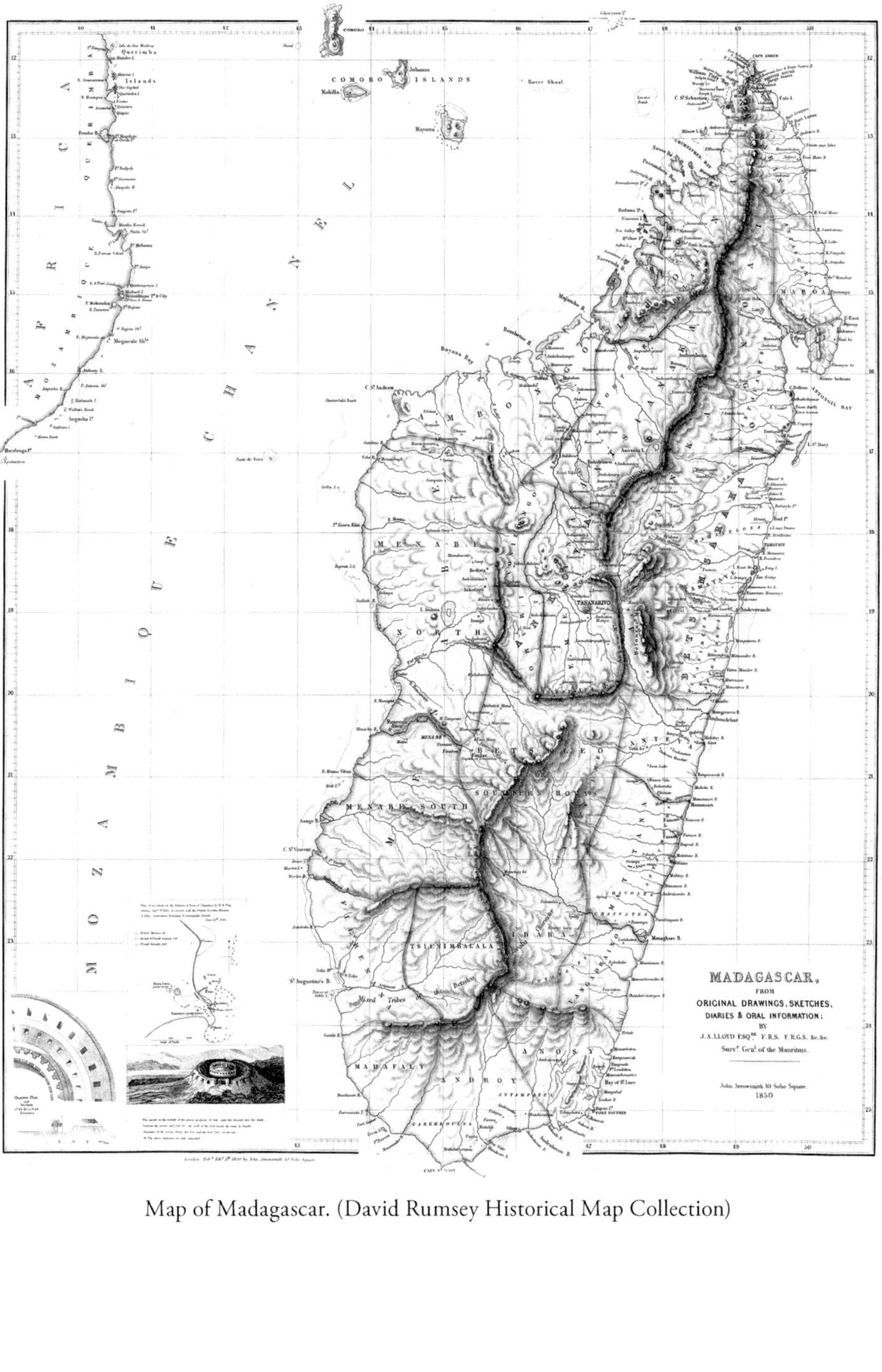


Map of Madagascar. (David Rumsey Historical Map Collection)

the 22nd took their place garrisoning the port.[49] Farquhar was elated, writing to the Secretary for War and the Colonies, the Earl of Liverpool, 'This has freed these seas from the last French flag, and secured to us an unmolested traffic into the fruitful and abundant island of Madagascar.'[50]

Whilst the landing had been smooth, the occupation proved to be a nightmare. As was the case in most tropical postings, disease quickly decimated the ranks of the 22nd Foot. Worse followed in the spring of 1811, when a squadron of French frigates surprised Wilson's detachment and imprisoned them. Fortunately, relief was at hand when on 20 May, Captain Charles Marsh Schomberg commanding HMS *Astraea* and a squadron of frigates encountered the French near Foul Point, off the coast of Madagascar. After a sharp action he captured the frigate *La Renommée*, before turning towards Tamatavé. Arriving at the port, Schomberg discovered another French frigate nestled amongst the reefs and ready to enfilade the passage into the harbour. Unable to take soundings of the passage, Schomberg could not force his way into Tamatavé; instead, on 25 May, he attempted to call on the French garrison to surrender.

After the previous action at sea, the French were in no position to offer resistance, and following negotiations, they capitulated and released the 22nd Foot. Schomberg described the detachment as 'being ill, of endemic fever of this country'. He took them aboard the captured French frigate *La Nereide* and, alongside the French garrison, conveyed them to Mauritius.[51] On 11 June 1811, Wilson died, another name added to the 27 privates who had fallen victims to the fevers on Madagascar.[52] For the remaining boys of the 22nd, 1/34th and 65th Foot, these small imperial expeditions were some of the last active service they saw as the Napoleonic Wars entered their twilight years.

49 Mervyn Brown, *Madagascar Rediscovered* (London: Damien Tunnacliffe, 1978), p.134.
50 Farquhar quoted in Brown, *Madagascar Rediscovered*, p.134.
51 C.M. Schomberg quoted in Nicholas Tracy (ed.), *The Naval Chronicle* (London: Chatham, 1999), vol.5, pp.54–56.
52 TNA: WO 17/2172: Mauritius Monthly Returns, 1811, July 1811.

# 13

# There and Back Again

As the drums of war faded across the Indian Ocean, so too did the boys of the 'experimental battalions'. As noted in Chapter 11, as early as 1806, less than a quarter of the rank and file of the 22nd and 1/34th were boys who had survived from the original enlistment in 1797–1800. With fresh campaigns, disease, and postings to tropical climes, that number continued to dwindle as the years slipped by.

This is clearly demonstrated in March 1810, during a review of the 65th Foot conducted by Major General the Honourable John Abercromby. The battalion had returned from the anti-piracy operations in the Persian Gulf, when Abercromby observed 'that in point of discipline, interior economy and arrangement, it [the 65th] surpasses any of the Batts. of H.M. service', laying particular emphasis on Smith's tireless command of the battalion. It was, however, a small battalion, with only 446 rank and file, hardly at half-strength, and a far cry from the 854 boys who had sailed from the Downs in 1800.[1] Abercromby particularly feared the 65th's continued reduction would eventually render the battalion 'of little service'. This was especially distressing as, in addition to the 65th's firm discipline, the soldiers were also 'particularly healthy', despite their return from active service. Indeed, Abercromby was so impressed he thought 'this little Batt. to be capable of undergoing, any reasonable degree of fatigue ... in this climate.'[2] Inspection reports like Abercromby's highlight the continual drain on men in the British Empire's tropical possessions during the Napoleonic Wars, where many battalions experienced severe losses during their tour of duty. Although for the surviving boys in the 65th they were lucky enough to become 'salted' to the climate, enduring great hardship and adapting to the rigours of campaigning in India.

Whilst the 65th became accustomed to seaborne raiding, the 1/34th passed the last years of the Napoleonic Wars in garrison. Following their bloodless campaign against Amir Khan, the battalion was posted to Jalna. Inspections were considerably delayed, as the 'Heavy rain and the peculiar nature of the Soil around us renders Military Exercise almost impossible'.[3] By June 1811, the battalion had left Jalna and joined the Hyderabad Subsidiary Force, posted at Secunderabad. Like the 65th, the ranks of the 1/34th had

1 TNA: WO 17/185: 65th Foot Monthly Returns, 1763–1812, November 1800; TNA: WO 27/98: Inspection Returns to 90 Foot, 1810, 23 March 1810.
2 TNA: WO 27/98: Inspection Returns to 90 Foot, 1810, 23 March 1810.
3 TNA: WO 27/102: Inspection Returns to 90 Foot, 1811, 01st April 1811.

been significantly depleted by their time in India, with only 515 rank and file remaining. Amongst the numbers of lost boys was their former protector, Colonel Dickens. He had lived long enough to earn the rank of brevet Major General before his death on 29 April 1808. Despite his demise, when the battalion was inspected on 17 March 1813, the new commander, Major John Matthias Everard, was commended for lavishing 'the utmost attention to the welfare of the Corps'.[4] Everard had joined the 1/34th as a lieutenant in 1798 and fought in eastern Ceylon in 1803. The Major's lengthy career with the 1/34th seemingly imbued him with the traditions and practices established in Dickens' day.

The 1/34th remained with the subsidiary force until 19 June 1814, when the battalion set off for Seringapatam. They spent a year in Mysore, but sickness continued to plague their ranks until the battalion moved to Vellore, in October 1815, searching for a hospitable posting.[5]

Meanwhile, Smith and the 65th continued to receive glowing praise for their discipline and bearing. On their return from Mauritius, they had been temporarily detained at Point de Galle, Ceylon, in expectation of joining the 1811 expedition to Java. However, they were not sent east, returning to Bombay on 21 April 1811. The regiment's sojourn in barracks was brief, and in December 1811, Smith was given command of an expedition to assist the Company's ally the Gaekwad of Baroda against the rebellious chief of Nownugger in the Kathiawar peninsula.[6]

Sailing on 21 December 1811, Smith's force included the 65th, which landed at Porbandar. By 21 February 1812, the expedition had reached Nownugger, their ranks swelling with reinforcements from their Barodian allies. Skirmishing took place on the first day of the siege, but as the troops erected batteries, the chief offered to capitulate. Smith accepted, and the expedition spent the next two months flying the flag across Kathiawar, finally embarking for Bombay in April 1812.[7]

Two years later in November 1814, the regiment, now commanded by Lieutenant Colonel Colin James Milnes, sailed again to Gujarat. This time to serve as an army of observation first at Baroda, and later moving to the borders of Gwalior ruled by the Company's ostensibly erstwhile enemy Scindia. At the time, the Company was embroiled in the Gurkha War with Nepal, where the fighting was primarily focused. Although the *Maharajdhiraja* of Nepal was keen to distract the British, and he attempted to encourage Scindia and other Maratha rajas to join an anti-British coalition.[8] Receiving intelligence of the Nepalese overtures, the 65th and the observation force watched Scindia from January 1815, hoping to dissuade him from throwing his lot in with the Nepalese. By May, this looked extremely unlikely, and the observation force was disbanded.

The 65th did not have long to rest and recuperate as they were ordered back to Kathiawar for an expedition against the Kingdom of Kutch, in Northern Gujarat. During their march, they became some of the first British troops to cross the salt marsh called the Rann. Upon entering Kutch, the expedition took the fort of Anjar before

4 TNA: WO 27/116: Inspection Returns to 90 Foot, 1813, 17th March 1813.
5 Noakes, *A Historical Account of the Services of the 34th and 55th* Regiments, p.58.
6 Broughton, *Memoirs of the 65th Regiment*, p.16.
7 Broughton, *Memoirs of the 65th Regiment*, p.16.
8 Chaurasia, *History of the Marathas*, p.141.

advancing on the kingdom's capital Bhuj, where they imposed terms on the Kingdom of Kutch, including the occupation of Anjar. The 65th eventually withdrew on 25 January 1816, but as they tried to march back to Company territory, they encountered numerous diversions, initially with local pirates at Okamandel and then a force of Arabs who had attacked Nownugger. They finally returned to Bombay on 20 May 1816.[9]

These minor actions built up to a final crescendo in 1817 with the outbreak of the Third Anglo-Maratha War. The Company had been concerned with the predatory behaviour of the roving bands of *pindaris* for some time, and Governor General Francis Rawdon-Hastings, Marquess Hastings, made it his goal to remove the threat of the horsemen's raids from Central India. Hastings planned to lead an expedition against the *pindaris* and orchestrated a series of treaties to tie the rajas of India closer to the Company and stop them from lending any support to the roving *pindaris*. The principal treaty concluded by Hastings was the 1817 Treaty of Poona, which forced the Peshwa, Bajirao, to hand over several key fortresses.[10] Concerned about the loss of prestige the Treaty of Poona forced on him, Bajirao was determined to throw off the British yoke. The Peshwa struck whilst Hastings was distracted fighting the *pindaris*. The subsequent war drew in most of the Maratha rajas and saw both the 1/34th and 65th Foot take part in the campaign.

Both battalions served in the many flying columns which criss-crossed Central India, hunting down *pindaris* and Maratha armies alike. The war eventually came to an end in 1819, although fighting persisted into the 1820s, with the 1/34th employed against some refractory forts until their return to England, sailing up the Thames in July 1823.[11] The 65th's time in India was also running out, but before they left, they had some old scores to settle. In 1819 and 1821 the 65th were sent back to Arabia to help finish the war against piracy they had started a decade before. Eventually, just like the 1/34th, their time in the east came to an end, in 1822, when they embarked for Britain. As they departed, the Governor in Council in Bombay offered his compliments to the 65th; 'The whole period since the arrival of the 65th Regiment has been an almost uninterrupted course of active employment … [the 65th] has proceeded on various distant expeditions by land and sea and has shared in some of the most arduous marches and of the several conflicts recorded in the military history of the East.' He continued that the regiment's behaviour and service 'entitle it to the highest testimonies of respect and applause.'[12] The 65th finally landed at Gravesend on 22 January 1823, after over two decades involved in some of the most unhealthy and brutal conflicts of the early nineteenth century. It is hard to determine how many of the original boys remained with the colours when the 1/34th and the 65th finally returned home, because aside from the 1806 Statement of Service, the British army did not conduct another wholesale review of the rank and file during the Napoleonic Wars. Despite this lack of evidence there is a high chance that

9 Broughton, *Memoirs of the 65th Regiment*, p.17.
10 Duff, *History of the Mahrattas*, vol.3, pp.396–397.
11 Noakes, *A Historical Account of the Services of the 34th and 55th Regiments*, p.71.
12 Donald Creighton-Williamson, *The York and Lancaster Regiment: 65th and 84th Regiments of Foot* (London: Leo Cooper, 1968), pp.44–45.

a handful of former boys may have still been with their regiments and the 22nd Foot provides two prime examples.

Following the conquest of Mauritius, the 22nd spent the end of the Napoleonic Wars in garrisons in the Mascarene Islands, with part of the regiment stationed on Mauritius whilst a sizable detachment went to the Île de Bourbon. During their time on the islands, Mansfield complained that the battalion was plagued with cholera. The sickness was so serious that in 1815, the Mauritius detachment was turned out of their barracks in Port Louis and had to camp 7 miles away from the town. Mansfield claims he staved off the illness by using a local remedy recommended by an old Frenchman; 'a third of a Bottle of Rum, honey and hot water mext [sic] and drinked it every night before bedtime'.[13] Meanwhile Plummer busied himself with setting up prayer rooms, first in Port Louis and then St Denis on Bourbon.[14]

In addition to the two survivors from the boy soldier days of the regiment, several other familiar faces remained with the 22nd Foot. Kelso was now a lieutenant colonel and commanded the regiment in Mauritius. Beside him, despite his missing leg, was Lindsay, who had rejoined the 22nd Foot. During his absence from the 22nd, Lindsay had become a major on 18 July 1807, and appears to have enrolled in the Senior Department at the Royal Military College at High Wycombe to be trained in the duties of a staff officer, as he is listed as a student in the regimental returns in October 1808.[15] He rejoined the 22nd Foot at Berhampore on 12 December 1808, in time to take part in the expedition to Mauritius, but when he arrived on the island he spent very little time with the regiment. Instead, Lindsay served as Deputy Adjutant General for Mauritius from 17 September 1812.[16] McNeight, now a brevet major, was away in Britain recruiting, and sadly the redoubtable Mercer was no longer with the regiment as he had died in Perth on 26 April 1809. For the boys who had served in their ranks, these officers had been a central feature in their lives for nearly 20 years.

Like Lindsay, Mansfield, one of the former boy soldiers, made a significant step in his career when, on 21 April 1811, he was appointed regimental quartermaster. His role made him responsible for managing the lodgings and the routes of march for the regiment, at a mere 29 years old.[17] Mansfield and the 22nd filled their days on Mauritius clearing paths through the hills, until 29 August 1819, when the regiment set sail for Britain.[18] They finally landed in Portsmouth in November of the same year. On his return Plummer complained of a recurrent illness and was sent to Chatham where he was eventually discharged on 22 March 1820. Plummer decided to retire to Norwich, 'with a view to spend the remainder of my days in ease and quiet'.[19] Upon his arrival he discovered that his parents had died, and he felt a certain amount of guilt for causing them stress by becoming a soldier, which he believed had ultimately shortened their lives.

13 CMM: 0003.01/16: Personal reminisces of QM William Mansfield, 1798–1834, p.15.
14 Plummer, *The Journal of Samuel Plummer*, p.77.
15 TNA: WO 17/124: 22nd Foot Monthly Returns, 1 October 1808.
16 Brown, *King George's Army: Volume 2*, p.288.
17 TNA: WO 65/63, Army Lists 1813, p.153.
18 Rigby, *Ever Glorious*, p.142.
19 Plummer, *The Journal of Samuel Plummer*, p.83.

Whilst Plummer retired to Norfolk, Mansfield soldiered on, spending 1820 in Newcastle with the 22nd Foot before setting sail for Ireland, where they were posted to Kilkenny. Here the 22nd faced scuffles with the Whiteboys, a secret agrarian movement that defended tenant-farmers. Mansfield recounted his experience of 'the whiteboys out every night burning farm houses and Corn Stacks. I have counted seven fires of a night'.[20] This 'very hard duty' lasted from 1821 to 1826, when the regiment was sent to the West Indies, arriving in Jamaica on 7 February 1827. It was in Jamaica, 31 years after their predecessors in the regiment had been decimated by yellow fever on Saint-Domingue, that the virus struck again. Mansfield recalled with horror how, 223 men were lost in six weeks. Eventually he was also struck down and, on 15 March 1828, he left Jamaica and parted with the 22nd forever, after spending 30 years with the regiment. He was treated in London by Sir James McGrigor, Wellington's former surgeon general in the Peninsular War. Mansfield's treatment lasted from May to July 1828, when McGrigor told the former boy soldier he could retire wherever he wished, although he recommended 'the North for he said Essex where I was born would not agree with me for my blood was too thin being so long in a hot country'.[21] Mansfield fully retired on 9 April 1829 and received a pension for 31 years, three months and nine days military service; he was 47 years old.

There is one other boy who has not been mentioned, who left an enduring legacy through the memoir he published. Following his promotion to lieutenant in 1805, the irrepressible Shipp embarked for Britain, in charge of a group of invalids, many of whom were casualties from the Second Maratha War.[22] In Britain, he became a darling of the Wakefield gentry, even acting as a second during a matter of honour between an officer and a civilian. Sadly, his youth and inexperience left Shipp vulnerable as he fell into debt and lost most of his money through the machinations of a serjeant and open theft by his servant. He was forced to sell his commission, and in Westminster he reenlisted as a trooper in the 24th Light Dragoons and left for India on 8 January 1808. Due to both the 22nd Foot and the 24th Light Dragoons long service together in Lake's Grand Army, Shipp was quickly recognised and immediately promoted to serjeant.[23] He rose to the rank of regimental serjeant major and spent the next seven years with the dragoons. In 1815, he wrote a letter to Governor General Hastings, which was accompanied by a recommendation from his officers. His solicitation proved enough for Shipp to add an unprecedented laurel to his career, when he was awarded an ensigncy in the 87th (The Prince of Wales's Irish) Regiment of Foot by Hastings. This meant Shipp had jumped from the ranks twice by the age of 31. Fortunately, or rather unfortunately, this was just in time for Shipp to take to the field again, this time against the Nepalese in the Gurkha War, in 1816.[24]

After the Gurkha War, Shipp saw out the 1810s fighting the Marathas and *pindaris* during the Third Maratha War, eventually becoming a lieutenant in 1821. Despite a

20 CMM: 0003.01/16: Personal reminisces of QM William Mansfield, 1798–1834, p.17.
21 CMM: 0003.01/16: Personal reminisces of QM William Mansfield, 1798–1834, p.19.
22 Shipp, *The Extraordinary Military Career*, p.97.
23 Shipp, *The Extraordinary Military Career*, pp.102–104.
24 Shipp, *The Extraordinary Military Career*, pp.118–126.

career that would give the fictional Richard Sharpe a run for his money, Shipp's time in India sadly ended in ignominy when he was dishonourably discharged from the army over a scandal involving racehorses. In April 1825 Shipp left India for the last time. By 1829 he had written a couple of melodramas and his memoirs. Looking for employment in 1830, Shipp like many other Napoleonic veterans, enrolled in the newly established London Metropolitan Police, founded the year before. Shipp was made an inspector and quickly came to the notice of the Peninsular and Waterloo veteran and one of the heads of the Metropolitan Police, Charles Rowan. Rowan introduced Shipp to Lieutenant William Parlour who, in 1830, was recruited as Superintendent of the Liverpool Night (or Town Watch). Within a few months, a vacancy for superintendent in the Liverpool Night Watch became available, and Parlour offered Shipp the role.[25] Like London, Liverpool was in the midst of trying to organise the often confused state of the city's law enforcement. When Shipp arrived, the city was policed by a Corporation Constabulary run by the town council, which only patrolled during the day, avoiding the docks. Men in the Night Watch, like Shipp, provided nighttime patrols. They were issued with a lamp and a rattle; Shipp added a heavy stick to his arsenal before he set out to patrol the streets and called the hours of the night.[26] As superintendent, Shipp's role included setting the watch for his men before undertaking his own patrol to check that the watchmen were performing their duties. During his career with the watch, he claimed to have saved at least one young lady from would-be kidnappers. Following his retirement from the watch, in a strange twist of fate, Shipp ended up back where he started in the Poor Law system, as a governor of a workhouse in Liverpool where he died on 27 February 1834.

Shipp's career may have been exceptional, but his life, like that of his comrades in the boy regiments, was an extraordinary example of their role in this unique experiment in the British Army. The boy battalions demonstrated the mettle of these lads, some drawn from extreme poverty, who subsequently rose to the occasion in the face of daunting odds, whether on the battlefield or in the barrack room.

25 Shipp, *The Extraordinary Military Career*, pp.286–287.
26 Mick Macilwee, *The Liverpool Underworld: Crime in the City, 1750–1900* (Liverpool: Oxford University Press, 2011), pp.14–15.

A portrait of John Shipp from the frontispiece for his memoirs, depicting the boy soldier in later life as an officer. (Public Domain)

# 14

# The Boys and Child Soldiery

Children have always been a part of the army, either born into a regiment or enlisting as drummer boys. What makes the boy battalions unusual was that for the first time in the history of the British Army, children were the focus of the recruitment drive. The unprecedented mass enlistment of boys was born out of the tempestuous years of the 1790s, when Britain's regiments found themselves spread increasingly thinly across the globe. Concerned by the decimation of the British Army's battalions freshly returned from the West Indies, the Duke of York and Sir William Fawcett authorised the depleted regiments to commence enlisting boy recruits for their long-term recovery. Recognising that these lads needed time to mature and become soldiers, York encouraged the boy battalions to establish regimental schools, which aimed to create a generation of NCOs equipped with skills in numeracy and literacy. By the end of the war, this educational programme had produced men including Shipp and Mansfield, who both served in positions of authority; in Shipp's case, this enabled him to become a commissioned officer on two occasions and an author during his retirement.

Building on his success with the boy regiments, York ordered the creation of regimental schools across the entirety of the British Army in 1811. Describing his reasoning behind the schools, York emphasised they were 'to give to the soldiers the comfort of being assured, that the education and welfare of their children are objects of their sovereign's paternal solicitude and attention; and to raise from their offspring a succession of loyal subjects, brave soldiers, and good Christians.'[1] York's pioneering regimental schools became the first state-sponsored educational bodies in Great Britain and an initial step towards government-organised and funded education across the country.

The mass enrolment of boy soldiers at the turn of the century was an isolated experiment, and the army did not witness such a concentration of boy soldiers – like the recruits of the 22nd, 1/34th, and 65th Foot – again. This was due to the time it took to train the battalions, which prevented them from being quickly deployed to Europe, as this theatre of operations required flexibility and the rapid deployment of battalions. Rather, the number of boys in the army remained small, as stricter stipulations were enforced on the enlistment of boys, when compared to their forebears. For instance, in 1812, boy enlistees were required to be over 16 and at least 5 feet (1.52m) tall. Professor

1 Clarke, *Redcoats in the Classroom*, p.63.

Kevin Linch compares the restrictions imposed by the army to the norms found in the British labour market at the time, where boys were apprenticed from 14, and children could work from as young as six, and suggests the Army was 'quite protective' in comparison.[2] Stricter recruitment measures ensured the numbers of boys in the Army remained a minority, with only 13,700 boys enlisting between 1808 and 1815.[3] Whilst more research is required to assess how many boys enlisted outside of the boy battalions before 1807, if the rank and file of the three boy soldier battalions are included in the total for the last eight years of the war, the figure would be closer to 15,000. This figure gives a sense of how rare it was for boys to enlist during the Napoleonic Wars, particularly as the army's overall enlistment was over 800,000 men during the entire conflict. Whilst the recruitment of boys continued, it was at a reduced scale due in part to the experience gained from the boy battalion experiment and York's continued efforts to refine his plans for the training of underage recruits.

In addition to recruitment stipulations and educational opportunities, the boy battalions continued to set precedents for child recruits who enlisted after 1807. After the boy battalions, York added further refinements to his boy enlistment programme, allowing regiments serving in India to recruit up to 100 boys, although this was later reduced to 50 in 1812. Similar to the original boys, these later enlistees spent long stretches travelling to the east and were usually in their late teens by the time they reached the garrisons of the subcontinent.[4] Additionally, posting boys to the East Indies became common practice with the HEIC's European regiments, which also recruited children into their ranks. In the Army Lists for the HEIC, there is a return of enlistees transferred from the British Army to the Company's depot on the Isle of Wight from 19 August 1802 to 24 April 1803. During this period, 607 recruits were sent in total and of this figure, 50 percent were under 18, and some were as young as 13 when they were recorded in the Army List.[5] These figures suggest the enlistment of boys developed into a response to meet growing imperial commitments in the East Indies and the requirement for longer deployments abroad, as younger recruits would have more time to train and then serve in the colonies.

Whilst Britain's boy battalion experiment inspired programmes for education and remained wedded to the concept of voluntary enlistment, child soldiery across the world was not imbued with the same principles. Over a hundred years later, Nazi Germany experienced a dearth of manpower following the disintegration of the *Wehrmacht* in the face of the rolling steel of the Allied and Red Armies. This led to many *Hitlerjugend* – Hitler Youth – chapters being thrown into the frontline after September 1944. Unlike the boy battalions, the *Hitlerjugend* boys were sent straight into battle to forestall the Allied and Soviet armies. Some of these boys were often younger than 14 and armed with a *Panzerfaust* anti-tank weapon, they were sent to the front with minimal training and orders to ambush enemy tanks.[6]

2 Linch, *The British Army*, p.182.
3 Linch, *The British Army*, p.182.
4 Linch, *The British Army*, p.181.
5 BL: IOR/H/502: Military establishments, pp.63–70.
6 Hans Holzträger, *In a Raging Inferno* (Warwick: Helion, 2024), pp.66–67.

More recently the desperate and brutal use of children in war has been instigated by non-state and some state actors, with well-documented examples on the continent of Africa. Children are kidnapped, cut off from their community, and brutalised into becoming child soldiers and are forced to commit murders, mutilation, and sexual assault. For instance, the Lord's Resistance Army (LRA), a former non-state actor in Northern Uganda, set quotas of children, which raiding parties were ordered to bring back.[7] Additionally, in Asia, the Liberation Tigers of Tamil Eelam in Sri Lanka (LTTE) were adept at indoctrinating children by fostering an 'us vs. them' mentality, with child recruits shown videos of dead women and children and told the government were responsible. This not only imbued a hatred of the Sri Lankan government's forces, but it also made violence casual and an obsession for these children.[8]

Children of the Royal Military Asylum, 1812. (National Army Museum)

7 P.W. Singer, *Children at War* (Berkeley: University of California Press, 2006), p.58
8 Singer, *Children at War*, p.72

York and Fawcett's programme in comparison, aligns with the many state youth organisations, which steadily appeared across Europe during the nineteenth and twentieth centuries. For example, in Britain, the Royal Military Asylum, which eventually became the Duke of York's Royal Military School, provided an education for the sons of British veterans.[9] Indeed, both Britain and France continued to offer voluntary pre-military training to youths well into the twentieth century. In contrast during the inter-war years of the twentieth century, Poland's State Department for Physical Education and Military Training came under the control of the War Department, which made pre-military training compulsory for all 16-year-old Polish children.[10] Similarly, Nazi Germany, Fascist Italy, Hungary, and the Soviet Union had compulsory youth programmes, which were in direct contrast to the voluntary principles of Britain's youth initiatives.

Today Britain continues to give adolescents, as young as 15 years and seven months, the opportunity to start the process of applying for the army. These young recruits are a link to York and Fawcett's boy soldier battalions established two centuries ago. Some of the restrictions set down by York survive, with underage recruits required to spend several years training before they can be deployed in a combat zone at the age of 18.[11] The connections between the Napoleonic boy soldiers and their modern counterparts illustrate how the British Army has adapted York's idea during the last 200 years. Initially, the boy battalions were a useful testing ground for the birth of a state-sponsored school system in the military. Their deployment to India alludes to the future primary role of the British Army in the nineteenth century as imperial commitments grew and British regiments were forced to adapt to warfare across the globe from frigid prairies to the tropics. The Napoleonic boy soldiers were pioneers who endured conquest, war, famine, and disease, repeatedly rising to each challenge and in the process becoming the soldiers York had always envisioned they would be, despite subsequently falling into historical obscurity. For the few surviving boys who returned to Britain, some after 20 years abroad, the army had become integral to their identity. Amongst the veteran boy soldiers, it is fitting to finish with Shipp's thoughts upon his own retirement from the army, 'I was no longer a soldier, I felt a weight at my heart that sunk me almost to the earth.'[12]

9 Cockerill, *Sons of the Brave*, p.78.

10 Holzträger, *In a Raging Inferno*, p.8

11 Defence Statistics, 'Deployment of children (under 18)', *Ministry of Defence*, <https://assets.publishing.service.gov.uk/media/5c87b59d40f0b636981e0b76/12590.pdf>, 31 January 2019, accessed 23 August 2025.

12 Shipp, *The Extraordinary Military Career*, p.282

# Bibliography

## Archival Sources

*British Library (BL)*

IOR/F/4/173/3033, Detachments of H.M. 10th and H.M. 22nd Regiment of Foot, the Bengal Marine Regiment and a Company of Artillery are ordered to embark for service in Cuttack, India Office Records and Private Papers, July – August 1803

IOR/F/4/174/3086, General Orders issued in consequence of the victories obtained by Generals Lake and Wellesley over the Marathas, September 1803 – February 1804

IOR/F/4/293, Report of a Native Infantry Battalion to attack the His Majesty's 34th Regiment

IOR/F/4/322/7378, Discontent of the rank and file of HM 22nd Regiment of Foot at Muttra, September 1806 – November 1807

IOR/F/4/343/7962, Operations of the Naval and Military forces employed against the Joasmee Pirates

IOR/H/595a, Correspondence regarding Ameer Khan and the Raja of Berar

IOR/H/MISC/479, Wellesley Papers

IOR/HOM/MISC/502, Army Lists

IOR/H/622, War against Sindhia and Rajah of Berar

IOR/HOM/MISC/626. Papers concerning the war with Holkar, Raja of Bharatpur, Sindhia and Raja of Berar

IOR/L/MAR/B/170C, Journals, Ledgers and Pay Books of the *Henry Addington*

IOR/L/MAR/B/222-I, Journals, Ledgers and Pay Books of the *Ocean*

IOR/L/MAR/B/307C, Journals, Ledgers and Pay Books of the *Preston*

*Cheshire Military Museum (CMM)*

0003.01/16: Personal reminisces of QM William Mansfield, 1798-1834

*The National Archives (TNA)*

WO 1/1068, General Correspondence: (b. Series II correspondence, B). 1794

WO 1/1078, General Correspondence: (b. Series II correspondence, R-S). 1794

WO 1/1079, General Correspondence: (b. Series II correspondence. S-T). 1794

WO 1/1083, General Correspondence: (b. Series II correspondence. B). 1795

WO 1/1119, General Correspondence: (n. Miscellaneous In-Letters). 1809

WO 3/16, Office of the Commander-in-Chief, General Letters: (series 1-1767-1800) 1st November 1796 – 30th April 1797
WO 3/17, Office of the Commander-in-Chief, General Letters: (series 1-1767-1800) 1st January 1797 – 28th February 1798
WO 3/18, Office of the Commander-in-Chief, General Letters: (series 1-1767-1800) 1st February 1798 – 30th September 1798
WO 3/19, Office of the Commander-in-Chief, General Letters: (series 1-1767-1800) 1st October 1798 – 31st July 1799
WO 3/20, Office of the Commander-in-Chief, General Letters: (series 1-1767-1800) 1st July 1799 – 30th November 1799
WO 3/31, Office of the Commander-in-Chief, General Letters: (series 2-1765-1801) 1st January 1797 – 28th February 1798
WO 4/170, War Office, Secretary-at-War, General Letters 1797 Oct. – 1798 March
WO 12/3321, Commissary General of Musters Office and successors. General Muster Books and Pay Lists, 16th Foot 1st Battalion, 1787-1797
WO 12/3322, Commissary General of Musters Office and successors. General Muster Books and Pay Lists, 16th Foot 1st Battalion, 1798-1799
WO 12/3873, Commissary General of Musters Office and successors. General Muster Books and Pay Lists, 22nd Foot 1st Battalion, 1785-1797
WO 12/3874, Commissary General of Musters Office and successors, General Muster Books and Pay Lists, 22nd Foot 1st Battalion, 1798
WO 12/3875, Commissary General of Musters Office and successors, General Muster Books and Pay Lists, 22nd Foot 1st Battalion, 1799
WO 12/3876, Commissary General of Musters Office and successors, General Muster Books and Pay Lists, 22nd Foot 1st Battalion, 1800-1801
WO 12/3877, Commissary General of Musters Office and successors, General Muster Books and Pay Lists, 22nd Foot 1st Battalion, 1802
WO 12/3878, Commissary General of Musters Office and successors, General Muster Books and Pay Lists, 22nd Foot 1st Battalion, 1803
WO 12/3879, Commissary General of Musters Office and successors, General Muster Books and Pay Lists, 22nd Foot 1st Battalion, 1804
WO 12/3880, Commissary General of Musters Office and successors, General Muster Books and Pay Lists, 22nd Foot 1st Battalion, 1805-1806
WO 12/3881, Commissary General of Musters Office and successors, General Muster Books and Pay Lists, 22nd Foot 1st Battalion, 1807-1808
WO 12/3882, Commissary General of Musters Office and successors, General Muster Books and Pay Lists, 22nd Foot 1st Battalion, 1809-1810
WO 12/3883, Commissary General of Musters Office and successors, General Muster Books and Pay Lists, 22nd Foot 1st Battalion, 1811-1812
WO 12/3884, Commissary General of Musters Office and successors, General Muster Books and Pay Lists 22nd Foot 1st Battalion, 1813-1815
WO 12/4867, Commissary General of Musters Office and successors, General Muster Books and Pay Lists, 34th Foot 1st Battalion

WO 12/4868, Commissary General of Musters Office and successors. General Muster Books and Pay Lists, 34th Foot 1st Battalion, 1798
WO 12/4869, Commissary General of Musters Office and successors, General Muster Books and Pay Lists, 34th Foot 1st Battalion, 1799
WO 12/4870, Commissary General of Musters Office and successors, General Muster Books and Pay Lists, 34th Foot 1st Battalion, 1800
WO 12/4871, Commissary General of Musters Office and successors, General Muster Books and Pay Lists, 34th Foot 1st Battalion, 1801
WO 12/4872, Commissary General of Musters Office and successors, General Muster Books and Pay Lists, 34th Foot 1st Battalion, 1802
WO 12/4873, Commissary General of Musters Office and successors, General Muster Books and Pay Lists, 34th Foot 1st Battalion, 1803
WO 12/4874, Commissary General of Musters Office and successors, General Muster Books and Pay Lists, 34th Foot 1st Battalion, 1805
WO 12/4875, Commissary General of Musters Office and successors, General Muster Books and Pay Lists, 34th Foot 1st Battalion, 1806
WO 12/4876, Commissary General of Musters Office and successors, General Muster Books and Pay Lists, 34th Foot 1st Battalion, 1807
WO 12/4877, Commissary General of Musters Office and successors, General Muster Books and Pay Lists, 34th Foot 1st Battalion, 1808
WO 12/4878, Commissary General of Musters Office and successors. General Muster Books and Pay Lists, 34th Foot 1st Battalion, 1809
WO 12/4879, Commissary General of Musters Office and successors, General Muster Books and Pay Lists, 34th Foot 1st Battalion, 1810
WO 12/4880, Commissary General of Musters Office and successors, General Muster Books and Pay Lists, 34th Foot 1st Battalion, 1811
WO 12/4881, Commissary General of Musters Office and successors, General Muster Books and Pay Lists, 34th Foot 1st Battalion, 1812
WO 12/4882, Commissary General of Musters Office and successors, General Muster Books and Pay Lists, 34th Foot 1st Battalion, 1813
WO 12/4883: Commissary General of Musters Office and successors. General Muster Books and Pay Lists, 34th Foot 1st Battalion, 1814
WO 12/4884, Commissary General of Musters Office and successors, General Muster Books and Pay Lists, 34th Foot 1st Battalion, 1815
WO 12/7378 Commissary General of Musters Office and successors, General Muster Books and Pay Lists, 65th Foot 1st Battalion, 1783-1797
WO 12/7379, Commissary General of Musters Office and successors, General Muster Books and Pay Lists, 65th Foot 1st Battalion, 1798-1799
WO 12/7380, Commissary General of Musters Office and successors, General Muster Books and Pay Lists, 65th Foot 1st Battalion, 1800
WO 12/7381, Commissary General of Musters Office and successors, General Muster Books and Pay Lists, 65th Foot 1st Battalion, 1801
WO 12/7382, Commissary General of Musters Office and successors. General Muster Books and Pay Lists, 65th Foot 1st Battalion, 1802

WO 12/7383, Commissary General of Musters Office and successors, General Muster Books and Pay Lists, 65th Foot 1st Battalion, 1803-1806
WO 12/7384, Commissary General of Musters Office and successors, General Muster Books and Pay Lists, 65th Foot 1st Battalion, 1807-1808
WO 12/7385, Commissary General of Musters Office and successors, General Muster Books and Pay Lists, 65th Foot 1st Battalion, 1809-1810
WO 12/7386 Commissary General of Musters Office and successors, General Muster Books and Pay Lists, 65th Foot 1st Battalion, 1811-1812
WO 12/7387, Commissary General of Musters Office and successors, General Muster Books and Pay Lists, 65th Foot 1st Battalion, 1813-1814
WO 12/7388, Commissary General of Musters Office and successors, General Muster Books and Pay Lists, 65th Foot 1st Battalion, 1815
WO 17/110, Office of the Commander in Chief Monthly Returns to the Adjutant General for the 9th Foot 1759-1802
WO 17/118, Office of the Commander in Chief Monthly Returns to the Adjutant General for the 16th Foot 1791-1812
WO 17/124, Office of the Commander in Chief Monthly Returns to the Adjutant General for the 22nd Foot 1766-1812
WO 17/143, Office of the Commander in Chief Monthly Returns to the Adjutant General for the 34th Foot 1759-1799
WO 17/144, Office of the Commander in Chief Monthly Returns to the Adjutant General for the 34th Foot 1800-1812
WO 17/170, Office of the Commander in Chief Monthly Returns to the Adjutant General for the 55th Foot 1785-1812
WO 17/185, Office of the Commander in Chief Monthly Returns to the Adjutant General for the 65th Foot 1763-1812
WO 17/260, Office of the Commander in Chief Monthly Returns to the Adjutant General for the 11th – 23rd Foot. 1813
WO 17/261, Office of the Commander in Chief Monthly Returns to the Adjutant General for the 24th – 34th Foot. 1813
WO 17/264, Office of the Commander in Chief Monthly Returns to the Adjutant General for the 60th – 69th Foot. 1813
WO 17/275, Office of the Commander in Chief Monthly Returns to the Adjutant General for the 11th – 23rd Foot. 1814
WO 17/276, Office of the Commander in Chief Monthly Returns to the Adjutant General for the 24th – 34th Foot. 1814
WO 17/279, Office of the Commander in Chief Monthly Returns to the Adjutant General for the 60th – 69th Foot. 1814
WO 17/291, Office of the Commander in Chief Monthly Returns to the Adjutant General for the 14th – 27th Foot. 1815
WO 17/292, Office of the Commander in Chief Monthly Returns to the Adjutant General for the 28th – 41st Foot. 1815
WO 17/294, Office of the Commander in Chief Monthly Returns to the Adjutant General for the 60th – 71st Foot. 1815

WO 17/1159, Office of the Commander in Chief, Monthly Returns to the Adjutant General, General Returns
WO 17/1160, Office of the Commander in Chief, Monthly Returns to the Adjutant General, General Returns
WO 17/1161, Office of the Commander in Chief, Monthly Returns to the Adjutant General, General Returns
WO 17/1318, Office of the Commander in Chief, Monthly Returns to the Adjutant General, Bengal, 1811
WO 17/1320, Office of the Commander in Chief, Monthly Returns to the Adjutant General, Bengal, 1813
WO 17/1431, Office of the Commander in Chief, Monthly Returns to the Adjutant General, Bombay, 1811
WO 17/1432, Office of the Commander in Chief, Monthly Returns to the Adjutant General, Bombay, 1812
WO 17/1433, Office of the Commander in Chief, Monthly Returns to the Adjutant General, Bombay, 1813
WO 17/1434, Office of the Commander in Chief, Monthly Returns to the Adjutant General, Bombay, 1814
WO 17/1435, Office of the Commander in Chief, Monthly Returns to the Adjutant General, Bombay, 1815
WO 17/1585, Office of the Commander in Chief, Monthly Returns to the Adjutant General, Cape of Good Hope, 1799
WO 17/1586, Office of the Commander in Chief, Monthly Returns to the Adjutant General, Cape of Good Hope, 1800
WO 17/1587, Office of the Commander in Chief, Monthly Returns to the Adjutant General, Cape of Good Hope, 1801
WO 17/1588, Office of the Commander in Chief, Monthly Returns to the Adjutant General, Cape of Good Hope, 1802
WO 17/1589, Office of the Commander in Chief, Monthly Returns to the Adjutant General, Cape of Good Hope, 1803
WO 17/1647, Office of the Commander in Chief, Monthly Returns to the Adjutant General, Ceylon, 1804
WO 17/1747, Office of the Commander in Chief, Monthly Returns to the Adjutant General, East Indies, 1801
WO 17/1748, Office of the Commander in Chief, Monthly Returns to the Adjutant General, East Indies, 1802
WO 17/1749, Office of the Commander in Chief, Monthly Returns to the Adjutant General, East Indies, 1803
WO 17/1750, Office of the Commander in Chief, Monthly Returns to the Adjutant General, East Indies, 1804
WO 17/1751, Office of the Commander in Chief, Monthly Returns to the Adjutant General, East Indies, 1805
WO 17/1752, Office of the Commander in Chief, Monthly Returns to the Adjutant General, East Indies, 1806

WO 17/1753, Office of the Commander in Chief, Monthly Returns to the Adjutant General, East Indies, 1807
WO 17/1754, Office of the Commander in Chief, Monthly Returns to the Adjutant General, East Indies, 1808
WO 17/1755, Office of the Commander in Chief, Monthly Returns to the Adjutant General, East Indies, 1809
WO 17/1756, Office of the Commander in Chief, Monthly Returns to the Adjutant General, East Indies, 1810
WO 17/1986, Office of the Commander in Chief, Monthly Returns to the Adjutant General, Jamaica, 1794
WO 17/1987, Office of the Commander in Chief, Monthly Returns to the Adjutant General, Jamaica, 1795
WO 17/1988, Office of the Commander in Chief, Monthly Returns to the Adjutant General, Jamaica, 1796
WO 17/2062, Office of the Commander in Chief, Monthly Returns to the Adjutant General, Madras, 1811
WO 17/2063, Office of the Commander in Chief, Monthly Returns to the Adjutant General, Madras, 1812
WO 17/2172, Office of the Commander in Chief, Monthly Returns to the Adjutant General, Mauritius, 1810–1811
WO 17/2173, Office of the Commander in Chief, Monthly Returns to the Adjutant General, Mauritius, 1812
WO 17/2174, Office of the Commander in Chief, Monthly Returns to the Adjutant General, Mauritius, 1813
WO 25/944: 22 Foot. Statements of the Periods of service of all NCOs and Men
WO 25/964: 34th Foot, 1st Battalion. Statements of the Periods of service of all NCOs and Men
WO 25/1017: 65 Foot. Statements of the Periods of service of all NCOs and Men
WO 27/73, Office of the Commander-in-Chief and War Office, Adjutant General and Army Council, Inspection Returns, Irish, 1792
WO 27/81, Office of the Commander-in-Chief and War Office, Adjutant General and Army Council, Inspection Returns, General Inspection Returns, 1798
WO 27/82, Office of the Commander-in-Chief and War Office, Adjutant General and Army Council, Inspection Returns, General Inspection Returns, 1799
WO 27/83, Office of the Commander-in-Chief and War Office, Adjutant General and Army Council, Inspection Returns, General Inspection Returns, 1800
WO 27/98: Office of the Commander-in-Chief and War Office, Adjutant General and Army Council, Inspection Returns to 90 Foot, 1810
WO 27/102: Office of the Commander-in-Chief and War Office, Adjutant General and Army Council, Inspection Returns to 90 Foot, 1811
WO 27/111: Office of the Commander-in-Chief and War Office, Adjutant General and Army Council, Inspection Returns, To 30 Foot, 1812 2nd Half-Year,
WO 27/116: Office of the Commander-in-Chief and War Office, Adjutant General and Army Council, Inspection Returns to 90 Foot, 1813

WO 121/78, Royal Hospital, Chelsea, Discharge Documents of Pensioners

*Clifton Park and Museum*

York & Lancaster Regiment Museum: 578-K/2/5/1: Administrative and financial records of Major William Augustus Bygrave, 29 November 1797.

*The National Army Museum (NAM)*

8703-67, Two letters with John Henry Fraser, 1804

9204-121, Journal of Lt. Charles Stuart, 3rd Bengal Light Cavalry, 1803-1805

9211-93, Photocopy of a letter written by Pte. Thomas Allen Brown, 1812

**Newspapers**

*Calcutta Gazette*
*Exeter Flying Post*
*Government Gazette* (India)
*Hampshire Chronicle*
*Ipswich Journal*
*Madras Courier*
*The Oxford Journal*
*Sherborne Mercury*
*Stamford Mercury*
*Sun (London)*

## Primary Published Sources

Blacker, Valentine, David C.J. Howell (ed.), *War Without Pity* (Warwick: Helion, 2018)

Hickey, William, Peter Quennell (ed.), *Memoirs of William Hickey* (London: Purnell Book Services Limited, 1975)

Howard, Thomas Phipps, Roger Norman Buckley (ed.), *The Haitian Journal of Lieutenant Howard, York Hussars, 1796-1798* (Knoxville: The University of Tennessee Press, 1985)

Pester, John, *War and Sport in India 1802-1806 an Officer's Diary* (London: Heath, Cranton & Ouseley, Ltd., 1913)

Plummer, Samuel, John Riles (ed.), *The Journal of Samuel Plummer: Private in the 22nd Regiment of Foot* (London: T. Cordeux, 1821)

Shipp, John, *The Extraordinary Military Career of John Shipp: The Experiences of a soldier in the Kaffir, Mahratta, Ghurka and Pindari Wars of the Early Nineteenth Century* (Driffield: Leonaur, 2010)

Skinner, James, *The Recollections of Skinner of Skinner's Horse* (Driffield: Leonaur, 2006)

Thorn, William, *Memoir of the War in India conducted by General Lord Lake, Commander-in-Chief and Major-General Sir Arthur Wellesley, Duke of Wellington; From its commencement in 1803, to its Termination in 1806* (London: Military Library, 1818)

Vandeleur, John Ormsby, *Duty of Officers Commanding Detachments in the Field* (London: T. Egerton, 1801)

Wylliams, Cooper, *An Account of the Campaign in the West Indies in the Year 1794 Under the command of their Excellences Lieutenant-General Sir Charles Grey, K.B. and Vice-Admiral Sir John Jervis, K.B.* (London: T. Bensley, 1796)

## Secondary Sources

Ackroyd, Peter, *London: The Biography* (London: Vintage, 2001)

Al-Qāsimī, Sultan Muhammad, *The Journals of David Seton in the Gulf 1800-1809* (Exeter: University of Exeter, 1995)

Al-Qāsimī, Sultan Muhammad, *The Myth of Arab Piracy in the Gulf* (Abingdon: Routledge, 2016)

Anderson, W.H., *The History of the Twenty-Second Cheshire Regiment 1689-1849* (London: Hugh Rees, Limited, 1920)

Anon., *Naval Chronicle*, vol.5, (1801)

Anon., *The East India Military Calendar* (Uckfield: Naval and Military Press, 2007)

Ball, Philip, *Neither Up Nor Down: The British Army and the Flanders Campaign 1793-1795* (Warwick: Helion, 2020)

Bamford, Andrew, *Sickness, Suffering, and the Sword: The British Regiment on Campaign, 1808-1815* (Norman: University of Oklahoma Press, 2013)

Bamford, Andrew, *Gallantry and Discipline: The 12th Light Dragoons at War with Wellington* (Barnsley: Frontline Books, 2014)

Barnard, Lady Anne, Margaret Lenta and Basil Le Cordeur (eds.), *The Cape Diaries of Lady Anne Barnard, 1799-1800* (Cape Town: Van Riebeeck Society, 1999)

Bayly, C.A., *The New Cambridge History of India: Indian Society and the Making of the British Empire* (Cambridge: Cambridge University Press, 2010)

Bishara, Fahad Ahmad, and Risso, Patricia, 'The Gulf, the Indian Ocean and the Arab World', in J.E. Peterson (ed.), *The Emergence of the Gulf States* (London: Bloomsbury Academic, 2016)

Briggs, Jimmie, *Innocents Lost: When Child Soldiers Go To War* (New York: Basic Books, 2005)

Broughton, E.C., *Memoirs of the 65th Regiment: 1st Battalion the York and Lancaster Regiment 1756 to 1913* (London: William Clowes & Sons, 1914)

Brown, Mervyn, *Madagascar Rediscovered* (London: Damien Tunnacliffe, 1978)

Brown, Steve, *By Fire and Bayonet: Grey's West Indies Campaign of 1794* (Solihull: Helion, 2018)

Brown, Steve, *King George's Army British Regiments and the Men who led them 1793-1815:* (Warwick: Helion, 2024–2025)

Buckle, E., J.W. Kaye (ed.), *Memoir of the Services of the Bengal Artillery* (London: Wm. H. Allen & Co., 1852)

Buckley, Roger Norman, *The British Army in the West Indies: Society and the Military in the Revolutionary Age* (Mona: University of the West Indies Press, 1988)

Burns, Sir Alan, *History of the British West Indies* (London: George Allen & Unwin Ltd., 1965)

Campbell, Gwyn, *An Economic History of Imperial Madagascar 1750-1898* (Cambridge: Cambridge University Press, 2005)
Cannon, Richard, *Historical Record of the Ninth, or the East Norfolk Regiment of Foot* (London: Parker, Furnivall & Parker, 1848)
Cannon, Richard, *Historical Record of the Sixteenth or the Bedfordshire Regiment of Foot* (London: Parker, Furnivall, & Parker. 1849)
Cannon, Richard, *Historical Record of the Twenty-Second or the Cheshire Regiment of Foot* (London: Parker, Furnivall, & Parker. 1849)
Cannon, Richard, *Historical Record of the Thirty-Fourth, or the Cumberland Regiment of Foot* (London: Parker, Furnivall, & Parker. 1849)
Cannon, Richard, *Historical Record of the Eighty-Sixth, or the Royal County Down Regiment of Foot* (London: Parker, Furnivall, & Parker. 1849)
Cantlie, Sir Neil, *A History of the Army Medical Department* (Edinburgh: Churchill Livingstone, 1974)
Cardew, F.G., *A Sketch of the Services of the Bengal Native Army to the year 1895* (Uckfield: Naval and Military Press, 2005)
Cavalicro, Rodcrick, *Strangers in the Land* (London: I.B. Tauris, 2002)
Chartrand, René, *Napoleon's Overseas Army* (London: Osprey, 1989)
Chaurasia, R.S., *History of the Marathas* (New Delhi: Atlantic Publishers and Distributors, 2004)
Clarke, Howard R., *Redcoats in the Classroom* (Warwick: Helion, 2021)
Cockerill, A.W., *Sons of the Brave: The Story of Boy Soldiers* (London: Leo Cooper, 1984)
Colley, Linda, *Britons: Forging the Nation 1707-1837* (New Haven: Yale University Press, 2012)
Colley, Linda. 'The Reach of the State, the Appeal of the Nation: Mass arming and political culture in the Napoleonic Wars', in Lawrence Stone (ed.), *An Imperial State at War: Britain from 1689 to 1815* (London: Routledge, 1994)
Collins, Alan, *Contemporary Security Studies* (Oxford: Oxford University Press, 2016)
Cooper, Randolf G.S., *The Anglo-Maratha Campaigns and the Contest for India: The Struggle for Control of the South Asian Military Economy* (Cambridge: Cambridge University Press, 2003)
Cordiner, James, *A Description of Ceylon* (London: Longman, Hurst, Rees and Orme, 1807)
Copestake, Andy, *'Their Infantry and Guns Will Astonish You'* (Warwick: Helion, 2021)
Creighton, J.N., *Narrative of the Siege and Capture of Bhurtpore, in the Province of Agra, Upper Hindoostan* (London: Privately Printed, 1830)
Creighton-Williamson, Donald, *The York and Lancaster Regiment: 65th and 84th Regiments of Foot* (London: Leo Cooper, 1968)
Dallas, R.C., *The History of the Maroons* (London: T.M. Longman and O. Rees, 1803)
Dalrymple, William, *The Anarchy: The Relentless Rise of the East India Company* (London: Bloomsbury Publishing, 2020)
Davidson, Basil, *People's Cause. A History of Guerrillas in Africa* (Harlow: Longman Group Limited, 1981)

Davies, Huw J., *The Wandering Army: The Campaigns that Transformed the British Way of War* (New Haven: Yale University Press, 2022)
Divall, Carole, *General Sir Ralph Abercromby and the French Revolutionary Wars 1792-1801* (Barnsley: Pen and Sword Military, 2018)
Dubois, Laurent, *Avengers of the New World: The Story of the Haitian Revolution* (Cambridge: Belknap Press, 2004)
Duff, James Grant, *A History of the Mahrattas* (Calcutta: R. Cambray & Co., 1912)
Duffy, Michael, *Soldiers, Sugar, and Seapower: The British Expeditions to the West Indies and the War against Revolutionary France* (Oxford: Clarendon Press, 1987)
Esdaile, Charles, *Napoleon's Wars: An International History, 1803-1815* (London: Viking, 2007)
Fergusson, William, *Notes and Recollections of a Professional Life* (London: Longman, Brown, Green, and Longmans, 1846)
Franklin, C.E., *British Napoleonic Uniforms* (Stroud: Spellmount, 2010)
Fortescue, J.W., *A History of the British Army* (London: Macmillan and Co. Limited, 1915)
Fosten, Bryan, *Wellington's Infantry (1)* (Oxford: Osprey, 2008)
Fowler, Simon, *The Workhouse: The People, The Places, The Life Behind Doors* (Barnsley: Pen and Sword History, 2014)
Gates, David, *The British Light Infantry Arm c.1790-1815* (London: B.T. Batsford Ltd. 1987)
Glover, Richard, *Peninsular Preparation: The Reform of the British Army 1795-1809* (Cambridge: Cambridge University Press, 1963)
Gordon, Iain, *Bloodline: The Origins and Development of the Regular Formations of the British Army* (Barnsley: Pen and Sword Military, 2010)
Gordon, Stewart, 'War, the Military, and the Environment: Central India, 1560-1820', in Richard P. Tucker and Edmund Russell (eds), *Natural Enemy, Natural Ally: Toward an Environmental History of Warfare* (Corvallis: Oregon State University Press, 2012)
Grieve, Hilda, *The Sleepers and the Shadows* (Chelmsford: Essex County Council, 1994)
Hall, Christopher D., *British Strategy in the Napoleonic War 1803-15* (Manchester: Manchester University Press, 1992)
Haythornthwaite, Philip, *British Napoleonic Infantry Tactics 1792-1815* (Oxford: Osprey, 2008)
Haythornthwaite, Philip, *Redcoats: The British Soldiers of the Napoleonic Wars* (Barnsley: Pen & Sword Military, 2012)
Heathcote, T.A., *The Military in British India: The Development of British Land Forces in South Asia 1600-1947* (Barnsley: Pen & Sword Books Ltd., 2013)
Hibbert, Christopher, *King Mob: The Story of Lord George Gordon and the London Riots of 1780* (Cleveland: The World Publishing Company, 1958)
Hibbert, Christopher, *The French Revolution* (London: Penguin Books, 2001)
Holmes, Richard, *Redcoat: The British Soldier in the Age of Horse and Musket* (London: HarperCollins, 2001)
Holmes, Richard, *Wellington: The Iron Duke* (London: HarperCollins, 2003)

Holmes, Richard, *Sahib: The British Soldier in India* (London: HarperCollins, 2005)
Hoover, James W., *Men without Hats: Dialogue, Discipline and Discontent in the Madras Army, 1806-1807* (New Delhi: Manohar Publishers & Distributors, 2007)
Holzträger, Hans, *In a Raging Inferno* (Warwick: Helion, 2024)
Houlding, J.A., *Fit for Service: The Training of the British Army, 1715-1795* (Oxford: Clarendon Press, 1981)
Howard, Martin R., *Death Before Glory! The British Soldier in the West Indies in the French Revolutionary & Napoleonic Wars 1793-1815* (Barnsley: Pen and Sword Military, 2015)
Howard, Martin R., *Wellington and the British Army's Indian Campaigns 1798-1805* (Barnsley: Pen and Sword Military, 2020)
James, Lawrence, *Raj: The Making of British India* (London: Abacus, 1997)
Johnston, Arthur, *The First Kandyan War: A Narrative & History of the British Conquest of Ceylon* (Driffield: Leonaur, 2014)
Keay, John, *The Honourable Company: A History of the English East India Company* (London: HarperCollins, 1993)
Knight, Ian, *Queen Victoria's Enemies (1): Southern Africa* (London: Osprey, 1989)
Knighton, William, *The History of Ceylon from the Earliest Period to the Present Time* (London: Longman, Brown, Green & Longmans, 1845)
Laurie, George Brenton, *History of the Royal Irish Rifles* (London: Gale & Polden, 1914)
Lawson, Joseph, *Letters to the Young on Progress in Pudsey during the Last Sixty Years* (Firle: Caliban Books, 1978)
Le Marchant, Denis, *Le Marchant: Wellington's Scientific Cavalry General: With a Short Biography by John William Cole* (Driffield: Leonaur, 2014)
Levine, Roger S., '"African Warfare in All Its Ferocity": Changing Military Landscapes and Precolonial and Colonial Conflict in Southern Africa', in Richard P. Tucker and Edmund Russell (eds), *Natural Enemy, Natural Ally: Toward an Environmental History of Warfare* (Corvallis: Oregon State University Press, 2012)
Lewis, J. Penry, *List of Inscriptions on Tombstones and Monuments in Ceylon* (Colombo: H.C. Cottle, 1913)
Linch, Kevin, *The British Army, 1783–1815* (Barnsley: Pen and Sword Military, 2024)
Lorimer, J.G., *Gazetteer of the Persian Gulf* (Calcutta: Superintendent Government Printing, 1915)
Low, Charles Rathbone. *History of the Indian Navy (1613–1863)* (London: Richard Bentley and Son, 1877)
Macilwee, Mick. *The Liverpool Underworld: Crime in the City, 1750–1900* (Liverpool: Liverpool University Press, 2011)
Marshall, J.D., *The Old Poor Law, 1795-1834* (Basingstoke: Macmillan Publishers Ltd., 1985)
Middleton, Richard, *Cornwallis: Soldier and Statesman in a Revolutionary World* (New Haven: Yale University Press, 2022)
Mikaberidze, Alexander, *The Napoleonic Wars: A Global History* (New York: Oxford University Press, 2020)

Milton, John, *The Edges of War: A History of Frontier Wars (1702-1878)* (Cape Town: Juta & Co, Ltd., 1983)

Mostert, Noël, *Frontiers: The Epic of South Africa's Creation and the Tragedy of the Xhosa People* (London: Jonathan Cape, 1992)

Moyse-Bartlett, H., *The Pirates of Trucial Oman* (London: Macdonald, 1966)

Münkler, Herfried, *The New Wars* (Cambridge: Polity Press, 2005)

Mutibwa, Phares M., *The Malagasy and the Europeans* (London: Longman Group Limited, 1974)

Noakes, George, *A Historical Account of the Services of the 34th & 55th Regiments* (Carlisle: C. Thurnam and Sons, 1875)

Parkinson, C. Northcote, *War in the Eastern Seas 1793-1815* (London: George Allen & Unwin Ltd., 1954)

Pearse, Hugh, *Memoir of the Life and Military Services of Viscount Lake Baron Lake of Delhi and Laswaree 1744-1808* (Edinburgh: William Blackwood and Sons, 1908)

Pearse, Hugh, *Lake's Campaigns in India: The Second Anglo-Maratha War, 1803-1807* (Driffield: Leonaur, 2007)

Provan, Joshua, *Bullocks, Grain and Good Madeira: The Maratha and Jat Campaigns 1803-1806 and the Emergence of an Indian Army* (Warwick: Helion, 2021)

Raikes, G.A., *Roll of the Officers of the York and Lancaster Regiment* (London: Richard Bentley & Son, 1885)

Reid, Stuart, *Armies of the East India Company 1750-1850* (Oxford: Osprey, 2014)

Reiter, Jacquline, *Quicksilver Captain: The Improbable Life of Sir Home Popham* (Warwick: Helion, 2024)

Richards, Eric, *Britannia's Children: Emigration from England, Scotland, Wales and Ireland since 1600* (London: Hambledon and London, 2004)

Rigby, Bernard, *Ever Glorious: The Story of the 22nd (Cheshire) Regiment* (Chester: Cheshire Military Museum, 2010)

Rodger, N.A.M., *The Command of the Ocean: A Naval History of Britain 1649-1815* (London: Allen Lane, 2004)

Roworth, Vivien, *Not So Easy, Lads: Wearing the Red Coat 1786-1797* (Warwick: Helion, 2023)

Sardesai, Govind Sakharam. *New History of the Marathas: Sunset Over Maharashtra* (Bombay: Phoenix Publications, 1968)

Selvon, Sidney, *A Comprehensive History of Mauritius* (Port Louis: Mauritius Printing Specialists Ltd., 2005)

Smithers, A.J., *The Kaffir Wars 1779-1877* (London: Leo Cooper, 1973)

Snell, K.D.M., *Parish and Belonging: Community, Identity and Welfare in England and Wales 1700-1950* (Cambridge: Cambridge University Press, 2006)

Simpson, Frank, *The Cheshire Regiment, or 22nd Regiment of Foot* (Great Britain: G.R. Griffith, 1905)

Singer, P.W., *Children at War* (Berkeley: University of California Press, 2006)

Singh, Patwant, and Rai, Jyoti M., *Empire of the Sikhs: The Life and Times of Maharaja Ranjit Singh* (London: Peter Owen Publishers, 2013)

Steenkamp, Willem, *Assegais, Drums & Dragoons: A Military & Social History of the Cape* (Johannesburg: Jonathan Ball Publishers, 2012)
Stone, Lawrence (ed.), *An Imperial State at War: Britain from 1689-1815* (London: Routledge, 1994)
Sutherland, Douglas, *Tried and Valiant: The History of the Border Regiment, (the 34th and 55th Regiments of Foot), 1702-1959* (London: Leo Cooper, 1972)
Taylor, Stephen, *Storm & Conquest: The Battle for the Indian Ocean, 1809* (London: Faber and Faber Limited, 2007)
Theal, George McCall, *History of South Africa* (London: Swan Sonnenschein & Co. 1891)
White, A.C.T., *The Story of Army Education 1643-1963* (London: George G. Harrap & Co. Ltd., 1963)
Wilson, Ben, *Decency & Disorder: The Age of Cant 1789-1837* (London: Faber and Faber, 2007)
Wilson, W.J., *History of the Madras Army* (Madras: E. Keys, 1883)
Winterbottom, Derek, *The Grand Old Duke of York: The Life of Prince Frederick, Duke of York and Albany 1763-1827* (Barnsley: Pen & Sword Military, 2016)
Zamoyski, Adam, *Holy Madness: Romantics, Patriots, and Revolutionaries, 1776-1871* (London: Weidenfeld & Nicholson, 1999)

## Journal Articles

Chopra, Preeti, 'Free to move, forced to flee: the formation and dissolution of suburbs in colonial Bombay, 1750-1918', *Urban History*, vol.39, pp.83–107
Palmer, Stanley H., 'The Military, the Law, and Public Order in England, 1650-1850', *Journal of the Society for Army Historical Research*, vol.56, no.228 (Winter 1978), pp.198–214
Tylden, G., 'The Third Kaffir War, 1799-1802', *Journal of the Society for Army Historical Research*, vol.37, no.150 (June 1959), pp.72–82
Sumner, Percy, 'Army Inspection Returns – 1753 to 1804', *Journal of the Society for Army Historical Research*, vol.4, no.17 (1925), pp.104–116

## Online Sources

Children and Armed Conflict, 'The Paris Principles', *United Nations*, <https://childrenandarmedconflict.un.org/publications/ParisPrinciples_EN.pdf>, February 2007
Defence Statistics, 'Deployment of children (under 18)', *Ministry of Defence*, <https://assets.publishing.service.gov.uk/media/5c87b59d40f0b636981e0b76/12590.pdf>, 31 January 2019
Becker, Jo, 'This is our opportunity to end the Taliban's use of child soldiers,' *Human Rights Watch*, <https://www.hrw.org/news/2021/09/20/our-opportunity-end-talibans-use-child-soldiers>, 20th September 2021

David Howell, 'The British Conquest of Ceylon and the Massacre at Kandy 1803'. *The Napoleon Series*, <https://www.napoleon-series.org/military-information/battles-and-campaigns/the-british-conquest-of-ceylon-and-the-massacre-at-kandy-1803/>

## Unpublished Theses

Geggus, David Patrick, *The British Occupation of Saint-Domingue 1793-98* (PhD thesis, York University, 1978)

Linch, Kevin Barry, *The Recruitment of the British Army 1807-1815* (PhD thesis, University of Leeds, 2001)

Pitre, K.G., *The Second Anglo-Maratha War 1802-1803* (PhD thesis, University of Poona, 1984)

Ray, Bhabani Charan, *The British Conquest and Administration of Orissa, 1803-1819* (PhD thesis, University of London, 1956)

Sivapragasam, Michael, *After the Treaties: A Social, Economic and Demographic History of Maroon Society in Jamaica, 1739-1842* (PhD Thesis, University of Southampton, 2018)

Western, J.R., *The Recruitment of the Land Forces in Great Britain, 1793-99* (PhD thesis, University of Edinburgh, 1953)

# From Reason to Revolution – Warfare 1721-1815

http://www.helion.co.uk/series/from-reason-to-revolution-1721-1815.php

The 'From Reason to Revolution' series covers the period of military history 1721–1815, an era in which fortress-based strategy and linear battles gave way to the nation-in-arms and the beginnings of total war.

This era saw the evolution and growth of light troops of all arms, and of increasingly flexible command systems to cope with the growing armies fielded by nations able to mobilise far greater proportions of their manpower than ever before. Many of these developments were fired by the great political upheavals of the era, with revolutions in America and France bringing about social change which in turn fed back into the military sphere as whole nations readied themselves for war. Only in the closing years of the period, as the reactionary powers began to regain the upper hand, did a military synthesis of the best of the old and the new become possible.

The series examines the military and naval history of the period in a greater degree of detail than has hitherto been attempted, and has a very wide brief, with the intention of covering all aspects from the battles, campaigns, logistics, and tactics, to the personalities, armies, uniforms, and equipment.

**Submissions**

The publishers would be pleased to receive submissions for this series. Please email reasontorevolution@helion.co.uk, or write to Helion & Company Limited, Unit 8 Amherst Business Centre, Budbrooke Road, Warwick, CV34 5WE

**You may also be interested in:**

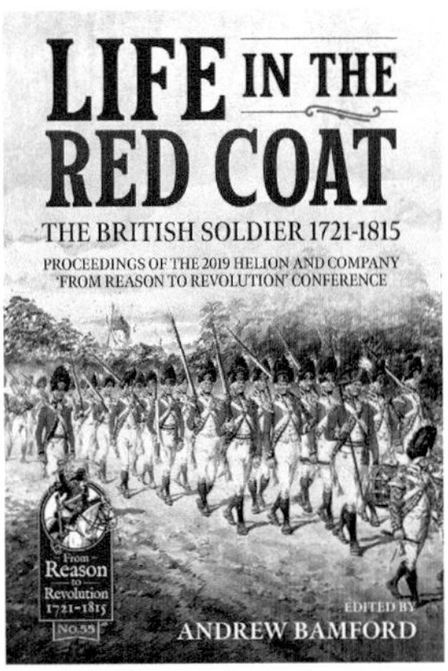

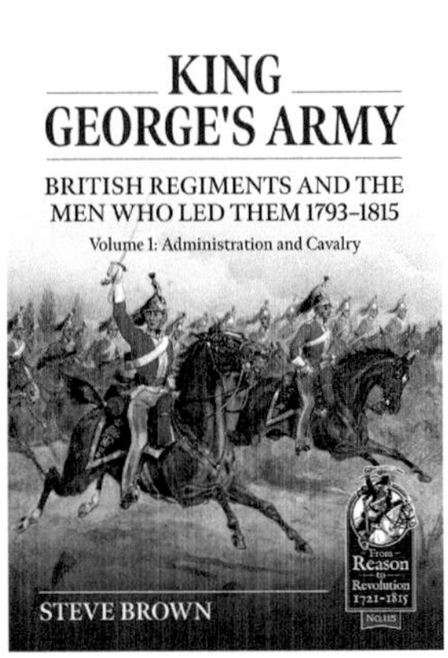

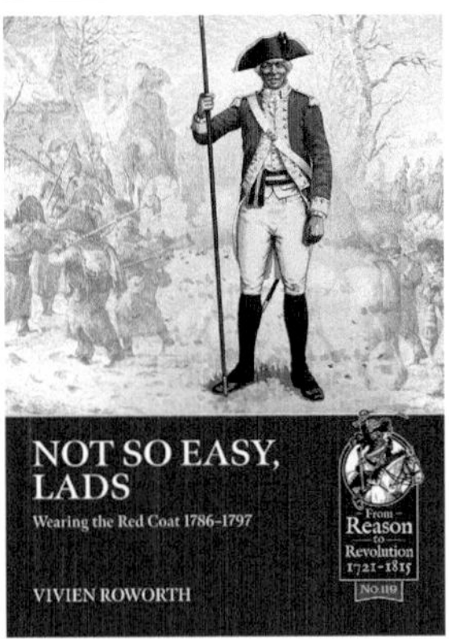

- From -
Reason
— to —
Revolution
1721–1815

In the 1790s, Great Britain faced a recruitment crisis. Swathes of men had been called up to fight Revolutionary France. This left the British Army thinly stretched, especially in the garrisons scattered across the British Empire. With a recruitment crisis brewing, the army resorted to recruiting boys aged between 13 and 16. Three regiments were designated 'experimental' battalions: 22nd (The Cheshire), 34th (Cumberland) and 65th (2nd Yorkshire, North Riding) Regiments of Foot. These regiments recruited boys who were destined to grow up in the army before being sent east to serve in the burgeoning empire of Britain's Honourable East India Company.

*Boys in Red Coats* is the first full-length study to examine the recruitment, training and deployment of these boys. The war with France was a catalyst for the Commander-in-Chief of the British Army, the Duke of York, to future-proof recruitment in the army and provide a source of manpower fit for the far reaches of the British Empire. Some parishes across England seized the opportunity to reduce the growing cost of poor relief and to relieve unrest in the counties, actively encouraging boys to join the army. As a result, a number of young boys raised in these battalions were sent to fight Xhosa warriors in South Africa, indefatigable Maratha defenders in the great citadels of India, and French and Arabian pirates in Mauritius and the Persian Gulf. Those boys who survived and returned home were veterans of some of the harshest fighting conditions in the nineteenth century.

---

**Owen W.H. Davis** has maintained a lasting interest in military history. He studied War Studies and History at King's College, London, and has served as Membership Secretary for the Waterloo Association since 2017 and as Editor of the Association's YouTube channel since 2020. Owen's main focus is the British Army during the Napoleonic Wars and the British Empire. He has written articles on the Scots Greys for Waterloo 200 and has subsequently contributed to the Age of Revolution. An editor on the Napoleon Series, Owen reviews the latest research and books on the Napoleonic Period.

ISBN 978-1-806722-61-7

9 781806 722617

HELION & COMPANY

www.helion.co.uk

helionbooks